# FORGIVE ME FATHER FOR I HAVE SINNED

## AN AUTOBIOGRAPHY

Pastor Phillip Aguilar
Email: setfreephil@aol.com
Phone: 714-400-4573
Office: 714-520-4122

Web-sites

- ● Setfree.org
- ● Setfreesoldiers.com
- ● Setfreehiphop.com

- ● Myspace.com/setfreephil
- ● Facebook
  - o Phillip Russell Aguilar
  - o Phil-Aguilar-Life-Story

CREDITS

**Edit**

Matthew Aguilar
Veronica Montenegro

**Graphics and design**

Matthew Aguilar
Roc Aguilar

FORGIVE ME FATHER FOR I HAVE SINNED

# Dedication

To my beloved wife Sandra Jean Aguilar
who I love with all of my heart!
You are the virtuous woman that Proverbs
31 speaks about. You are Saint Sandra and I
am ravished with your love always.

# Contents

FORGIVE ME FATHER FOR I HAVE SINNED

# Special Acknowledgement

*I would like to thank all my children for the joy you have brought into my life.......*

To my grandchildren Lil MJ, Serena, Jesse, Christian, Santino, Sophia, Ava Joy, Jaden, Brody, Xavier, Michael, Taylor, Landon, Jacob, Ashaya, Moshe, Brooklyn, Giana, Leila, I love you very much.   To my oldest son Geronimo *(Pastor G)*, I am proud of you for continuing to fight the good fight for Jesus and I thank God for bringing you back into my life. MJ *(Pastor MJ)* for being that golden boy in my life, thank you for always serving me faithfully.  Chill *(Phillip Jr.)* you have blessed me and your mom with the best worship music in the world.  Trinajoy, thank you for bringing me the best gift ever, twin grandsons, and for unconditionally standing by me throughout the years. Roc, *(aka Hebrew)* I love you for making the last part of my life so exciting, you truly bring joy to my life.  To my daughter-in-law's, I thank you for being faithful wives who have made my son's so very happy. To my son-in-law Michael, I know God is raising you up to preach to millions, I believe in you.

I extend my special thanks to those Set Free Soldiers in Orange County, Phoenix, Great Falls, and San Diego, who have remained loyal no matter what the cost.  You have shown me that there is still honor among men. To my Set Free church family in beautiful downtown Anaheim, we are the Last one's left and I love you for that.

To the multitudes of you who have given your life to Jesus at Set Free Worldwide ministries from1982–2010, thank God for saving a wretch like me! You have truly blessed my life.

To all the Set Free pastors that have been part of my life I honor you for choosing Set Free to be your name. To those Set Free Pastors who have left our fold, I love you with the heart of Jesus. To the men and women that have given their time, talent and treasures for our ministry I pray God's best for you, it is through your commitment that Set Free remains alive.

To Reverend Glenn Morrison who led me to Christ, I thank you for being faithful to Jesus and introducing me to my PaPa. To Pastor Herb Sokol thank you for teaching me about the gift of inconvenience, without it I would not have been blessed with the 1000's of people whom have lived in our Set Free homes. To Pastor John Lyle for sending me to Bible College and teaching me to be a soul-winner. Last but not least to my father Gilbert who will be celebrating his 87th birthday this year. I love you very much dad and look forward to eternity with you in Heaven. To my mother Celia the mother of the year, my helper, my friend and my most loyal supporter, I love you mom. To my brothers Bert (R.I.P.) you are missed by so many, Billy you are a great brother, Mel you are #1 , Milton I love you sooo much, Eddie my baby brother I love you,  and to my favorite sister Elizabeth I love you so much. To those of you that I have offended and not lived up to being the Pastor I should have been, I ask for your forgiveness and prayers. Last but not least, to those of you that have chosen not to forgive me, I pray blessings on your life. To you who have spoken these words to me "Till death do us Part" I will never forget your love.

# PREFACE

That August morning in southern California was unusually cool. At 5 a.m. in the morning, it was still dark outside and most of us were in our deepest sleep. Little did I know that a SWAT team, federal agents, and hundreds of other law enforcement officers were wide awake and preparing to raid my home. On August 6, 2008 at approximately 5:45 a.m. in the morning a loud speaker screamed out, "This is the Anaheim police department, come out with your hands up". I hadn't heard those words in over thirty years. There was a loud bang that got me out of bed fast and, all of a sudden, the smoke from the flash grenades began to fill my home. I see men climbing over my back walls, I hear the choppers and I am blinded by the bright lights beaming through the windows. Again I hear, "Come out with your hands up!"

My wife, scared and confused, hands me my bathrobe and says I should go out there and see what's going on. So after a short prayer I walk towards the light and I wondered to myself what could have possibly happened. I had no clue, but as soon as I stepped outside a chill came over me and I knew that this would be the biggest trial of my life! I saw dozens of little red dots all over my body, the bright lights from circling choppers nearly blinded me. The angry voices of law enforcement surrounded me, and yet by far the worst thing of all…I had to see my own family: wife, kids, and even grandkids on the curb, handcuffed. They had a look of sadness and confusion I will never forget! But before I get ahead of myself and share with you one of the darkest days of my life, let me take you to the place where it all started, beautiful downtown Anaheim, California!

CHAPTER 1

# I WAS ONCE A GOOD LITTLE BOY

This is a true story about my wonderful, wild, and crazy life! Well, at least as I see the truth through these wicked and fleshly sinner's eyes. It all started back in the late forty's when a child named Phillip Russell Aguilar was born in a small German town called Anaheim.

Anaheim is a city located in Southern California, not far from Newport Beach. Anaheim was run by predominately white, right wing, John Birch type of people. Good old conservative Republican type of politicians. Anaheim is a German word that means "Anna's house." In my adolescent years I realized I was born into a white world. All of my elementary school pictures showed this dark kid in the middle of a white cloud.

My family was of Mexican/ Native American decent. My mom and dad were both from Anaheim and graduated from Anaheim High School. My parent's generation went through some tough racial experiences. My mother had to try harder than the Anglo kids, and was even told by one of her school teachers that she would get straight A's if she wouldn't hang out with Mexicans. After Pearl Harbor was attacked, the Japanese-Americans became targets of the U.S. Government, and my mom saw many of her classmates relocated to internment camps. My dad, like all young men, was drafted into the armed forces. He married my mom before he went overseas to fight for his country. It's hard to believe the town that made Disneyland so famous was also racist at one time—there were no black or Asian people to speak of in our city. I didn't understand the racism, nor did I realize it was happening to me. I was an odd commodity in this white world, where the only gang in town was the Mickey Mouse Club.

During my first five years we lived in a little barrio *(neighborhood)* named La Colonia Independencia *(Independence Colony)*, situated in an unincorporated part of Anaheim. My mom was born there in an unpainted little home that my grandfather built right before her birth. It was a small, tight-knit community of Mexican people who had a hard life but a lot of love. As much as my mom cherished her life in La Colonia, my parents knew that our neighborhood was not where they wanted to raise their children. Poverty surrounded us, and due to a lack of parental supervision, some of the kids were getting into drugs and being sent to Juvenile Hall. It was 1952 *(President Harry Truman is in office and we are in the middle of the Cold War)* and my parents decided to move to another part of Anaheim where it hopefully would be a better environment for us all. It was a small three-bedroom home that cost my parents about eight thousand dollars to purchase.

Everyone spoke Spanish in La Colonia, but in our new neighborhood it was mostly Anglo people with little Spanish being spoken. While my parents spoke fluent English and Spanish, my siblings and I were told that Spanish wasn't important for us to know because it would soon become a dead language.

I can remember my mother showing me my birth certificate that read I was of the Caucasian race; the only races recognized back in those days were Anglo, Black, Red, and Oriental. The city of Anaheim had no idea how much things would change over the years. Our new house had a front yard and right across the street was a gigantic orange grove. Caddy corner from our house was an elementary school that we would be attending, since I was only going in to kindergarten it was a great time to move to a new area.

We had an old freight train that ran down the middle of our street three times a day. I can recall the way it made our house rattle and vibrate every time it passed by. My dad would head off to work every day and my mother would take care of business at home. In many ways I felt like I was living the perfect life with a great mom and dad. I assimilated quite easily with my new friend's' at the elementary school and wanted to be like them so badly, to the point of even wanting to be white. One day I asked my mom if she could get us better soap, thinking that would lighten up my skin color. My dad was my hero and my mom was my provider and I was enjoying such a great childhood.

I had four younger brothers and one beautiful sister. There was my brother Bert, my brother Billy, Milton and Melvin (the twins) and my sister Elizabeth. I was the big brother to all of them and I realized at a young age I was a natural born leader, I would later realize that where I led people would raise a lot of eyebrows. My mom would let me invite my friends over after school to play games, and she always had some hot buttered tortillas for us to munch on. Soon, our house became the headquarters for the whole neighborhood.

I can remember watching all of my favorite television show's in black and white. *The Lone Ranger, Popeye the Sailor Man, Beaver Cleaver, I Love Lucy Show, Father Knows Best,* and so many more. My dad was a hard working bricklayer who I respected very much, but he never seemed to have time to talk to me. I have seen pictures of him hugging me, but I don't remember any warm embraces, or any I love you from him. Yet, I knew he was a good dad because of the financial support he gave to me and our family. My mother was the one who met my needs when it came to showing me love and concern for my life. It was a little taste of the Beaver Cleaver lifestyle that I enjoyed so much. I knew we had a roof over our head and plenty of food to eat. We ate a lot of beans and rice but I knew it was made with lots of love. I have nothing but sweet memories of my preteen years, but my little dream world had a huge wake-up call when I turned 13.

My mom always had a nanny or some type of helper living with us to clean house, babysit and run errands. One day I walked in our home and I saw my father holding hands with this so called nanny, and I soon came to understand that my father loved this woman more than he did my mother! My dad was always the most popular guy around his circle of friends, funny, good looking and always dressed to kill. When weekends came around he was always out with his pals, and when he did stay home he would throw parties at our house. He was the life of the party and I admired that part of him very much, probably too much. It seemed like all of his friends loved having him to themselves and as I watched I realize how much I was starving for my dad's attention. When he was drinking alcohol he would be extra nice to me, so I didn't care how drunk he was because I wanted his love and attention so very much.

One day I started to notice that my dad was becoming short with my mom quite often. One night I witnessed him pulling my mom by the hair while she begged him to stop. I remained in denial about it, and considered this to be my parent's problem and obviously things just got worse, very much worse. The big day finally happened and I knew my dad was gone for good! I was so messed up in my mind that I actually blamed my mom for this, thinking maybe she could have done something, *anything* to stop him from leaving!

I didn't have any religious upbringing in my life. I don't recall my mom or dad ever reading the bible or going to church; however, my mom did sign us kids up at a local Nazarene church for Sunday school. Every Sunday morning the bus would pick us up, and I remember hearing about God and Jesus, and the church people were very nice, but I just felt nothing but anger towards God. My view of life became very coldhearted and I was filled with bitterness, I struggled to understand why this was happening to our family because divorce was very rare in those days and definitely rare in our neighborhood.

My whole life seemed to be self destructing right in front of my eyes. I felt as if I was on a rollercoaster ride to hell! As I tried to reason things out in my young mind, I became convinced that it was all God's fault. After the divorce, my mother became a very independent woman and she refused to go on welfare. Instead, she got two jobs and went to college to learn more. She focused on the material things that our family needed, but at the same time, did not understand the emotional wreck I was becoming! I loved my brothers and sister very much, being the oldest I felt that I should help but I had no guidance tips for them whatsoever. I had to accept that my dad had a new woman, and that he was raising two stepchildren. The thought of that other woman brought hatred to my mind. My dad moved nearby, but spent all of his free time with this lady and her two children, and to make things even worse, I heard he was a good step- father, now that really pissed me off! I was just beginning junior high school and not happy with my life, looking for a place to fit in and be accepted by the new friends I had met at school.

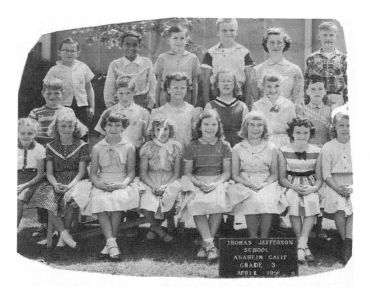

**My 3rd grade class. I am the tall dark handsome one.**

I decided to associate myself with others experiencing the same sick family issues as me. I felt comfortable around them and not embarrassed of my parents. Trouble was easy for me to find even at such a young age because I was mad and I wanted everyone to know. As I look back now I realize I had a big chip on my very small shoulder, but in spite of this, God was definitely watching out for me through my most rebellious times. I started feeling very distant from my mom, my brothers and sister, and I entered a new world where it was all about me and my friends.

**Me on the top right, at 10 yrs old with my sister and brothers**

I only liked school for the social part of it, and I never ever remember doing homework. Fortunately, I did seem to catch on quickly which was my saving grace. As I stumbled along life's path trying to make the best choices on my own, I clung real close to my friends; I enjoyed them because they understood me. We were just a bunch of regular kids trying to make it through the day. In junior high school I started making out with girls and felt my hormones kick in, and at the age of 14 my attitude started to go downhill real fast. My mom completely lost control over the way I was living. I started ditching school, getting loaded on pot, pills, and booze. I even started my own gang and called it "The Olive Street Crew," (which was the name of the street we lived on).

I began utilizing my natural born talent to be a leader in a very negative way. We started by painting graffiti on all our local walls, stealing cars, and this was the beginning of many dumb things we would do. I remember the Olive Street Crew getting drunk and loaded one night in front of my house, and we got this stupid idea to rob the freight train that came down our street.

Here came this old freight train that just carried sugar beets, so we hopped on board and told the conductor to stop. He stopped the train and could not believe we would do something so dangerous and yelled at us for being such stupid kids. To us it was just fun; we were bored and couldn't think of anything better to do with ourselves, after all, during those times we didn't have cell phones or video games to keep us entertained. I was also picked up by the Anaheim police for vandalism quite a few times. I just had this thing in me that made me want to start trouble anywhere and everywhere.

It was now 1963 (*The Beatles release their first album, Please Please Me*) I was in the 10th grade, time for me to get ready to make my move to high school. Anaheim High School was located in the downtown area of Anaheim directly across the street from a hamburger joint called Tastee Freeze.

Tastee Freeze was the meeting place before and after school for some of the groups of people I hung out with. I was considered to be a Chicano *(Mexican America from Southern California)* to most of my Anglo peers, yet I had a strong attraction to hang out with mostly Gavachos *(white boys)*. I was considered a Coconut *(brown on the outside, white on the inside)* by most of my friends and some of my Chicano friends didn't like me running with the white boys. They referred to me as a Chicano Falso *(fake Mexican)*. I was living one of those "dammed if I do, dammed if I don't lives."

In the early 60's we had 5 major clicks in our high school. We had the jocks that played sports. Then there were the white greasers who took on the James Dean, Elvis look. Next there were the band geeks, who were very studious. My favorite looking crew was the Pachucos. *(Pachucos were a subculture started in the late 1930s also called zoot suitors and distinct way of dressing)*. They wore shinny French-toed shoes and their clothes were all creased down. They had rain drain, and pompadour hair dos,' they didn't just walk down the hallways at school; they had to have the coolest stroll of all.

I was still a square peg trying to fit in a round hole so I ended up hanging out with the Anaheim bad boy surfers. What in the world was a young Mexican guy like me doing hanging out with surfers? I just thought the blond haired, blue eyed, sun tanned girls looked so fine. I was digging all the surf music that was on the scene, and I loved hanging out at the Beach. I can remember hanging out on 15th street in Newport at a place we called "The Wall". Everyone would lay out in the sun and put coco butter on them so they could get a nice dark tan. Their skin went red/brown and my mine went jet black. The next thing all my surfer buddies did was peroxide their hair, theirs went blonde and sure enough mine turned to orange.

We partied at a place in Anaheim called the Harmony Park Ballroom. The entertainment was Dave Myers and the Surftones, Dick Dale and the Deltones who played there weekly. We did a dance called the "surfers stomp" all night long and I was pushing the envelope in every direction. I was a fifteen year old Chicano surfer boy with long orange hair; I mean was I trying to fit in or what? I'm sure that I was quite a sight to see but I didn't care because I loved giving people something to talk about since I unofficially belonged to the bad boy surfers of Anaheim High School.

The jocks at Anaheim High school painted a beautiful sign in the lunch area; it read "Colonist spirit knows no Limit". One night the Olive Street Crew went and painted the words "bullshit says the Olive Street Crew." It was plain to see that my whole world view was upside down during that time as I started developing my own sick thoughts of what was right and wrong.

I use to stop at Taste Freeze each morning on my way to high school and I would see the older guys who had cars ready to hit the beach with their surf boards. I had to make the big choice each morning to go surfing or go to school and, yes, most of the time surfing won the coin toss. My mom always took care of my everyday needs in life so I just needed money to buy my marijuana and booze. I started stealing stuff out of cars, garages, and breaking into homes.

At 16 I was getting busted for being drunk in public quite often so my mom decided to buy me a car, being the enabler she was. It was a pink and white Rambler with a continental kit on back. It was not a cool looking car to have in the 60's, and I really wanted a Chevy Nomad surf mobile type of ride. The only thing cool about my pink and white Rambler was the tilt down reclining seats, for the purpose of kissing and hugging, and a radio. I was heading down to Newport Beach more than ever now and I was racking up one parking ticket after another.

One day, the police showed up at my house to arrest my mom for all those parking tickets since the car was registered in her name. She told the police that she never illegally parked anywhere and if the cops wanted to take her in they would have to take all of her six kids with her. Sure enough they left and asked her to please pay the tickets; I caused my mom a lot of grief and gave her most of her grey hair.

One night coming home from a party my driveshaft broke, I told my mom I needed to have my car and that it needed to be fixed ASAP. She told me she didn't have the money at the time to fix it, I was so irritated that she didn't see the importance of repairing my car right away I decided to take matters into my own hands and recruited two of my pals to help me steal a driveshaft. There was a car lot located on Anaheim Boulevard, just down the block from my house, and in the back row of the lot was another car just like mine.

I told my two buddies to stand watch as I crawled underneath the car and told them to give me a sign if they saw any police in the area. I crawled underneath the car and took a look at the part I needed, not really having a clue what I was doing. I was driven by anger to go out and show my mom that I needed it now and I was gonna get it with or without her help.

I had this big pipe wrench in my hand and as I started to wrench away I could hear footsteps running away from the car and realized my buddies deserted me. I was now just as upset with them as I was with my mom, now even my own partners had ranked out on me. I was already thinking of payback for them as I stayed frozen underneath the car and then I heard the voice of a cop named Babcock calling my name. Anaheim was a small town and we all knew each other, well kind of like Mayberry with Andy Griffith *(The Andy Griffith Show)*, and this cop really reminded me of Barney Fife *(character from the Andy Griffith Show)* by his appearance and actions. Officer Babcock yelled at me and told me to come out. Obviously, I was just trying to buy a little more time so I could make up a story. It was then that I saw his long skinny arm reach for me, and I grabbed it with my hands full of grease as he pulled me out. I soiled his pretty little shirt and he got frantic. I ended up going to juvenile hall for some kind of thievery; they gave me 90 days and 2 years probation. I felt like I had a badge of honor given to me so I gladly did my time.

My mom always blamed the cops for picking on me. I am sure she was motivated by guilt as she raised us six kids. I lived my life in depression, trying to kill the pain of my father leaving me. I was dying daily of a broken heart because of my broken dreams, and I should have known the *Ozzie and Harriet* show wasn't real life. I should have learned by now that father doesn't always know best. I just kept bumping my head over and over in life. However there were a few times when it seemed that life had something to offer me.

I was almost seventeen when I met a young girl named Annie. She was the cutest little red head, but she was from the other side of the tracks. Her brothers were star football players at Anaheim High School and she was the leader of the drill team, I was just another loser from the wrong side of town. I would walk Annie part way home after school as often as she allowed; she said she wasn't allowed to date, and for sure not a guy like me. We hit it off right off the bat and I asked her a whole lot of questions about her life and what she liked to do for fun. I asked her if there was any way possible for me to spend time with her on the weekends. She told me she had an older brother that she baby sat for on Friday nights and I could tell she liked being sneaky just like me. She would call me and tell me when her brother left the house and I would then slip over there and bring a six pack of beer with me. Our babysitting nights were the best times ever; we kissed, hugged, and got a little drunk while talking dirty to each other. It was pretty innocent, but it was so special. I enjoyed the thrill of sneaking over to Annie's house with the chance of maybe getting caught.

A year went by and we saw each other almost every weekend. My mom hooked me up with a cool Thunderbird that was one of the nicest cars around. I would pick Annie up in the mornings down the street from her home and give her a ride to school every day. I had a record player that played 45s and we listened to those oldies but goodies as we cruised the streets of downtown Anaheim. I knew back in the day that a girl's ears were the most sensitive part on their body so I would call her up every single night and say sweet nothing's in her ear. I was so very much in love with Annie, I mean it was wonderful, and I finally found what I was looking for. The Bible call's it *sick with love*.

**Finally the day came when Annie told me she loved me.**

I had worked so hard to win her love and now she was mine. We had to keep it a secret so her parents wouldn't find out but my mom knew all about her, and of course I talked my mother in to buying a very expensive promise ring for her to show my affection. My mom had no choice but to make her little baby boy Phil happy. Annie and I had carried this underground love affair for a long time now; I was eating from the forbidden fruit tree, and I was loving it. All I've got to say for now is "payback is a mutha." I was on top of the world again and ready for more. The Bible teaches that "where your treasure is, there will your heart be also!" My first treasure was my dad, and when he left he broke my heart, now I had a second chance to give my heart to someone. I believed in my little Annie so very much. She promised to be true and never do me wrong like my father had. Don't forget I was only 16 years old.

When I gave her the friendship ring the following week she was thrilled beyond words. It was a very pricey piece of jewelry, and it meant a lot to me that my mother would give up her hard earned money to please her son. So here I am living the life again, got a girl, got purpose, and got hope! You have no idea what I was about to experience next. I was hanging out in front of Tastee Freeze one day with my friends waiting for school to end—guess who came riding by? I looked out of the corner of my eye and I see this 1955 Chevrolet surf wagon coming down the street and the driver was one my best friends. Seated right next to him was my little red headed Annie!

In those day's you didn't have many cars with bucket seats, they were bench seats where the girl would slide up right next to her man.  She would then put her arm around his shoulder as they cruised down the boulevard of life.  My heart dropped to the ground as I turned a lighter shade of grey.  Annie was posted up so close to my good friend, before that day, life seemed so good again, and I was starting to believe that there might be a God.

Yes, my little Annie, the cutest red head in the world, had betrayed me.  My heart was in the front seat of that car driving away from me.  From that moment on I knew I would never love again, trust again, and never care again about anyone or anything ever!  First my father betrays me, then my girl betrays me…I had to find something to kill the pain.

# CHAPTER 2

## ETERNAL HIGH

I went and met some of the older fellows in the neighborhood that night to get some good drugs. I was so down-trodden and depressed with this whole stinking world, and I just went full throttle looking for some way to kill my pain. I had contracted the disease I refer to as "Victimitis".

*(According to the Urban Dictionary, Victimitis is a disease that makes the person inflicted with it a victim in every situation. Common symptoms for Victimitis are the feeling that no one understands, frequent pity parties and last, it would be better if you just left this cold cruel world because everyone's against you).*

I was throwing pity parties day and night; I knew that misery loves company so I had a lot of followers joining. I was back in the fast lane of life, riding my rollercoaster ride to Hell! I spent the next couple years of my life just destroying any good habits I had developed.

**On a "trip" in Mazatlan MX**

It was 1965 *(Malcolm X is assassinated, musician Bob Dylan releases his influential album Highway 61 Revisited, featuring the song "Like a Rolling Stone")* and I was supposed to be graduating from high school. I was truant so often that I failed my junior year and I was now officially a high school dropout. The Vietnam War busted on the scene and many of my older buddies were getting drafted into the military. The college kids were having protests against the war, and it seemed the whole country was in a state of turmoil. And me, I was still hanging out at Tastee Freeze doing the same old thing.

One day while hanging out at Taste Freeze, a group of fellows caught my attention. These bad boys were always getting into fights with someone and I personally had a few run-ins with them myself. I admired the violent part of their lifestyle and watched them turn the all American one-on-one fight game into something quite different. Anytime one of them got into a fight, the whole group would join in. It was an "all for one, one for all" philosophy, you know, group therapy on anyone who dared to mess with them. That meant no more good old fashion John Wayne honorable fighting; once they knocked someone to the ground they just kept on pounding them 'til they were done.

After watching how they carried themselves and witnessing the violent acts they had committed, I was awestruck as I watched their whole disposition go in another direction. They were becoming soft-spoken, kind to people, and downright peaceful. I knew something had changed their way of thinking and I became quite curious about what they were all about. I pulled one of them aside and asked him what was up! He explained how they had joined a movement called the Brotherhood of Eternal Love.

"What in the heck is the Brotherhood of Eternal Love"? I asked

*"The group was founded in Laguna Beach, California. They had headquartered in the Mystic Arts bookstore on Pacific Coast Highway. Timothy Leary, the excommunicated Harvard psychology devotee of free love and author of "turn on, tune in and drop out," became the godfather of the group. The group was composed of surfers, drug users and rich kids from Orange County, LA and the Pasadena area. The Brotherhood was a rag-tag crew of very young street toughs in, California - in a poor neighborhood - who in the course of smoking multiple kinds of vegetation and swallowing random available pills for recreational purposes, accidentally encountered LSD. At least a half-dozen of them found their lives transformed by that experience. They tended to wear simple cotton garments, sometimes robes. Most were vegetarians, and they daily spent considerable time in prayer and simply doing good deeds. Many of them continued to practice their own version of Christianity while opening research into Hinduism, Buddhism, and indigenous and Eastern religions as Brotherhood members happened to find them."*

He told me it was a new spiritual movement being headed up by a man named Dr. Timothy Leary and invited me to join them on a trip they called a spiritual journey. He described Dr. Timothy Leary as a Godly enlightened Guru who had discovered a way to have peace and harmony in one's life. He went on to tell me that Dr. Leary was a professor at Harvard University, so I figured since Dr. Leary went to Harvard University he must know what he was talking about. In the Bible God says, "We are all like sheep being led astray". I jumped in with both feet, and I was ready to take a big leap of faith into this new found trail.

● ● ●

My new friend told me that the Brotherhood took what was called "acid trips" every Sunday morning. This drug that they took which put them on this spiritual journey was called LSD. LSD is a hallucinogenic drug that alters your mind and makes you see things that aren't necessarily there, or maybe they are? I was hell-bent on finding out more about this drug LSD and how it was changing people's lives. I was always looking for a place and people to fit in with. The burdens I was carrying were way too much for me to bear, always feeling like some kind of outcast on this planet and wanting and needing someone who understood me. Therapists often refer to this as codependency!

The seekers in this acid trip movement chose nature to be the backdrop for taking their trips on LSD. A lot of young people were doing this drug for fun and pleasure, but I had made my mind up that I was going to give this religious experience thing a chance. The following Sunday morning I was on my way with these Brotherhood people to the mountains of Palm Springs California. We headed out early that Sunday morning to seek what they called a Holy trip. Upon arriving we parked our vehicles and unloaded our gear and then hiked up to a spot called Tahquitz Falls.

I had a sleeping bag in one hand, fresh fruit in the other and I so looked forward to what was in store for me. The journey began at 3:00 a.m. on a Sunday morning, and the hike was about three miles up a very rocky mountain. They chose to start hiking early so we could catch the sunrise at about 6:00 a.m. I had never been hiking before or done any type of camping out. My father never took me anywhere, come to think about it. After arriving at our destination, we laid our sleeping bags on the ground and ate some of our fruit, and then we prepared ourselves mentally for what would turn out to be a life changing experience. There was someone in the group that referred to himself as a guide, who instructed us to take this capsule of Sandoz, a pharmaceutical acid, and then lay down on our sleeping bags. What the hell was I thinking?

Approximately 30 minutes later I started to feel some strange things happening to my mind and body. Our guide began reading to us from the Psychedelic Prayer book which was an off shoot of a book called *The Tibetan Book of the Dead.* Its teachings were taken from monks in the Middle East who had meditated their way to a place they called Nirvana. The Buddha described Nirvana as the perfect state of mind that is free from craving, anger and other afflictive states. It is also the "end of the world," there is no identity left and no boundaries for the mind. The subject is at peace with the world, has compassion for all and gives up obsessions and fixations. The first words that came out of our guide's mouth were, "Flow into this mystery of mysteries, through this gate of all wonder, nameless, timeless, speed of light." As soon as he finished the first sentence, I was on a cosmic jet flying through the universe in a time capsule!

I was now on an out-of-body mind experience that took me to places that I cannot begin to describe with the English language. I began to notice I was breathing in unison with the mountains around me and nature had become a living organism. The countless stars were so big and bright and as the sun rose it was a never-seen-before sight that thrilled me beyond belief. I looked deep into that gigantic ball of fire with no fear of anything. Through the next several hours I listened to frogs croak like bass trombones, I heard the birds sing heavenly songs--it was all so unbelievable. I felt like I could kiss the sky forever. It was joyous, it was sensational, and it was out of this world!!

Before I knew it I felt like a voyager in the deep beyond. It was far out man, totally groovy. I had never really looked at a sunrise before, or at least paid full attention to it. The sheer beauty and magnificence of this ball of energy seemed to radiate a majesty that was picture perfect. The sky was made up of so many colors of blue and the mountain tops glistened like they were adorned with diamonds and pearls. Then I heard the voice of our guide saying that God created this universe perfect. He told us that it was up to us to become one with all creation and explained to us that the universe was made of electrical energy, and we needed to flow with it.

He spoke to us about a death that needed to take place in our lives. Our ego must die so we could fully appreciate God's universe. I needed to kill my fleshly desires and live for God. I needed to forget about the world of materialism and focus on the God of nature.

I felt myself starting to surrender to the feelings I was experiencing under this drug, my heart's doors opened to the truth being revealed. I then rose to my feet and, as I walked along the way, I saw a small stream flowing with crystal clear water. I enjoyed its tranquility and the way it flowed so gracefully. Whenever I would witness a stoppage of the water by rocks, debris or something else, I would feel a blockage in my spirit.

The world was becoming a reflection of the inner me and the way I looked at things. When I felt that beautiful peaceful feeling inside, the world appeared beautiful and peaceful, too.  When I allowed some negative thought to enter my thinking, the world became distorted and ugly.

My mind was being journeyed through with a fine-toothed comb and I didn't like a lot of what I saw inside my inner being.  About six hours had passed and I was just gazing into the vastness of all my eyes could see when I heard our guide's voice summon us to come together for further instructions.  He shared with us that many had traveled these roads of their inner minds.  He told us about many great prophets of the past and their infinite wisdom they had learned from becoming one with nature and that all paths lead to just one Universal God.  He then gave us some truths to be aware of on our journey back home.

> #1 "Turn on" that meant to smoke marijuana as a sacrament daily, and have a religious experience on LSD every Sunday.
> #2 "Tune in" to be aware of what we learned while under the influence of LSD,
> #3 "Drop out" to become disconnected with society

and all its worldly morays.

Later that evening, we marched down that mountain with new goals in mind.....I felt a new calm within myself and believed I was ready to begin a brand new life.  When I got home, my newfound friends and I would faithfully smoke pot every day, and Sundays go back to the mountains for another LSD trip.  My music changed from the rock n' roll of the Rolling Stones, to Ravi Shankar and his Middle Eastern sitar music.  My food changed from burgers and fries to salads and fruit.  I abstained from sex and became like a monk living in a monastery.

My life has always been a reflection of my addictive personality, so when I do something, I go all the way. My violence ceased, and my attitude made my altitude soar high like an eagle. I enjoyed this new lifestyle for about six months, but the newness wore off quickly--life sure has a lot of dead end streets. People started cutting the drugs with other chemicals and our trips started becoming ugly. I saw people's behavior starting to resort back to the old days. So here I go again looking for love in all the wrong places.

# CHAPTER 3

## GO DIRECTLY TO JAIL FOOL

Later that year, I heard about a big movement going on in San Francisco called the Hippies. So once again, I journeyed on to find a higher level of understanding of life taking a good friend with me named Freddie. We headed on up to San Francisco, California to the Haight Ashbury District. It was one long street with a park at the end of it called Golden Gate Park; it was famous for all the free concerts by big name bands. These bands represented all the LSD, peyote, mescaline, and pot-smoking people across America. This neighborhood was the home of the Grateful Dead, Jefferson Airplane, Country Joe and the Fish, Janice Joplin, Jimi Hendrix and so many others. Freddie was always hooking up with people in the mix, so when we arrived in town we went over to the Grateful Dead's home.

 A man named Pig Pen from the band opened the door and invited us in and offered us a shoe box full of big rolled marijuana cigarettes to smoke.

There were thousands of long-haired hippies who lived and squatted on this big main street in downtown San Francisco.

**Being perfectly normal....on LSD**

Everyone was so nice and they all shared not only their drugs, but their women, too; I felt right at home right away. I picked up a newspaper called the Free Press that was distributed to all the Hippies with the front page reading, "Mayor of San Francisco stages war against 500,000 Hippies." The front page also had the headline, "500,000 Hippies stage war against the Mayor." I loved the philosophy and was ready to put stakes into the ground and call this place home. The hippies prided themselves in being free from the capitalistic, materialistic society we lived in. They wore bell-bottom pants, tie-dye shirts, and put flowers in their hair. It was such a cool sight to see multitudes of young people all gathered up and down the street shouting "peace and love!" It was great. I loved it, and I wanted in on the action. Everyone was sharing their marijuana and giving the sign of peace to one another.

I started growing my hair and participating in what Hippies do: get high, listen to music, and make love. The Hippies came up with a saying "do your thing." So I got busy doing *my thing*. I partied 'till the wheels fell off. I saw a whole city of people that appeared to be just like me, they were all looking for love and acceptance. I declared myself to now be a full blown hippie--smoking pot, hashish, peyote, and dropping LSD.

I was sleeping everywhere and anywhere commune-style. I thought life should be just one big slumber party. I was living a life full of complete selfish indulgence.

After a month or so in San Francisco, I headed home to Southern California with the intentions of spreading the Hippie movement. I got involved with selling kilos of Marijuana to support my new lifestyle. During that time, law enforcement looked down upon marijuana like it was heroin or some other dangerous drug. In Anaheim, they were even stricter because it was home to Walt Disney and the famous Disneyland flagship project. It is then that I realized, I was making some okay money, but I wanted to get more involved in large quantities of dope trafficking. I started making trips to Tijuana, Mexico and meeting up with drug lords. I made a few runs across the border and started making good money, but the biggest problem I faced was that I was my best customer

One night in downtown Anaheim, I got loaded out of my mind and was picked up by the Anaheim Police for being under the influence. I was taken to the Anaheim Police station and booked. After hours of interrogation by the detectives they sent me to my jail cell where I met another inmate who seemed like a real cool dude. He was tattooed up and seemed to be my type of people. We talked about life and what we were all about.

He asked if I would be interested in meeting with him when we got out to set up a drug deal. In those days even the drug dealers and users had a code of ethics we lived by, anyone who decided to tell on someone was looking for serious retribution. Most people who looked like this guy were definitely not the type you would ever imagine being a snitch.

When I was released a few days later, we set up our appointment, and I told him to meet me at one of my favorite places called the Bean Hut in downtown Anaheim. I was only interested in selling large quantities of dope so I just brought a sample of the marijuana to give him a taste of the top quality dope I had. We met and said our hellos to one another, had some small talk and then got down to business. As I handed him the dope to sample, he handed me some money. I explained to him that this was just an opportunity for him to try it out before buying some, but he seemed insistent on giving me the money so I figured why not. I took the money and said "give me a call if you're interested in doing business." I made a big mistake that night and didn't realize that I was being set up by the Anaheim Police!

The police didn't come to arrest me for about ninety days--I guess they were waiting on me to do some more drug deals. When I got arrested I was still thinking like a Hippie with thoughts of just getting high. I had sold the snitch about one ounce of marijuana. The maximum sentence for sales at that time was five years in state prison; I couldn't believe that it was such a serious crime for ten lousy dollars of dope.

The attorney the court appointed for me said the best deal they could give me was one year in the county jail. Now what's a young teenage boy like me going to be doing locked up in jail? I took the deal, because I was guilty and caught red-handed...I didn't know what my future was going to be like but I knew it would be different. I left the party scene, and traded it for a cell block full of older men with very violent backgrounds.

My first night as a long-haired hippie in jail was scary as hell. I noticed right away that the inmates were running the cell blocks and it was all about only the strong surviving in the jailhouse. I had a juice card of some sorts for being a Chicano and knowing some of the OG's in the cell block. I had an old friend of mine who got me moved to his cell block so he could hook me up (a hook up is extra food and protection). It only took me about a week in jail to realize I didn't like the place.

It was about the second week in jail when I witnessed what appeared to be a very feminine looking young kid thrown into our cell block. With no hesitation a group of inmates tossed this kid in a cell and began to rape him repeatedly!

He was crying and screaming and shouting out that he wanted to kill himself, so the men raping him obliged him and gave him a razor blade. He slit both his wrists right there in the midst of all of us...and that was just the beginning of my next year in jail.

**When I was known as King Cobra**

Fortunately, I was shipped out to what they called the Honor Farm in El Toro, California. It was a real farm with pigs, chickens and lots of vegetation. There were two big bunk houses on the property. One was for what they called "winos," those who were dealing with alcohol related problems.

The other bunk house was full of drug addicts of all sorts and there were approximately 150 men in each bunk house. The guy that snitched me off had also turned informant on about another 30 inmates, so I was locked up with a whole bunch of my pothead friends from the streets.

While incarcerated, I went to some bible studies, AA meetings, and tried a few other things to change my way of

* * *

thinking. There was only one little piece of hope in my life at that time, an old high school friend who had a crush on me. Her name was Karen and she heard that I was locked up in jail and had real concern for me. I don't know why I never gave her the time of day, but now I needed

a friend. My mom, of course, was there for me as usual. Karen wrote me regularly and visited me often during my stay at the Orange County Honor Farm. She was a beautiful Jewish blonde-haired, blue-eyed woman. We bonded through all of our jail house letters, the things you can write when you have nothing but time to do so. I must say I fell in love with the beautiful heart she had and I felt that God in some way sent her to me.

I was busy doing what farmers do while I was locked up. We woke up early in the morning and headed out to our assignments. My first job was picking weeds in the strawberry fields. Once again my leadership skills came into play and I got moved to the poultry ranch, then the nursery, and then the top job on the farm. I became the head irrigator, taking care of about 100 acres of vegetation. I was definitely one of those people who rose to the top quickly. I knew I had potential but just couldn't harness it for good. I met this Samoan fellow in jail who taught me martial arts and I began exercising daily and became a pretty good fighter. I became one of the top handball players and seemed to get along well with others. Now feeling all around very good about myself and getting encouragement from Karen, I felt I would make good upon my release. The day of my departure had come and, sure enough, Karen was patiently waiting for me outside the gates.

# CHAPTER 4

# KAREN, KARATE AND GERONIMO

Karen picked me up at the Honor Farm, and we headed right out to a motel. We spent the entire evening in the motel room talking about the future. I couldn't understand why God sent me such a wonderful woman. I always waited for everything good in my life to go sour--it seemed like she was the perfect person for me. I didn't love her in the same way I loved Annie, but she was so gentle, kind and trustworthy. Karen was a hardworking lady with a very good job so she didn't need me, but I sure did need her.

**Me and my first wife, Karen**

We found ourselves a little apartment and moved into it right away. I enjoyed Karen's love that she showed me in every way. I became even more aware of how beautiful she was inside and out; however, the Bible says the eyes of man are never satisfied or full. Now I knew I had the best lady, but I just wanted more out of life and I started getting the single life itch again and needed my space. I believe success is much harder to handle than failure. When you begin to prosper in your life, it comes with responsibilities and concern for others. Being a failure only requires a real bad attitude, and a bad attitude is easy to acquire, and easy to keep.

My mindset was always looking for the next adventure in life like a kid at Disneyland that was riding the Matterhorn, but thinking about the Monorail ride.

Then along came my cousin Jerry, he gave me a call one day. The last time I heard about him he was a Jehovah's Witness preacher. He said he was now taking up martial arts and wanted me to join up with him. It was early in 1970 *(Rev. Jim Jones leads hundreds of people from the U.S to establish a Utopian Marxist commune in the jungle named Jonestown)* when I headed down to his Karate and Jui Jitsu studio to begin my training.

I just knew I needed something different in my life. I couldn't handle trying to be a homebody one more day; I had to tell my beautiful lady Karen I needed some excitement. After all, I was only 20 years old and had my share of life's disappointments and heartaches.

It was now time for me to go another path, so I entered into a hardcore physical training regimen at my cousin's martial arts studio. The head Sensei (Japanese title used to refer to a teacher) was a man named Tom Crites. His assistant was my cousin and friend Jerry Piddington. It was such a good feeling getting out on the mats and training hard. Jerry was a natural fighter from the get-go and I had some skills but it took a lot of hard work for me to excel in Karate

*"Jerry Piddington was described in an article by his fellow karateka as one crazy dude, an animal, and a crazy animal that you needed a chair and a whip to fight. A lifelong rebel who purportedly won one match by flustering his opponent with a kiss"*

After one month of Karate training, I entered my first fighting tournament--just a local tournament where I got to test my skills against others. My first match had my adrenaline at an all-time high, I faced off my first opponent and this is where my hard training paid off. I won a 2$^{nd}$ place trophy and walked away with my head held high, now drug-free and loving this new season of my life. I had done well and felt a sense of accomplishment for all the work I put in. After my first taste of victory, I got addicted to fighting and entered in every tournament I could. There I went again with a new trip and a new high in my life.

Karate was at its heights in popularity when I got involved. Bruce Lee was at the top of the martial arts world. Jerry started training under another Grand Master named Mike Stone, who was the light heavyweight champion of the world and also famous for dating Elvis Presley's wife Priscilla. Jerry took me under his wing and worked me harder than all of his other students. As usual, I went all the way and I trained and trained hardcore for my future in

Karate tournaments. I started traveling up and down the state of California fighting in one tournament after another.

One day, I showed up late for a tournament and was not allowed to fight in the beginners division anymore. Jerry said, "I want you to fight in the Brown belt division with the very experienced fighters." I told him "You gotta be kidding me Sensei, they will kill me." I felt that I was not able to fight at their skill level with the short amount of time I had been training. Reluctantly, I ended up doing what my Sensei Jerry told me and fought guys who had been fighting for years. I quickly found out fighting more skilled fighters will make you a better fighter and make you take it much more seriously. The Bible says, "iron sharpens iron, so does a brother sharpen the countenance of another." To my surprise, I ended up in the finals in the brown belt division and was on my way to the top.

From that day on, I was fighting with the big boys and enjoying every minute of it. I won the California Capital Championships and a lot of other tournaments as I worked my way up to becoming a Black Belt. I traveled the country making a name for myself in the martial arts world, along with getting a real sense of satisfaction in my life. At one time, I was one of the top twenty fighters in the lightweight division across the USA. During a six-hour workout, I was very surprised when Sensei Jerry awarded me my black belt and I became a loyal and dedicated friend and teacher, representing our new American style Karate.

With life going so well, I was unhappy to find out that my girl friend Karen became pregnant (just one year into our relationship). That was the last thing I wanted to happen to her. In those oldie-but-goodie days, it was a disgrace to see a girl pregnant who wasn't married, and not even engaged.

I wasn't ready for that type of responsibility, so her family sent her to New York with relatives to hide out and have our baby. I told Karen to name the baby Geronimo if it turned out to be a boy, because Geronimo was one of my favorite Indian heroes. I was so into my Martial Arts world that it didn't seem realistic for me to have a kid, settle down, and support my own family. I was very involved with a team of famous fighters and looked at Karate as my career and livelihood until I was old and grey.

A few months later, I was invited by Cousin Jerry, who was now the head black belt instructor, to open up Karate franchises on the east coast with our own style being taught. This was a great opportunity for me to do what I loved and to make a living at something that people admired. I told Karen I would be heading to Baltimore, Maryland while she was in New York having our child and preparing for what lay ahead.

**The eyes say it all**

The next thing you know I am leaving my home in Anaheim to a city that would prove to be a major test of my character. When we arrived in Baltimore, I was amazed at what a big and crazy city it was. There were so many people and so many hotels and apartments stacked one on top of another. It was a loud city, with people up at all hours of the night doing their business in public view. My new residence was a basement apartment right in the center of downtown Baltimore, about a block away from the famous John Hopkins University Hospital. The homicide rate in Baltimore is nearly seven times the national rate, six times the rate of New York City, and three times the rate of Los Angeles. Here I was coming from sweet and lovely rural Orange County…it was definitely a culture shock to a man who thought he had seen it all. There were about twenty of us black belts that moved into our new training headquarters. It was definitely a ghetto-fabulous place we were living in but I made the best out of it.

We borrowed the sale's techniques from the Arthur Murray dance studios and we planned to open Karate franchises everywhere. This was so different to us from the way our Karate schools were run back in California with training and dedication being of the utmost importance. In the old school days, you would train people hard and teach them fighting moves that really worked on the rough streets and not just for show. In this new franchise setup it was all about selling them colored belt programs and just making it something fun for the whole family to enjoy.

It was all about making money and building more schools to accommodate people that had no real dedication to the Martial Arts as a way of life.

Our head instructor in Baltimore was heavyweight kick boxing champ of the world, Joe Lewis. We became very successful in our business endeavors and prospered rapidly. Before I knew it we had opened three Karate studios in three different cities throughout the state of Maryland. Time was flying by and I forgot all about my girlfriend being pregnant in New York and the fact that I was really going to be a father soon. We were so focused on our work and enjoying the fruit of our labor that we became consumed with making money and enjoying ourselves.

We had been working hard for a good while, so we thought it would be fun to see the town and get a taste of the nightlife. In California we had beer bars, pool tables and maybe a juke box to get our parties going. On the East coast they had nightclubs everywhere and they're open every single night of the week--I mean dancing, partying, get down nightclubs that people got all dressed up for.

This place we were headed to was called Club Villa, in a suburb of Baltimore named Parkville. Our bodies were clean and drug-free so it wasn't going to take much booze to get our party on. We got wasted on whisky and started doing a Karate dance in the middle of the dance floor, throwing kicks, and punches all over the place. We were showing off all of our Karate skills that we had learned over the last year of training. We were pretty cocky and arrogant fellows thinking we could just walk in for the first time at this club and just take it over. We thought we were Batman and Robin, an unstoppable team who didn't care what anyone had to say.

The bouncers came out to put an end to our foolishness as we laughed our heads off and disrupted everything going on in the club. Jerry and I went back-to-back, ready for combat, but to our surprise the owners and the bouncers asked us if we would like to do security for them. I looked at Jerry as he gave me the heads up and we said, "Sure, we would love a job here." We decided that on weekends we would take the job so that we could practice some of our fighting moves on real people to find out which punches and kicks worked best on real live human beings.

We started working at the club every Friday and Saturday nights running the doors and making sure there was no drama happening inside or outside the establishment. I was mainly a beer drinker on the west coast, but part of our pay was a complimentary all-you-can drink pass. It's cold and windy a good part of the time on the east coast, so I started hitting up a lot of tequila and whisky to keep warm. Going to work at the club was like getting paid to run the party and enjoy all the delicacies that go along with the job. It was a pleasant sight to my eyes watching all these beautifully decked-out chicks come walking in. We made the choice of who was let in, or who to kick out of this establishment....so; we slowly sought to take control of the place.

It was a two-story nightclub with live bands and about a 1,000 people attending nightly. I got to meet lots of ladies, and fell in love over and over again as I was doing this kick-back job and actually getting paid for it. It was sin city for me, and I took full advantage of the position I was given to keep the peace.

There was just one problem, I was the biggest troublemaker in the place; add that with some firewater (*A common name among Native Americans for a strong alcoholic beverage*) *and* it just meant things would get worse. Under the influence of all the hard liquor I was consuming trouble was a common occurrence. I would wear white shoes when I was bouncing and try to paint them red with the blood of people who I felt needed a ass whipping! I was on my way to another wreck and it seemed like I didn't even give a rip about the consequences that would befall me.

One night while one of my Karate students named Bunkie band was playing I hit up on his girlfriend and asked her out and she was all for it. Once again, I didn't care about anyone but myself. I gave her the nickname, "Bunkie" in memory of the guy I stole her from, he was in her fourth year at a prestigious university in Baltimore and was close to graduating. I threw a song and dance routine that knocked her off her feet and right into my wicked arms. They had a hot pants contest at the club one night and she won hands down, I mean, she was a beautiful woman. She was my new love and I couldn't wait to take her to see California and introduce this hot thing to all of my friends; this would surely impress them all.

Now, Karen never even crossed my mind as I got mesmerized by this young beautiful, intelligent girl. My Bunkie made the mistake of telling me she had $4,000 in the bank and was ready for me to show her around California. At this point she didn't care about finishing school, or anything that her family or friends counseled her on. She thought I was the man that walked on water, and that I was going to part the Red Sea for her. Next thing you know we were on an airplane to beautiful downtown Anaheim, the happiest place on earth.

Even though I always knew I had a strong effect on people, I was aware it wasn't always for the best. We spent about a month in California, and I could tell that she had had enough of me and my evil ways. She was ready to head back home into the wonderful arms of her family and back to her good old boy Bunkie the 1st. I went back to Baltimore and continued with my Karate training, looking for something new to entertain me as I wrestled with my failure to settle down and make something good out of my life.

News came that my child was soon to be born at the Queens hospital in the Bronx, I actually felt a little bit guilty and ashamed that I was partying while my girlfriend was away having our baby. I headed up to New York a few weeks later and to my surprise I heard my son had been delivered and was a healthy baby boy. I went to the

Riverdale section of the Bronx to Karen's aunt's home to get a visit with Karen and my son.

Seeing Karen for the first time in so long was quite strange and as I looked at her I felt guilty living as a tramp with a variety of women in my life. She was looking so beautiful and I wanted so much to see our baby boy Geronimo and kiss him on the lips and tell him how much I loved him. I really did love him.

When I asked Karen where our child was, she delivered some real bad news. She thought it was best that she give Geronimo up for adoption so he could have two parents that would nurture him and spend time raising him. He was now living with a wonderful family who had wanted a baby boy and who had promised to take great care of him. I told Karen I want to see my baby boy now, and as I grew angry I shouted in her face that it wasn't fair and I wanted to see my baby.

She said the hospital counselors were handling the adoption and only they could approve of me visiting my son. Karen went on to tell me that the new parents had already changed his name to Scott, Scott?

I headed down to the Queens Hospital and made an appointment with the people in charge of adoptions, convincing them that I was going to marry Karen and be a good father, spending the rest of my life raising him up right. The hospital was a Jewish hospital in Queens, New York and the hospital staff was mainly concerned that he be brought up Jewish. It didn't matter to me what he was brought up, so I gladly agreed and assured them they were making the right decision by allowing me to take him home. They brought Geronimo back to the hospital where Karen and I were jumping for joy, looking forward to a beautiful future for the three of us. The family that had Geronimo wanted to keep him badly, but not at the expense of having his real father miss out on the opportunity to become a wonderful father to his son.

I told Karen to take our son back to California and I would meet her there in a few weeks. She did as I instructed and moved home to be with her parents. Karen had a wonderful mom and dad who loved her very much. She informed them that I was ready to take the step of marriage. I left for California and as soon as I arrived at Karen's parents' home they were ready to take us to get married. A few days later we were on our way to Las Vegas with her parents, we were hitched up in one of those chapels that are meant for people just like Karen and me.

I was trying to please Karen. I was trying to please her parents, I was trying to please Geronimo, but it still wasn't enough for me to settle down for good. No matter how hard I tried to be that great father and husband, my thinking was too jacked up and I wasn't able to keep a commitment. I still had nothing but making money and partying on my mind.

So, we moved out of the little apartment that we had rented, and I decided to become a Disneyland dad *(also known as a weekend dad)* to my son. I would visit all the time and continued to be intimate with my wife, but I knew there was no turning back for me. I was done with my scene on the East Coast, so I bought a Harley Davidson motorcycle and started frequenting the biker bars around town. It was easy for me to gravitate towards trouble and that's just what I did. Getting deeply involved in the biker world and spending most of my time hanging with the fellows and causing lots of drama everywhere I rode. I wasn't done with my rollercoaster ride to hell yet. I wanted one more for the road, pedal to the metal, full throttle ahead.

I waited until Geronimo was about three years old to give him my last farewell. Karen was visiting at her mother's house when I pulled up on my chopper to see my son Geronimo for what I thought would be the last time. Karen walked him to the front yard so I could say some departing words. Since I felt like a leaf in the wind that was never gonna settle down and I was definitely a rolling stone, I believed the best thing I could do for my son and wife was to leave them. I did care for them after all.

I told Karen that I was sorry for the life I had dragged her through and for not being the father that I should have been, but I said I didn't know how to help myself. I told her to divorce me and get it over with, and she did. I was self-destructing and I didn't want anyone to get hurt in the explosion that would become my life. I told Geronimo that I needed to get in the wind and hopefully I would see him again someday. The goodbye would be the last time I saw my son for the majority of his youth. I started up my bike and rode off into the sunset...of Hell.

**Me at 23 with my first born (Geronimo) and his first beer**

# CHAPTER 5

# DR. "PHIL-GOOD"

I stayed in Anaheim and opened up a Karate studio of my own to stay in shape, keep my mind occupied and try not to get myself into too much trouble. I was always stirring up trouble so I named my Karate Dojo "American Jumpin Jack Flash Karate." knowing it would upset most of the other masters who tried to keep their karate studios named after ancient training methods and famous instructors from the Orient.

*"Jumping Jack Flash: Jagger said in a 1995 interview with Rolling Stone that the song arose out of all the acid of Satanic Majesties. It's about having a hard time and getting out. Just a metaphor for getting out of all the acid things."*

I was training hard by day, partying hard by nights, getting on my Harley and hitting the biker bars. I decided to get involved part time smuggling drugs from Mexico to California once again.

I had family in Sinaloa, Mexico that I would visit often, so I made some special visits to some of the marijuana farmers to do a big operation from Mazatlan to La Paz, and then to southern California. I was now involved in the biker world and we had a biker code that forbid any kind of opiates or drugs because it would alter our riding skills and could cause injury to our fellow riders. My goals were making some good money and acquire a few toys along the way, without getting busted and going to jail.

The violence in my life was just a bunch of good old bar room fights that made for some good fun and for the most part no one was hurt badly. I rented a singles luxury apartment in one of the most exclusive spots in town with lots of amenities like tennis courts, pool tables, and a big swimming pool with a Jacuzzi. There were so many frills that made it appear I was living in paradise.

I entertained people at my house every night of the week to keep my busy mind occupied. I felt like I had the drug thing in my life harnessed down and I was now getting involved with people who ran companies and were into legit pursuits in their lives. I was pretty proud of what I had accomplished and hit this comfort mode that made me feel that I was doing everything right.

At that time one of my brothers was working as a psych tech at a local hospital in the city of Orange, California and selling drugs to some of the doctors on staff. He told me about a psychiatrist who worked there named Dr. Marilyn who was interested in meeting me. For some unknown reason Dr. Marilyn was interested in doing some cocaine with me. I told my brother to hook me up and give her my number so we could set up a time to hang out and maybe do a little cocaine together. I had an impressive lay out in my home, surround sound, a big television, and lots of expensive gadgets throughout the entire quarters. It appeared I had it together financially, was in top physical shape and by own accounts looking sharp.

Dr. Marilyn gave me a buzz and we set up a blind date at my little bungalow of love. The minute I answered the door and escorted her in, I fell in love with her looks, style, wit, and knowing she wanted to get high on cocaine. Cocaine was always looked on as an aphrodisiac that would make intimacy a 100 times better than on any natural high.

It was the first time I found myself hanging out with a professional woman, unlike all the biker mamas and rehab women that I had grown accustomed to running with on those days. I had always liked the kind of women that been around the block more than once. I always wanted action with my ladies, not games, phoniness, or pretending, just plain old let's get down and dirty. So here I am now, in my little palace, sitting face-to-face with a lady who is educated and makes big money helping people get their lives back on track again, a stone cold fox.

To be completely honest, I was feeling a little intimidated by this beautiful woman who had an aura and confidence about her that was a threat to my ego. She was cool and calm and straight to the point, let's do some cocaine together. I was use to being the one on top, me Tarzan you Jane, I would run the show, and this time she was pulling my strings. It was like a lamb being led to the slaughter. I loved every minute of her looking at me with those big brown longing eyes of hers. I pulled out my best Bolivian coke and put out some lines on my silver platter, rolled up my hundred dollar bill, as I handed it to her without hesitation she leaned her head down and snorted up a couple of big ones. She got down and dirty real quick.

Cocaine is a rush, a deep flood, a fast trip to the moon with no stops in between. I fell into narcotic love with that woman and we partied till the sun came up in the morning. When she left the next morning I had no idea if I would ever see her again. She was very business-like and didn't talk like a girl who wanted to fall in love and get married some day. It was a new experience in my life and I was cherishing the thought that one time with her was enough for me to live on for a while. She called me again a week or so later and suggested that we go out on a date and do something interesting and fun. I had a good lawyer friend of mine who I respected and always had a good time with. He had invited me over to his house for a political function. He was deeply entrenched within the Democratic Party in Orange County and was a highly educated fellow who did his graduate studies at the University of Southern California. He had the coolest house and grade "A" parties where people from every walk of life attended.

This one night in particular he had Jane Fonda as a special guest and gave me an invitation so I thought Dr. Marilyn would mix well with these people. We headed on over to the party and enjoyed a wonderful night of mixing it up with some of Orange County's beautiful people. The night went smoothly, and later we left and hopped into her new Range Rover and drove out to her home in Laguna Beach. Dr. Marilyn had a beach house overlooking the Pacific Ocean, it was beautiful. I felt like I was being entertained by a princess and she was making all my dreams come true. As she opened the door and invited me in I started getting these funny fuzzy feelings in my gut....could she keep me there all night? I was getting kidnapped and I wasn't about to try and escape from her clutches as I was a willing participant in this crime.

The waves were crashing in the back ground as I spent another extremely blessed night at my favorite doctor's house. We seemed to be getting along well and enjoyed getting high together from time to time with no expectations other than to enjoy the moment and let destiny run its course. Then one night she asked me a strange question about doing a certain drug she had heard of. The drug was Heroin. She asked if I could score some and if we could do it just one time together. I had heard that the devil came in many disguises, but never as a beautiful doctor. I said to myself, this just can't be true.

I saw how Heroin had ruined people's lives over the years and always said to myself at a very young age I would never try it, not even once. I witnessed men and women rob their own families of all their dearest possessions just to get a fix. What I knew about Heroin was that it was one of the most addictive drugs available to humankind. Everyone I knew that did Heroin told me it was like having a gorilla on your back that you could not get rid of on your own. I knew that I could never, ever put a needle into my arm full of Heroin or any other drug for that matter. Some of my close girl friends sold their bodies, and did other things that I won't mention just to get well from the side effects of Heroin. So upon hearing this request from a successful doctor that seemed so well adjusted, it really threw me for a loop. I finally got weak and said "the hell with it"; I am going to do it one time, get it over with and never do it again.

The Bible says the eyes of mankind are never satisfied or full. The forbidden fruit grows everywhere and anywhere to show us what we are made of; I had a lot riding on this baby. If I would have known how to pray I would have done so because this was an all or nothing proposition for me. A few days later I got on the phone with one of my connections and told him to bring me over a couple balloons of Heroin. He was shocked with disbelief that I was putting in an order of what he knew I thought was the drug for losers. I called Dr. Marilyn and said, "honey, I am ready to give it a shot," (excuse the pun) but that was one of the most difficult calls I ever made.

She showed up the following Friday night after work ready and willing to take this next step in our somewhat unique relationship. I was a nervous wreck as I contemplated what would transpire in just a short time after her entering my domain. I gave her a hug and kiss and was ready for act 2 in this complicated drama. I was in my mid 20s and I had been doing drugs for a good twelve years off and on. I knew good and well that Heroin wasn't any lightweight trip to be messing with. This little voice in my mind kept telling me to put an end to this madness that I was about to enter. The voice was telling me I was being set up by Lucifer himself and that I would come to regret my decision. Unfortunately, those thoughts vanished when I looked into Dr. Marilyn's eyes and felt she could do no wrong. It was all business for her, but I was so enamored by her that it was like a Sampson and Delilah love story.

I handed Marilyn the Heroin very reluctantly as my hands shook and trembled. My body was feeling sensations like never before and this foreplay was a big part of all drug addicts' game. When you get ready to smoke pot, you roll them, or season them before smoking. When you do methamphetamine you either smoke, shoot or roll your glass pipe and enjoy the time just preparing for your high. Heroin addicts had their own dirty dance before they injected the lethal drug of death into their veins.

I watched Dr. Marilyn pull out a leather bag full of medical goodie's that were part of her everyday practice. I knew doctor's give shot's all the time, but this was a first for me and I was like a little child going to the dentist for the first time. This coconut *(brown on the outside, white in the inside)* from Anaheim was deathly afraid of needles and didn't really want to play with Heroin. Her first weapon out of her bag of mass destruction was a new syringe all wrapped in plastic, then a large looking piece of stretch elastic, a bottle of alcohol and a small spoon with some stick matches. She started to fondle the syringe in a very seductive manner, and then poured some alcohol on a clean white cloth and applied it to the inner vein on the inside of my arm. She poured the contents of one of the balloons full of Heroin into the small spoon with a few drops of water. She would then strike one of the matches and place it under the spoon and started cooking the ingredients until it came to a boil. Then she put a small piece of cotton in the spoon and dipped the tip of the syringe into the spoon and drew up the Heroin into the body of the syringe. Then with her index finger she snapped the syringe until all the bubbles disappeared.

Next it was time to wrap the piece of elastic around my arm so my veins would protrude out and be ready to receive my medicine. My heart was pounding out of my chest as my mind wondered what it would be like to have this narcotic flowing directly into my heart. Marilyn looked at me with a look like I had never seen before from any woman I had ever met. Her eyes aflame and her smile was gigantic as she moved towards me with a loaded needle in her hand. She then grabbed my arm pulled it towards her took aim and watched me turn my head away from my body as she thrust the needle into my vein. I never even had a chance to count to one; I was on a trip to a place that I had never been before. The Heroin had rushed directly to my heart and I was entering this world of the damned!

From the very first moment I felt this drug I knew I was sold. It was like peace on earth, good will towards men. It can't be explain in words, I had opened the door to a living hell that most humans would never even consider to enter. For the next month this would be a journey that Dr. Marilyn and I would travel to every weekend then every other day, then every day. Our interests in seeing beautiful sunsets or feeling the ocean breeze or have intimate times were over. We didn't care about anyone or anything except putting that needle into our veins and enjoying the temporary relief from all of life's cares and worries. Of course all good things must come to an end eventually.

● ● ●

**Me and my biker buddy slingshot**

Dr. Marilyn was screwing up at work and was put on temporary probation, and since I have never had the joy of seeing her face again. I spent every penny I had on this new drug. I sold all of my valuable toys, even my Harley. My days of partying and enjoying the good life were now over. I started spending all of my time sticking that nasty needle into my veins. Heroin was like having a sin baby born into your life. At first the sin baby is small and you can hide it, but after a while the sin baby grows up and becomes a gorilla on your back. Your full time job becomes chasing that first high you had when you began injecting the deadly poison.

It didn't take me long before I had sold everything I had, done things that I never believed I would have ever do. I was a hope-to-die dope fiend that went looking for money to supply my needs anywhere I could get it. When you become an addict you start to live by faith. This means from the minute you wake up it's not about if you're able to get the money, it's about what means are you going to use to get it. I was now not getting high anymore, but trying to keep from getting sick. My insides felt like a thousand fingernails clawing down on a thousand chalk boards driving me absolutely insane!

During my travels to score dope from people I would occasionally get busted for being under the influence. I would get 90 days in the county jail, and as soon as I got out I went directly to the connection's house. I didn't care about women, didn't care about anybody but my miserable self and started stealing all I could from my loved ones. I finally got so desperate I decided to go rob my own drug connections and borrowed my brothers' sawed off shotgun to intimidate them and make them turn over all of their supplies.

I went from having a beautiful luxury apartment with all the toys to living in a dope fiend garage sharing the same dirty needle and dope with about 5 other losers like myself. My mother was always there for me, and so was the rest of my family even though I didn't deserve anyone loving or even caring about me. My mother had a group of relatives on her side of the family who became Jehovah's Witnesses. Most of them had treated me very well during all my youngster days but a lot of them had moved to Oregon to establish a Kingdom Hall for their worship. One of my uncles offered to let me stay at his home if I would go by the rules and promise to not get loaded on any drugs. The rule's were I had to go to five of their religious meetings a week and pass out their little magazines you see them holding on street corners. I didn't have any other open doors and there were lots of people trying to chase me down, so I went for it.

My mom flew me up to southern Oregon to a town called Weimer; about 16 miles from the city call Rogue River. Upon arrival at my Uncle Ray's home it was snowing and I guess to anyone else it looked beautiful, but to me it was just a white hell and nothing more. For the next two week's I had the worst nightmares and I wanted to kill myself, not caring if I ever saw another human being again. Through the love and patience of my Uncle Ray and my Aunt Teresa I was starting to get a few rays of hope coming back into my life. I started to care about my life again wanting to get a clean start and a brand new life. I started attending weekly meetings, reading the Bible and enjoying the company of this wonderful religious group of people who gave me another chance. The only problem I had in Oregon is that I brought myself with me!

I was doing well at the Bible Studies, and having a great time as I joined the Jehovah's witnesses at their weekly parties. I noticed that a few people were drinking beer as they ate that their food so I asked my uncle if that was allowed in their religion. He told me that you can do all things if it is done in moderation, I asked him what moderation meant and he said, "It means drink what you think you can handle." Well I felt like I could handle a case of beer and I was already looking for some loopholes in their church. The Bible says, "Bad associations ruin good habits" and life will show you that birds of a feather flock together. It didn't take long for me to find the bad boys and girls in the congregation.

One night at one of our church meeting's I caught the eye of this beautiful young lady named Teresa, so I asked my uncle and aunt who she was. . They let me know that she was the prize of the whole church and that her father who had been one of the leaders had recently passed away. It was very clear to me that all the church leaders had adopted her as their own, so the probability of me hooking up with her didn't look real promising. I talked to my uncle about the chances of me taking her out on a date sometime in the future. He said no one is allowed to date a lady in the church until they are a baptized believer and understand all the basic tenets of their faith. So, I got baptized.

I found out Teresa had an older brother named John, who with one look I could tell would be one of my followers. I was on a mission to get this girl and with my addictive personality it wasn't about if I could get her but what technique I would utilize to make it happen. She was gorgeous and I heard she was the virgin waiting on the perfect man to serve God with. That's just what a loser like me needed in his life, a wonderful Christian lady who was looking for a knight on a white horse. I got close to her brother and figured I could earn some brownie points. He helped me accomplish the necessary things for baptism and taught me the politics of the people in the congregation and who to butter up.

I was allowed to talk to Teresa in group settings only and the conversations had to be strictly about the bible. She wanted to date me and I was head over heels in love with her so the combination was just right. I still didn't have a clue what real love was but I knew she could help me find happiness through her faith in God. The time had come for all the Jehovah's Witnesses in Oregon to attend their meeting in Medford. I got baptized in Medford Oregon during the summer of 1976 and that same night I was allowed to date the love of my life for the very first time.

Teresa was the closest thing to my red-haired Annie that I had ever found. In life I have found that it is so much easier to pull somebody down than to pull somebody up. Teresa was a beautiful woman, inside and out who loved God. I was a confused, angry, bitter person who hated life but wanted so badly to love and to be loved.

Our first date was to a drive-in movie theatre with her brother John and his wife. Teresa didn't stand a chance with me as I sat next to her in the back seat of her brother's car. I had no self control and I had proven to her that I was not a knight on a white horse, but a man who still had to destroy a lot of demons in his life. That night when I took her home she was feeling very confused about our date and tried to comfort me and give me hope for the future still.

The next morning she woke up ill, and was on bed rest for a few days. Her brother told me that whenever she would get sick like that it meant she was making big decisions in her spiritual walk with God. I found out later that week she had decided to dump me. I was right about what a wonderful young lady she was. She knew better than wasting her time with a fool like me. I could see the handwriting on the wall once again and knew it was time to leave town.

# CHAPTER 6

## THAT'S AMORE

I had spent close to a year in Oregon and physically I was feeling real good. As for my love life and my personal choice's, I was still screwed up. I headed back to Orange County with the hopes of having a new life without drugs and alcohol. Before I left Oregon I had to have one last hurrah so I started trouble everywhere I could and even talked some foolish girl into giving me a ride back home to Anaheim. Ever since I got burnt by my red headed Annie I was getting even with women on every front of my life. I did all the religious stuff and it changed some of my actions for a while but it never did change my heart.

I dumped the wonderful girl that drove me back to Southern California the second I got home. I was leaving a trail of spiritual blood everywhere I put my foot on the ground. She was another great person that God sent into my life to give me a hand and I treated her like trash. I can never remember a year go by without some wonderful human being trying to help me with my struggles. Jesus was always hunting me down and I didn't even realize how blind I was.

When I pulled into town I hooked up with an old friend of mine named John, he gave me a place to stay and said he was interested in helping me out. I had cut my long hair, gained weight while in Oregon and I was actually looking pretty good. While trying to reconnect with my buddy John, he mentioned he was hungry and wanted to go out and get something to eat, so he took me to a new restaurant in town.

The establishment was called *De Falco's Italian restaurant.* De Falco's was a family own restaurant ran by a mom and pop along with their three daughters. It was a family of Sicilians who were originally from Chicago and had recently opened up this joint right in the middle of my old neighborhood. I learned that the head of the family was Papa John *(no connection to the franchise "Papa John's"),* and his wife was called Mama Rosa, two very nice and friendly people. They were terrific people who treated their customers with lots of love and I could personally tell they were sincere people. The family's three daughters were Joanne, Sandra and Suzanne, all who were very beautiful but the middle one is the one that caught my eye. I didn't care for the Italian food as much as I did for the one daughter whose name was Sandra.

I decided to ask her out on a date, and for some reason she said yes. I am aware that I am not that good looking, but in spite of that, I was able to score with women quite often. I told her to meet me at a bar called the Tiki Club where I was going be playing in a pool tournament. *(While I am writing this book, my wife is looking over my shoulder and correcting me about our first date. I'm sticking to my story!)*

*Sandra's version is that she told me that she was engaged and I had no chance of a date with her. She states that I pursued her over and over again. Sandra said she finally gave in because she felt sorry for me. but then again that's her story...*

Now, let's get back to my version of the story... Anyway, she went to the bar to meet me one night while I was in a pool tournament. There I was, playing pool in a real sleazy bar, and guess who comes walking in the door, all decked out like a Goddess? I told her I was busy playing pool, and maybe we could postpone our night out for some other time. She got so upset that she stormed out of that place spewing out venom like a scorned woman. I knew she was upset, but a few hours later I had a call from her telling me I was a rotten no good this and that. I knew I had her in the palm of my hand now because she wouldn't have gotten that angry if I didn't hit a weak spot in her heart. .

About a week later she called and invited me to go out to some dance place she loved to hang out at and enter dance contests. I wasn't into dancing, but I did want to take the opportunity to get to know her and spend some time seeing what she was all about. I had gotten back to hanging out with my biker friends causing nothing but trouble, drinking it up, fighting it up, and doing a little dope *(marihuana)*. The weekend came and she picked me up in her car, and we went out to this disco club called Mugsy Malone's near Disneyland.

When I got there I saw all these people doing this dirty dancing type of stuff and acting like they were Patrick Swayze or John Travolta. I told Sandra I didn't dance so she went on the dance floor without me and she looked like she was having the time of her life. I on the other hand was at the bar doing tequila shot's and before you knew it, I was standing on the bar taking my shirt off doing what I did best, causing a scene. The firewater was just too much for this crazy Mexican Indian and needless to say she wasn't very happy when she saw security kicking me out of that place. I know she felt sorry for this poor puppy dog, and for some reason thought she could fix me.

We made another attempt a few nights later and went to a club where her **"fiancé"** was playing music with his band. I think that's the night she told him to put things on hold and that's when I knew I really had my foot in her front door. We had a good time that night and I didn't cause any drama. Later that week, she said some of her friends from college were coming over to play volleyball and just chill in the back yard, would I come over.

I asked if I could bring some of my friends with me to enjoy the day. She responded with an apprehensive yes. Little did she know what was in store for her and friends? I showed up at her party with a half dozen biker buddies, sleeping bags strapped to their handle bars with a mindset to party all weekend long. She asked "why the sleeping bags?" and I told her we were spending the weekend and we proceeded to get our party on. In a nice way we took over her party and sweetly made sure all of her friends left the party. That poor girl had no idea that she was in for the ride of her life with no slowing down for danger signs or anything else.

Sandra reminded me of the Italian actress, Sophia Loren, she was full of class and beauty. We got along great and I moved in to stay with her and her son Christopher. I was doing just a little booze and dope *(marihuana)*, thinking to myself that I had my life under control. I was trying real hard to make this lady my last stop and tried to work out a long lasting relationship with her. I knew she was a one-of-a -kind woman and I didn't want to blow this one like I had so many others. However, I just couldn't get my act together and thought I could do anything to anybody and get away with it. I had a very suicidal attitude about life and I was stuck on stupid, trying to make sense of all my past affairs and how I could change things. It wasn't long before I was doing Heroin again. I was getting all messed up and my mind and body were deteriorating fast.

I was back to where I began, blaming God, blaming my dad, and blaming Annie for all the pain I was experiencing in my sick life. The Bible tells the story about Adam and Eve in the Garden of Eden and how they were given everything, but God said just stay away from the forbidden fruit. I just couldn't seem to keep away from that forbidden fruit in my life.

**Myself in dead center with my crew, the Boyz**

# CHAPTER 7

## JESUS SET ME FREE

I really did love Sandra and I wanted to do right by her, but I just couldn't stop getting loaded every single day and night of the week. I can remember on Sunday mornings watching church services on television and pondering the thought of God in my life wondering if I could fit in with all those good people. I knew I was a male whore, liar, and a deceiving sinner without a chance of forgiveness. I needed money real bad so my brother Bert gave me a chance to make some easy cash if I promised not to blow it. My brother was what I would call a good honest dope dealer who treated people right. . He believed that he would die one day with someone shooting at me, miss, and end up shooting him. Bert was always stopping me from killing myself from some violent action I was always taking. The bigger a guy was, the more I wanted to smash him to the ground. I got to the point when some one wanted to fight at a bar or some other hang out, I would put my cigarette out in their eye to get things going. I was definitely a suicidal man with major problems with drugs and violence.

Here was the deal….I was to transport a large amount of cocaine to a certain destination, just drop it off and nothing else, it seemed easy enough. So here I go again taking a the risk of possibly getting busted for a big crime and losing all possibility of a life with Sandra,   I took the job and once again I was on the highway to hell from Ojai, California to Orange County with a kilo of uncut Peruvian flake in my trunk. While I was driving to the delivery spot, my sick mind thought about burning the people, I could hear the cocaine calling my name and asking me to indulge for just a little bit. This was a very expensive shipment and I was dealing with the Cartel, a group you just don't mess with.

I knew I would have people out to kill me if I dared to not bring all of the stash to the assigned area. I just didn't care about what anybody might do to me and the fear of having someone want to kill me almost sounded like music to my ears. I was definitely suicidal in the way I had been living my life for a long time now. I didn't care about anybody but me and all my selfish desires my body was craving.

For all the pain and tragedy that I had been through, it still wasn't enough to make me slow down and process the thoughts I was having and realizing that this could end my life. I reasoned in my mind that I would just take a little of their dope and deliver the rest after I cut it with some lactose to make it appear untouched. What was I thinking? Like they wouldn't know what I had done, like they were new to this game?

I drove directly to Sandra's house to prepare for my next dope fiend move of cheating someone out of their livelihood. Sandra saw me come into the house carrying something that appeared suspicious to her and questioned me about it in kind of a stern way. I told her to stand back and let me do my thing. I reiterated, "I don't want to hear anything from you, leave me alone." At first I thought of just pinching a small portion to satisfy my needs for about a week but I changed my mind and said to my sick self I want it all.

This would turn out to be one of the worst decisions I had ever made in my life up to that moment. I had turned into a greed monster that had no respect for anyone including myself. Inside of my brain I could hear that voice that spoke to me every time I was about to do something down and dirty, asking me "What about Sandra?"

Misery loves company so I invited my brother Billy and a few other friends of mine to come over and party and here I go again leading even my own family down the path to hell. We were up for two weeks straight snorting, shooting cocaine, and going out of our freaking minds. I was getting paranoid and seeing shadows everywhere I looked and I needed something to bring me down. I made a call and traded a dealer I knew a load of coke for some heroin knowing that I had to come down from horrible speed trip. What was about to happen next would put the nail in my coffin and prove just how far I had gone downhill in my life. I knew deep down inside of my sick soul that I was heading for a gigantic train wreck but I just had no idea how this night would change my whole life forever.

Sandra, who had locked herself in the bedroom with her son during this time, got sick with stomach problems, most likely from the stress I was putting her through. Finally she decided to drive herself to the hospital and asked if I could watch her son. I wasn't able to watch myself, let alone a child. I didn't know a thing about kids and I didn't care about them either. I remember making statements in my life like "any man, woman, or child, who messes with me is asking for trouble." This night would prove that saying to be true.

While Sandra was at the hospital my mind started filling up with hateful thoughts towards so many people. Never in my sickest dreams did I ever think I would do what was about to happen Sandra's son came into the room I was in and I physically hit this young child for no reason whatsoever, and then went on to hurt others just for the fun of it. I had literally gone out of my mind and I was in a state of insanity.

Next thing I knew, the Anaheim Police were shouting over their loud speakers for me to come out of the house with my hands up. I ran to the bathroom and started flushing down all the dope I could before they found me. The police officers then chased me down and I was thrown to the floor with a cold barrel of a pistol touching the temple of my head. The police officer said, "Make a move Aguilar and I will kill you." My nightmare was finally coming to an end. I was thrown in the police car and taken to the Anaheim city jail. There was a sense of relief when they had handcuffed me and led me away for what I knew would be a long time.

Sandra came to the jail later the next day to question me about my actions and the charges that they had on me. When she asked me if it was all true, I looked directly into her face with tombstone eyes, and said, "I can't believe you would even think that I would do any of those things". I was in total denial of what I had done. I needed to be locked away for a long time and I deserved everything I had coming to me. I was actually happy that I was being put away for the safety of others and myself.

I spent the first couple of weeks in jail kicking heroin and finally understanding that it is the nastiest, dirtiest, meanest drug in the world. I was in a living hell and beginning to wake up and meet the real me who had been trying to hide under the disguise of drugs. In the county jail the courts gave me a lawyer named Lloyd Freeburg. I instructed him not to fight any charges and to get me sent away as quick as possible. I knew in my heart that I was a no good heartless human being who needed help so very badly and didn't know where to go for this kind of help. Drug charges were dropped but I was convicted of assault, with a sentence of 1 to 10 years in state prison. I got shipped out to Chino State Prison for evaluation and then would be transferred to the best place for me to do my time.

I finally got sober enough to deal with the issues in my life. I said I loved my family, but in reality I only loved myself and was starting to feel so much guilt and shame about how I hurt everyone I said I loved. I knew Sandra loved me, and I believed I loved her--she meant the world to me, but I knew I didn't deserve her.

Chino State Prison was a good place to get educated in "the school of hard knocks" and get the cool knocked out of you. When I got to Chino it was full of people who thought the same way as I did as far as being a gangster and not taking any disrespect from anyone. I had met my match as far as life is concerned and quickly found out there is a difference between stupid and crazy. I discovered that I was definitely stupid, but not crazy. .

I met people who didn't care if they ever got out of prison and was willing to spend their lives there for something they believed in. It was a huge wake up call for this young fellow and I learned real fast how to do my time locked up in those prison cells.

I hooked up with my brown brothers, and was ready to put in work for my people because I wanted to be able to walk out of prison one day, not shipped out in a plastic bag. No longer was my life about surfers, hippies, or bikers. It was all about *La Raza* and all of our people sticking together to back one another up as we tried to do our time without violence. I lived in a cell in a part of the prison named Cypress Hall where we were temporarily housed until they determined which prison we would do our time. While at

Chino State Prison I heard someone shout out chapel call for all inmates interested in hearing about Jesus, this was possible by volunteers from the streets who would come and share music and a message with the inmate's. They held chapel in a little room down the hall from our cell block so

**Me and Sandra at the visiting room, Vacaville State Prison**

I decided I was going to check it out and maybe get a glimpse of one of the women the inmates said came and sang occasionally about Jesus. I will never forget that Sunday morning as I walked down the hall and entered a tiny little room with about twenty-five other inmates patiently waiting for the visiting Christians to share their songs and message. I was always into Jesus whenever I was locked up, but mainly to ask him for help in getting me out of another jam.

A portly man named Glen Morrison stood up front that day to share a message about the forgiveness and love of God. He shared a simple story about the prodigal son and how God accepted his son back even when he went out and did drugs and hurt people. I raised my hand and asked the preacher if God could forgive me of all my horrible sins. He said Jesus love's you right where you are at. He said:
*"If you ask Jesus into your heart, he will completely forgive you of all your sins." And I said to myself: "This deal sounds too good to be true."*

Preacher Glenn next asked all of us inmates the question of the century--at least as far as I was concerned. He said:
*"If you would like to ask Jesus to come into your heart, please stand up and identify yourself so everyone will know that you are openly confessing that you want Jesus to take over your life."*

Immediately a battle began to rage within my soul. It told me that there was no way I was going to surrender to this Jesus, that I couldn't see, especially in front of a group of men that I could possibly be spending years with. I didn't want the word getting out that I was weak and needed Jesus to be my crutch. Pride is a *mutha,* and I fought back and forth within my self on what decision I was going to be making that day. I thought I would be giving so much up if

I gave my life to Jesus… but suddenly realized that I didn't have a *life*, and no one really cared about me. I was a 130lb and deathly ill with Hepatitis B. I knew that I better at least give this Jesus a chance. Finally through some inner power, which I now know was the Holy Spirit of God, I stood to my feet and said:

**"Yes! I want to surrender to Jesus."**

At that moment I knew a transformation was beginning inside of me, and that my life would be completely different in ways that I would never imagine! I knew I had nowhere to go but up. After I prayed the preacher hugged me. I went back to my cell and with a Bible the preacher gave me in hand, I started reading it like I was looking for hidden treasure. I wanted to know more about this heavenly father of mine and this Jesus he sent to die on a cross for me.

The days went by and every time the chapel doors were open I was there, hungry to hear a message that would make my time in prison worthwhile. I had now become one of those "born again Christians" on my way to heaven, full of joy and thanksgiving in the midst of the chaotic world I was sentenced to. I had no idea of what lied ahead of me in prison or life. About one month later I loaded up on the infamous Grey Goose bus *(the bus used to transport inmates)* going north to Tracy prison.

My next stop on this unique tour overlooking a beautiful bay was San Quentin prison. I was the perfect age and considered a southern Mexican who should be locked up there and do all of my sentence. They offered me a program if I was willing to go to do group therapy at Vacaville prison which has a medical facility attached to it that tried to help prisoners that had stinking thinking like me. Vacaville prison would be my final stop for my term of one-to-ten years in State prison unless I messed up again.

When I left San Quentin *(California's only death row for male inmates, the largest in the United States, is located at the prison)* and arrived at Vacaville prison, a volunteer chaplain named Herb Sokol introduced himself to me as he had heard word in the prison grapevine that I was a new believer, hungry for the things of God. He was an ex-con who served the Lord while in prison and he came into the prison every day to share the love of Jesus with all of us men. Herb became my mentor in my Christian walk. He taught Bible studies on a regular basis and did church services every Sunday for all the inmates.

I ended up so excited about this Jesus thing that I was telling everybody about what Jesus could do for them. I used to get everyone hooked on drugs and now I wanted them hooked on Jesus, and so began a little ministry of my own with some of the other men who wanted to give God a chance. .

God doesn't change our personality--he changes our heart and starts to soften you so you can be molded into something wonderful to be used as a tool in the hand of almighty God. My new little Gods gang crew was a little rough around the edges because we were still young Christians. However, we did our best to be a blessing to our new heavenly Father and to those we came into contact with. . We understood prison politics enough to be ready to throw down at any time if necessary, not looking for trouble but not running from it either. It took us quite a while to become the peace loving, turn-your-cheek-type of Christians that I knew God wanted us to become. I got taught a valuable lesson one day as I was walking down the mainline with my bandana over my eyes trying to look like a bad ass. One of the main officers asked me "where are you going Aguilar"? I told him it was none of his business! He got his big hand and wrapped it around my neck and I felt at least 6 inches off the ground and against the wall. It was definitely God telling me that I better recognize that all authority comes from God.

I had finally found a peace that passeth all understanding and I knew I definitely didn't deserve all this joy after the things I had done. Religion is all about trying to be good enough for God, but I learned from the Bible that we can't be good enough. It was all about how good Jesus is. I knew I had burnt many people for drugs and I had a lot of enemies that wanted to take my life, but I kept my eyes focused on the Lord in prison.

I had written my ex-girlfriend Sandra, many times during my first months of incarceration but she wrote me back a "Dear Phil" letter and told me to move on and stay out of her life. I sure couldn't blame her, even though my letters were filled with remorse and pleading for forgiveness. I really did love Sandra.

# CHAPTER 8

## SAINT SANDRA

By this time, all my so-called friends had now forsaken me, and all I had left was my wonderful mom, brothers and sister. I read in the Bible about a man named Abraham who put his son on an altar of sacrifice for God. God had instructed Abraham to sacrifice his son in order to test Abraham's faith. Similar, in my new relationship with Jesus I heard my heavenly father speak to me about my ex-girlfriend Sandra. I, too, was instructed by God to put Sandra on the altar and completely trust him for my future and happiness. I realized now I loved her so much, but I didn't feel worthy of having her back in my life after all the horrible things I did to her and her family. I was done with the lying and deceiving, so by faith I spoke to God and told Him that I was spiritually giving Sandra to Him and believing he knew what was best for my life and hers.

For once in my life I wanted Sandra to be happy, and my concern for her to have a rich and full life was more important than all of my needs and desires. It seems like it was just yesterday that I dedicated her to the Lord and was leaving the results completely up to God. I had a release inside my spirit and another gigantic weight had been lifted off my weak shoulders and given over to the strongest man in the universe. The Lord allowed me to write one last letter to Sandra, definitely not the kind I would have written before. Before, I would have attempted to get her back into my life by smooth talking her or by giving her some guilt trip.

When Sandra first wrote me, she said that she couldn't understand why God would forgive me and bless my life while she was left hurting and deeply depressed. The Bible says, "There is none righteous, no not one," and that "all have sinned and fallen short of the glory of God." The final letter I sent to Sandra was thirty-four pages long. I wrote what I thought would be my farewell message. I told her that I just wanted her to be happy and that she needed to give her life to Jesus. I remember dropping the letter in the prison mail box with a peace in my heart about finally doing what was right in God's eyes. The Bible tells us the first commandment is to love God with all of our heart, mind and soul, and to love our neighbor as ourselves. Before I asked Jesus into my heart, I didn't love God and I sure didn't love my neighbors at all. Now, I felt that peace of God that surpasses all understanding and now I was focused and going for the gold. My only concern in life was what my Father in Heaven wanted, everything else was secondary.

As God as my witness, on that very same day the letter was put in the prison mail box, I received a letter from Sandra telling me she had given her life to Jesus! You tell me, *is there a Lord or what?* Sandra said she would wait as long as it took for my release date to arrive. What a wonderful God, and what a wonderful Saint Sandra. So much hope was pumped into my veins that time just flew by. I knew I didn't deserve any of this, I should be sent to hell with no "get out of jail free card" for hurting Sandra and her family as badly as I did. God was giving me another chance.

Sandra and her son Christopher packed up their bags right away and headed north to find a place near the prison, and she was ready to fight the good fight with me. Her whole family and my whole family thought she was out of her ever-loving mind to follow me to prison just because I said I was into Jesus now. Everyone has heard someone tell the story of how they found Jesus in jail or some other type of tale like that. Sandra was stepping out in faith and she put her whole heart and soul into making our lives something beautiful.

Sandra found a cool set of apartments to move into, which was situated near the Prison. Several other wives of inmates who wanted to be close to their men lived in the same apartment complex. They decided to call their living quarters "Victory Village" because they were all learning to be over comers, waiting for their mates to return to them. They were all in love with Jesus, and in spite of realizing that their husbands were locked up in prison, they remained free in their spirit. My friend and mentor, Pastor Herb, conducted Bible studies for the prisoners' wives along with the studies he gave at prison chapel seven days a week.

At Vacaville State Prison, fellow inmates thought it was weird when I called my cell "my bedroom" and were intrigued when they witnessed me thanking God for all of my meals. They couldn't figure out why I was enjoying my time in prison when so many were downtrodden and depressed. I spent a lot of my time reading Bible stories about a man named Paul who wrote a lot of the books in the New Testament. It was during Paul's incarceration that God gave him the words to write—words for Christians to learn by.

I loved being locked up for many reasons, for example, being able to spend a massive amount of time studying God's Word, and having a captive audience to share Jesus with. The daily title of my message to my fellow inmate's was "how to be happy in prison". It may sound a little crazy but I praise the lord for prison, because that's where I found happiness and was given a brand new start on life. Prison is where I found wisdom *(my new love)*, and fell in love with her and prison is where I divorced my other girlfriend, foolishness.

While incarcerated I was assigned by Pastor Herb to be the head greeter at the chapel entrance for church on Sunday mornings. I took it as a great honor that I could make my inmate friends feel welcome and show them another way of life. My visiting time with Sandra was like having a honeymoon every weekend, as we shared all the neat things we were learning and the excitement of one day getting married. We were not allowed contact visits with our ladies, but whenever the guards turned their head we would sneak in a quick hug or kiss. Pastor Herb asked Sandra and me to spend some of our visiting time counseling other inmates and their wives. It was very difficult for us to give up our intimate times together as it was the best part of the week; however, it gave us the opportunity to learn all about the "gift of inconvenience." My time locked up would prove to be the key I needed to prepare myself for my release and my future life's work for God. My prison time flew by because I was so thankful to God for allowing me another shot. It was all a free gift from God above that no man could purchase at any store on earth.

Pastor Herb told me that if I wanted to get married I would need to submit myself to an extensive marriage counseling program. He informed us that he had never married a couple before because during counseling with various couples, he had not encountered a couple that he felt was ready to make a lifelong commitment. He assigned me scriptures on commitment, love, communication, and he trained me on how to love Sandra the same way Jesus loves us. I had made so many bad decisions in my life and I was ripe for good advice and accountability. Pastor Herb was no joke; he was one big bad dude you just didn't want to lie to. I chose to ask my Pastor to let me know when he thought I was ready for that big step of marriage. Pastor Herb worked with me for seven months, teaching and preaching about every aspect of being committed to one woman, for one lifetime. Pastor Herb finally told me he believed I was to ready to move on to the next chapter in my life and get married. That night I asked Sandra to marry me and she said "yes." The wedding was set for August 13 1977.

Getting married in prison is quite an ordeal and there are a lot of details to be followed in order to have permission to make a party out of it. The guards running the prison treated me great and said I could have the wedding in the prison visiting room. As far as the guest list was concerned, it was easy for us to invite my prison friends since they would not have much of a drive. On the other hand, neither of our families planned on attending. They thought we were crazy. I understood why our parents thought that our marriage would be a big mistake, and I could not blame them for thinking that way.

I mean who marries some guy in prison, especially the man who destroyed your life at one point--now they were becoming "one?" As it turned out, both of us had one representative from our families, one of Sandra's cousins, and my sister Liz. Our guest list included a big group of my Christian inmate friends along with good friends from all the clicks in prison.

On that warm August day, my heart leapt as I saw my Sandra walk into the visiting prison room. My saint was wearing a beautiful white summer dress with a "Jesus First" pin she proudly wore on her tiny spaghetti strap. I was so excited about getting married that I asked Jesus not to return until the honeymoon was over. The vows my pastor shared with us that day were hardcore and all about a lifetime commitment to each other with no divorce allowed. We also made another commitment that day, to making our lives 100% about sacrificing all comforts and pleasures for the sake of the ministry of reconciliation. It was a beautiful wedding, and my one and only sister, Elizabeth, gave her life to Jesus that day. The honeymoon happened 30 days later when we received our first trailer visit. My son Matthew John Aguilar was in the making thank you Jesus!!!!

**Sandra and I, getting married at Vacaville State Prison**

# CHAPTER 9

## FAMILY MAN

When sentenced to prison, I was sentenced under the Indeterminate Sentencing Law. This meant that upon entering prison, the inmate was subjected to the discretion of the Adult Authority, who would decide at what point the prisoner should be released prior to the expiration of the person's maximum sentence. Therefore, each year I would go before the parole board and they would determine my fate. After being in prison for less than two years, the parole board unanimously voted to **Set me Free!!!!!**

I was thankful to God for the experience that Sandra and I traveled through via the prison ministry, and my release day was similar to the parting of the Red Sea if you can imagine that. First of all, I was paroled back to Orange County—I was going home. Secondly, I walked out of prison happy to see my brother, Mel, who drove from Southern California to pick up my new family. My brother Mel treated us like royalty. Thirdly, Pastor Herb set me up to speak at a local church in Vacaville and to give my testimony about how God had changed my life. It was so cool being out with my wife and son (Christopher), serving Jesus and strategizing on the life ahead for us all. After my first weekend of release in Northern California we headed back to Orange County.

We moved in to my in-laws apartment for a new start and the beginning of showing my wife and my in-laws that I wasn't just another "I met Jesus in jail" story. I was so appreciative that they gave me the opportunity to prove myself to them, so I immediately went out and found work as a maintenance man in the local neighborhood. My brother, Bert, hooked me up with a fifty-dollar car--I was ready to do something good in this world. After working at my first job as a maintenance man, I enrolled in a training school to repair homes. I then applied and received a job as a street maintenance man for the city of Anaheim. Here I was back in Anaheim ready to rebuild my life, get my own place and assume responsibility for taking care of my family.

We rented a cool little apartment and started furnishing it with new inexpensive items that would meet our needs. During the consummation of our marriage at the "Vacaville Hilton," my wife had become pregnant with our first child. *(Vacaville Hilton was also known as the trailer visit yard for all inmates and their wives.)* I thought a lot about Geronimo as I prepared to be a parent again and bonded with my stepson, Christopher.

I was also on the hunt for a good church to worship the Lord with my family. I had only one friend who was a Christian, Greg Lyles, who invited me to his Baptist Church. I rolled up that first Sunday morning at a place called Central Baptist Church in Anaheim. The place was filled with people wearing suits and looking very conservative but quite friendly. It was quite a contrast to the prison dress code of Levis and blue shirts that inmates wore to chapel. I had to believe this is where God must want me to be because it all transpired so naturally.

The music was way new to me and to be honest, it was quite boring; with organ music and people singing what seemed to be very old hymns. I figured this is what Christ meant when he said there would be suffering in the Church.

When the church service was over I looked for information on when they were meeting again so I could get involved with others and have some accountability in my walk with God. The church brochure said that services were held on Sundays and Wednesdays with no other meetings in between. I was used to doing church every single day of the week in prison because we had nothing but time on our hands. I knew I needed church everyday to make it through the week, and two times a week just wouldn't work for me. The weeks went by and I faithfully went to church. I could see myself prospering financially, but in my spirit I was lacking the daily study of God's word.

I made an appointment to speak with the pastor, Dr. Bob Wells. I told him that I had this great hunger for the Word of God. He asked me if I thought I was *called* to preach. I didn't have a clue what he meant by that. Pastor Wells explained that "called to preach" means you feel that God has a call on your life to serve him full time. I told him that didn't know about all that; I just felt I needed the Bible seven days a week. He told me I that should enroll at a place called Pacific Coast Baptist Bible College in San Dimas, California, located about an hour away from Anaheim. It scared me because I was enjoying my job, the new apartment we had, and I didn't feel I was ready to give up the good life I was living. I was just getting my first credit cards and enjoying legal money for a change.

I shook off what Pastor Wells told me to do and continued to work hard at my new job. It was so cool working for the city of Anaheim, especially in light of the fact that I used to try and mess it up. Now I wanted to clean it up for Jesus.

Near the end of my wife's pregnancy I had an emergency call from home, left work and headed home to the shock of seeing my apartment on fire. When I arrived I saw my wife and Christopher standing outside and I felt so good to know that they were out of harm's way. Christopher had started a fire in the closet. A few hours later, I went in my apartment and saw all my belongings burnt to ashes. Everything that I had worked so hard for in my first year out was now a heap of ashes. I felt God was telling me to get busy about God's business--quit my job, enroll in Bible College, and prepare for *what God had for me*. I gave my employer's notice that I was quitting my job, one I had worked so hard to get. It was another very difficult decision in my life and I was learning that life has many opportunities; it's up to us to be courageous and step out in faith.

Each time we choose a certain path; we encounter new obstacles that we have to contend with, in order to be a fighter of our faith. My brother, Mel, had an old trailer in a city called Perris, about 45 minutes from Anaheim. He was willing to rent it to me for fifty dollars a month so I couldn't pass up that great opportunity. The trailer had no air or heating system other than a wood stove to warm the place up. It didn't matter, I was happy to have a roof over my family's head and to be in God's will. I packed up what belongings we had left in my old station wagon and headed out to Perris, California to my little trailer in the desert.

Later that same year (1978), Sandra gave birth to our first son. We named him Matthew John Aguilar and called him MJ for short. I was now a proud new parent of this wonderful baby boy who I loved so very much. I had messed up with Geronimo and now I was trying to be a good father to MJ and Christopher while at the same time following the Lord. I knew that God had sent me to Perris for a special reason—I just needed to figure out what it was. In the Bible God sent many men to the backside of the desert for spiritual training in order to sharpen their swords and get them ready for battle. We moved into the battle right away, and I was on a hunt for another good church.

**Me and my baby boy, Matthew John**

It didn't take long before I found Temple Baptist Church of Perris, California. The pastor's name was Reverend John Lyle, a loving fire-and-brimstone church leader that everyone loved. God was leading me, and I knew I needed some leadership in my life knowing that it takes a good follower to become a good leader. I introduced myself to Pastor Lyle my first Sunday at church and I told him that I felt called into the ministry in some capacity. I told him that I planned to enroll in this school called Pacific Coast Baptist Bible College. I volunteered to help at the church in any way he saw fit.

Pastor Lyle was a wonderful man who took the time to mentor me in my life as I searched for God's perfect will for me. Without hesitation he put me in charge of about 90 children, ages ten to twelve years old. My job was to teach them the Bible and counsel them about receiving Jesus, and loving and obeying their parents. My wife and I began to teach Sunday school to these children the very next week. Next Pastor Lyle enlisted me to drive the church bus and pick up kids on Sundays mornings and on Saturdays visit their parents if they had any. Pastor Lyle helped me find a job, paid my tuition for Bible College, and had the church missionary board give my family groceries on a weekly basis.

Pacific Coast Baptist Bible College was an affiliate school of Dr. Jerry Farwell's Liberty University in Lynchburg, Virginia, an ultra conservative fundamental Bible school. So Here I am now in Perris, California living in a trailer, chopping wood to keep my family warm, going to school full-time, working, and teaching little children at church. My cup was overflowing, my life was being blessed, and I could tell that everything happening in my life was destined to be.

# CHAPTER 10

# "PHIL" THE BAPTIST

I was learning that it is the tough times that make us stronger, and we are to not be weary in well doing. I wanted to make my mark on this world and leave a legacy for my children and their children. Life was going great and I knew I was in God's perfect will for my life as I served under my new Pastor and enjoyed the fruits of my labor. My wife got pregnant again, and I was excited about our new child that would enter this world and be raised up by us as we followed the Lord.

Shortly after learning about my wife's pregnancy we received some bad news in the form of Sandra's ex-husband wanting to have a custody battle over her son Christopher. We did all we could to keep Christopher but it was a losing battle because I was an ex-con. It was a very difficult trial, especially for my beautiful wife who loved her son so very much. I felt so much guilt and shame, and I knew all this wouldn't have happened if it wasn't for me.

My wife was a soldier for God and triumphantly kept her eyes on Jesus and never wavered with her love for me and her son. We moved ahead with God's plan for our lives with great determination and zeal. God wants us to just live one day at a time and has never promised us a tomorrow. School is always in session on planet earth and I was learning so many priceless lessons that would prove invaluable to me in so many ways.

* * *

It wasn't long before our next child came along, a wonderful boy I named Phillip Aguilar Jr. I now had two children, two jobs, full time school, and full time church work. I was a high school dropout and now here I was a fully fledged Bible College student taking English and Psychology classes, and training to be some type of full time church worker for God. I knew right from the start that God had to be hard-up if he would use someone like me to do his work.

I met many great professors and some really nice fellow students at Baptist College, who I enjoyed so very much. One particular professor was named Dr. Dan Davidson, my Psychology teacher. We hit it off right away, and he informed me that he was a pastor at a church in Anaheim California. It just happened to be located right down the street from my mother's house. What a small world we live in and God connects the dots anytime he chooses. Right after finishing my first semester at Bible College Dr. Davidson offered me a job at his church as an extended day school overseer.

**My life as a Baptist**

The job included a church parsonage to live in and free tuition for my kids at the Christian school on their campus. I left Anaheim the year before believing God had a wonderful plan for my life and now he was bringing me back home to work at Anaheim Baptist church.

I started my next semester at Baptist Bible College and I also enrolled in the International Bible Institute and Seminary, doing direct home study courses so I could work full time at the church. My wife Sandra was happy that we had a beautiful home and money to pay our bills. I started my new job at Anaheim Baptist church as soon as we moved our belongings to Anaheim. What can I say but I was so looking forward to another adventure in my walk with Jesus. I met a school teacher at the church who became one of my best friends. Her name was Holly Palmer and I developed a very good relationship with her that lasted for a long time. She shared how her husband was away from God and requested prayers to bring him back so they could serve the lord together. I can still remember telling Holly that one day I would be her boss, so she better treat me good. Holly was a multitalented person with a long track record in Christ, but was also very teachable.

In the next year-and-a-half, I worked every position possible at Anaheim Baptist Church, seeking exactly the calling God had for me. I was the youth pastor, evangelism director, young adults' teacher, outreach and mission's leader, etc. I finally became one of the co-pastors of the church along with my friend Pastor George Gilmour and my good buddy Doug Dorsey.. I continued with my Theology studies and earned a Bachelor's Degree and then went on to receive my Masters Degree in Bible Theology. I was also determined to one day earn my Doctor of Divinity Degree.

When I first arrived at Anaheim Baptist church it was a small congregation; however, through hard work, it became packed out with people and so many new converts coming to Christ all the time. Pastor Davidson and I had some great times together, and he taught me a lot about counseling and living a holy life. Our denomination was called the Bible Baptist Fellowship and my heroes of the faith were all fire and brimstone devil-chasing preachers. I had a preacher in particular that I was modeling my life after named Dr. Jack Hyles from Hammond, Indiana. He was the pastor of America's largest church in the 80s. I would travel to his yearly pastors' school and take classes on how to reach people in the inner city along with a number of other important issues.

In Bible College one of my professors had a lot to say about birth control and abortion. He taught me that any type of birth control was wrong, and that we should just trust God for how many children he wants to give us. Sure enough Sandra was now pregnant one more time and I was ready to deliver my third child with her. I was being fruitful and multiplying just like the Bible teaches. I was still in prayer for my son Geronimo to come to Jesus and I don't think a day went by when I wasn't lifting him up to the Lord. I kept my wife barefoot and pregnant for a long time and my new arrival was a baby girl we named Trina Joy Aguilar. I was delighting myself in the Lord and he was giving me the desires of my heart. Children are a blessing from the Lord so I knew God loved me and was blessing me to the max. It was now late in the year of nineteen eighty and I was officially ordained as a pastor at Anaheim Baptist Church. I loved working for Dr. Davidson and leading people in the right direction instead of the old trail that leads people to hell.

In prison I would describe myself as an on-fire loving Christian brother who wanted to spread the message of God's wonderful forgiveness. Now after entering Baptist Bible College I had become a lot more militant about my service to God and I was losing my sweet touch of love that I once had for Jesus. My new philosophy was "don't be concerned about what you're for, just know what you're against." I was turning in to a very oddball type of character as I traveled unchartered waters in my Christianity. I had to wear a suit everywhere I went as a Baptist preacher and our bylaws stated we could not go to the beach, movie theatres, or listen to rock music.

The only differences I had with most Baptists were the dress and music standards. I always questioned why the devil should have all the good music. I wanted to start doing music that people loved and enjoyed and that was not 100 years old. I believed that there should be no dress code for church and you should "come as you are" because Jesus always loved people no matter how they dressed or looked. In Bible College they taught me that God cannot use a man that doesn't wear a suit and tie along with many other manmade rules. I was also taught that if you had divorce in your background you couldn't be a Pastor or any other type of leader.

I have always felt that my forehead had an invisible sign on it that read, "all twisted up people come unto me." I seemed to attract the outcasts from every lifestyle possible that were financially ruined and needed lots of help and guidance. I was starting to raise a few eyebrows and bump a few heads at Anaheim Baptist Church when some of the elders told me I was bringing too many people without money. They said that I needed to look for -people who would tithe, give ten percent of their income to the church. I couldn't believe what I was hearing these deacons say to me. The Bible says bring the lame, blind and poor. Here I was a young pastor, surrounded by old time Christians who are judging the very people God sent us to.

God was definitely beginning to lead me in another direction than most of my fellow ministers who considered money to be a priority over people. I knew that I wanted to plant my own church one day and do my best to follow God's words, not mans. One of the biggest no-no's of the day was to not watch Christian television because it had different teachings than our church family. The list went on and on and on about all the do's and don'ts in Baptist life.

The beginning of the end for me as a Baptist preacher came when I turned on Christian television in rebellion to my pastor, Dr. Davidson. The program I watched was called the *Praise the Lord* show. The founders and spokespeople for the Christian network were a man and woman named Paul and Jan Crouch. These were some trippy looking people who had come from the Midwest and brought their country flavor with them. They announced on television that they were having a revival meeting in Hollywood at a night club called Gazzaris. I use to spend time in Hollywood going to the night clubs so I was familiar with all the hot spots around that town. They said a fellow named Arthur Blessit would be preaching what they called a rock 'n roll revival. Arthur was described as a long haired Southern Baptist evangelist who wore t-shirts and Levis. I was now opening the door to a flavor of Christianity that I had seen on television but never experienced in my Baptist circle.

I took my Biker brother Bert with me to hear this man share about Jesus, in a nightclub, of all places. I was a big part of my brother Bert coming to Jesus and now he was studying in Bible College alongside me. Bert was a big fellow who became the first "billboard" for Jesus in the world. He loved to wear shirts that said things like "turn or burn", "its hell without Jesus" and his favorite "Satan Sucks". Bert and I drove up to Hollywood. We actually "snuck" up there, knowing that our Baptist brothers were very much against these other Christians. When we arrived, I was looking like a Mormon at a Snoop Dog concert. The people there were all dressed very casually and they actually looked excited about being there and couldn't wait to hear this Arthur Blessit fellow. They looked nothing like the Baptist crowd I ran with and they didn't act like my friends either.

The meeting started with some great country gospel music and the crowd was fired up, dancing to the music as they waited for Arthur Blessit to ascend the stage. His appearance was everything thing I was being taught not to look like. He was a down- home, simple fellow who began to speak about the love of God and telling others about Jesus. While I was listening to him it was like I was hearing God speak directly to me and my heart became broken again as I felt God touching me like he did back in my prison cell. I was returning to my first love once again and realizing that although I was school smart, I had forgotten all about my love affair with Jesus.

When Arthur was finished preaching we all prayed together and I knew I was being refreshed as I shed tears of joy that hadn't come out in a long, long time. That night was being filmed for live viewing on the *Praise The Lord* show nationwide. Without me realizing it my brother, Bert, who is a huge-looking biker for Jesus, jumped on stage with Arthur so he could give him a hug. While being filmed, Arthur asked my brother Bert who he was and what he was doing there. My brother Bert began to tell him that he was with his brother Phil who is a Baptist Preacher. The cameras turned my way and sure enough I was being shown to the world on national television. Little did I know that back home at my church the worship leaders were watching me on this charismatic Christian Network.

On my way back home I began to ponder all the wonderful words I had heard. A few days later I was taken to the back room by my church elders who wanted an explanation why I was there on Sunset Strip with those people. I defended my actions by sharing with them how God had spoken to my heart while I was there. The leadership at our church was not budging on their stand against those types of Christians. I got myself a good tongue lashing and tried to mellow things out so I would not offend them anymore. I really did love my job and my wife and family had some security while I was employed at Anaheim Baptist church.

Things were going good for the next month or so but I couldn't stop watching the Praise the lord show. I was hooked on hearing all the guest speakers and hearing about lives being changed 24 hours a day. One night on the *Praise the Lord* show they announced a musical concert they would be having at a large amusement park in southern California. The group that was performing in the upcoming concert was called *Andre Crouch and the Disciples*. I knew I shouldn't do it, but I was like an addict who just had to have more Jesus.

Sandra and I drove about an hour-and-a-half to get there and it was all worth it. I rolled up my sleeves and pulled out my tucked in shirt, trying to fit in with this modern group of happy Christians. The Baptist group I hung with said they were happy, but I guess they never notified their face. We took our seats up in the grandstands as I tried to be low profile, like I was breaking the law or something. A few minutes later here comes this black fellow named Andre

Crouch and his group, singing the most beautiful worship music I had ever heard. I saw people lifting up their hands and standing as they sang along to the music. In my Baptist world we were not allowed to lift our hands or to act too emotional during our music time because they said it brought attention to ourselves and that would be prideful. I can still remember the words to the first song he sang:

*'"How can I say thanks for the things he has done for me, things so undeserved to prove his love for me, the voices of a thousand angels could not express my gratitude.".*

I was floating on air and so full of peace in my heart. My hands kept lifting up into the air to praise Jesus and I just lost control and shouted out loud that I was set free inside. When the concert was over Sandra and I drove home pondering all the beautiful feelings we were having. I knew our life was going to go through some big changes again, but I wasn't sure what they would be. The concert was on a Saturday night and on Sunday morning I was ready for a new day at church as I stepped up to the pulpit in my normal manner that Sunday morning.

It was my job at church to welcome everyone and give announcements for the week but I was so full of the night before that I just cut loose and shouted Jesus in the in the loudest voice. I was starting to act like those charismatic Jesus freaks on the *Praise the Lord* show. I was under the influence of the new wine and so very drunk in the spirit.

The Pastoral staff realized it was time for me to move on and do my own kind of ministry and church. I didn't feel ready to be on my own yet, but I knew it was my time! A few weeks later on a Sunday evening I shared with the congregation that God was leading me to start my own church. The congregation gave me a two hundred dollar offering and sent me on my way. The leadership was pretty much glad that I left, and so was I. Dr. Dan Davidson my pastor was a great pastor to me and my family. We just had some different ideas about how to do ministry. My Baptist church days were coming to an end and my Set Free days were just beginning.

# CHAPTER 11

# ISRAEL, HERE WE COME

It was 1982 *(The 54th Academy Awards are hosted by Johnny Carson and Michael Jackson releases "Thriller")* and I was raising three children and had no money, but I had a desire to win the world to Christ. I had a dear family who opened up their home for us to live in and I dug into the Bible and started teaching a group of about ten of us. My brother and sister in Christ, Wayne and Holly Palmer, and a small group of others helped me kick-off Set Free of Anaheim. After my encounter with the street Preacher Arthur Blessit, my spirit was renewed and I was excited about building a new ministry utilizing some different methods for the purpose of healing the sick and lost ones of this world. It was important for me to pick a name for our new church. I was inspired by the Bible verse John 8:32: "You shall know the truth and the truth will set you free."
Shortly after I started Set Free Baptist Church I had other pastors questioning the name on my church cards. The other pastors saw that I was bringing in new music and dress standards that didn't go along with the doctrines of my Baptist brethren. They encouraged me to take the name "Baptist" off all my cards and the new t-shirts I was making. So I changed the name to Set Free Christian Fellowship to try and keep the peace with the haters club. We met in homes, pizza parlors and anywhere else that someone would let us have church. It took us about six months to find a small facility to rent for the 35 plus people who were now attending Set Free Church. I needed to make money to pay the bills, so I used our church facility to start teaching Karate lessons like I did in the past.

One of my first students to enroll was a beautiful lady named Lois Trader, who lived in nearby Villa Park. She walked into to our facility sporting a football jersey with the Bible verse Isaiah: 53 printed on the front of it. Lois informed me that she was a born again Jewish believer in Jesus. Her interest at my place was to learn the martial arts, so she could protect her children from any harm. I received a wonderful education on Jewish people in our first encounter as I could tell she was very pro Israel. She told me her husband worked at Trinity Broadcasting Network as a camera man for Paul and Jan Crouch. It's a small world meeting someone whose mate was employed by the television network program that helped change my life.

She went on about all of her family being born again Christians who were raised up in the Lord at Calvary Chapel church in Costa Mesa by the founder and Pastor Chuck Smith., She said her family all loved the Lord but didn't go to church much anymore due to her husbands work schedule. Lois noticed people walking in and out of our little office space and mentioned that they all seemed poor and needed a place to live. I told her that I accept anyone that God sends my way. Whatever their situation is, I take it from the lord that God wanted me to minister to their needs. Lois was definitely from the high class part of town and I did not think she would fit into the Set free mold of people very well.

Lois recognized that I needed some help with all the people so she volunteered to help me do some office work. Once we started our martial arts training I could tell Lois was a natural athlete and she excelled very rapidly in her skills. We hit it off big time working out together and sharing the love of the Lord as we punched and kicked ourselves away. I remember her being a hard working, wonderful person who was looking for purpose in her life. She had a beautiful daughter and a wonderful mom and dad, and a great husband. Lois and I became so close she ended up leaving her job as a court reporter to work for me. I could only pay her with Jesus bucks at that time but I could tell she found her niche.

My family and I lived in other people's homes and garages for about a year, until we saved up enough money to rent a small house. It was just a matter of days after acquiring our new little home that we filled it with homeless people. From the very beginning of Set Free I had a burden for taking in those in need and give them a place to grow up with a spiritual father. I never had a father's guidance so I wanted to be able to help others along the path of life.

In the Bible there is a story about a couple named Joseph and his wife Mary who needed a place to stay. The Bible said everyone turned them down and said there was no room for them at the inn. Joseph and Mary had to sleep in a barn because people wouldn't make room for them. That night Joseph and Mary gave birth to the savior of the world. Think about having the Lord Jesus Christ being born in your home, my motto has since been, "we don't have room we, make room". Financially we didn't have much, but spiritually our bank account was overflowing while God was supplying all our needs.

Set free Ministry had a very dedicated group to start with and now Lois and her husband, Tim, were the icing on the cake. Lois never let up on telling me how much Christians should love the Jewish people. She taught me a whole lot about God's plan for the Jewish people and I learned that they were the apple of God's eye. Her favorite verse she quoted to me quite often was Genesis 12:3: "Bless the Jew's and you shall be blessed!!! Curse the Jews and you will be cursed." I shared with Lois that my first wife was a beautiful Jewish lady named Karen Bengeldorf. I told her I had a son named Geronimo who I hadn't seen since he was three years old. . She got so very excited and said that Geronimo is Jewish because the Jewishness comes from the mother's blood line. I didn't get all she was trying to tell me at the time but it turned out to be very important stuff.

Tim and Lois had recently come back from a month of living in Israel, hitchhiking the length and breath of it. Their stories about fishing on the Sea of Galilee and floating in the Dead Sea were thrilling to say the least. Lois was a workaholic and a bugaboo when it came to pushing her views, thoughts, and insights about everything. She inspired me so much when she described the nation of Israel and how it was the center of God's plan for the future of the world. I was chomping at the bit to go visit the Holy Land and visit all the places I had read about in the Bible.

Well the day finally arrived about 6 month later. With a little help from my friends, a ticket was purchased for me and my friend Tim (Lois husband). We flew on an airline called Royal Jordanian Airlines that first landed in Amman, Jordan then onto the land of Israel. From the moment we entered the airplane I felt like I was in another world. People were wearing head scarves and smoking some crazy types of tobacco. During the eighties lots American airlines were being hijacked so we decided that we might be safer if we flew on an Arab airliner.

The plane was now ready for takeoff and I was so hungry for what God was going to teach me. We were thirty thousand feet in the air, and heading out ten thousand miles away from home sweet home. The flight took about sixteen hours before we landed in Amman, Jordan. It was a grueling experience for my mind and body and I was so full of jet lag, yet so excited to get out of that plane and head out for adventure. We flagged down a cab, and the next thing you know were going a hundred miles an hour with no seat belts on. What a way to begin our trip on dry land to our hotel that looked a thousand years old and so very primitive.

Every square foot of ground we were treading on was marched on before by the 12 tribes from the nations of Israel in the Bible. Entering my hotel bed room I saw there was no traditional toilet, just a hole in the ground, with a hose next to it. All of my norms were being shaken and rattled as I entered this brave new world. It was now time to get some rest and be ready to enjoy our sightseeing adventures the next day. Early the next morning I heard the sound of loud speakers sending out Arabic prayers all over the city. I heard a lot of new strange sounds as I watched the masses kneeling for prayer. I learned real quick that I was not in my hood anymore as we joined with a group of other Christian pilgrims and headed out to a place called Petra.

Petra is recognized as one of the wonders of the world and rightly so when you climb down into it. It is a mountain with a city carved out right in the middle that you can ride in on horseback into the depths of this beautiful masterpiece of God. I began to feel so small in the deep valley as I looked up to the heights of this city. To me it was kind of like the first time I was at Yosemite Falls, knowing in your heart that it is a great big God who put this all together. There are so many Bible stories written about the ground we were standing on and the Bible tells us that there will be multitudes trying to escape to Petra during the tribulation period.

We were very worn out after the long flight and a full day of sightseeing and praising Jesus. It was time for us to go to our hotel and get some food and good rest. There was no Burger king or McDonalds in Jordan, so Middle Eastern food; here we come. The only food tip I was given concerning the food in Jordan was, "If you don't see fire underneath the food, don't eat it." Off to bed we went and once again early in the morning heard the sounds of prayers throughout the whole city. We got in our tour bus and drove by the Red Sea…come on, I mean the Red sea from the movie *The Ten Commandments*. It was just too awesome knowing this is where Moses and all the people of God crossed over while the Egyptians were chasing them down.

Next on our tour list for the day was a place called Mt. Nebo where Moses over looked the Promised Land, a place described as, flowing with milk and honey Later that afternoon we were on our way to cross the General Allenby Bridge, named after a famous military hero in the Middle East.

When we crossed this bridge—I am telling you the truth, the inside of my body felt a joy that I had never experienced before with out any drugs. The Jesus who lived in me was in his home land and Jesus was jumping for joy inside of my skin

We spent the next several days going to the empty tomb, Wailing Wall, church of the nativity and so many other great Bible sites as we read the Bible all along the way, singing praises to God. It is one thing to read about something in the Bible, but to see it with your own eyes is a true awakening. My time in Israel was another monumental time of my life and I couldn't wait to get home and tell everyone about all that I had seen and learned while on this journey. I purposed in my heart that I would make a pilgrimage to Israel every year.

# CHAPTER 12

## HOME IS WHERE THE HEART IS

Upon landing back into Orange County, I was so happy to see my family and friends from our Set Free Church. I spent time talking to Lois about all the wonderful experiences that I enjoyed, she was so happy for me, and I was once again renewed in my faith. The church started growing ever so slowly, but I was patient and just waited on the Lord.

I went back into the prisons as a chaplain to share with the inmates about my conversion to Jesus and give them the hope and encouragement I found in there. I was a hope-to-die dope fiend for many years and related well with those that were incarcerated. I understood their plight and offered my hand of friendship and hope to them. There is a saying, "once a dope fiend always a dope fiend." I wanted the prisoners to see living proof that you can reverse the curse in your life. I was taking people in my home, feeding the hungry and doing all I could to help the poor, as I had been helped by others who had received the Lord.

I needed to find a bigger place for our congregation to meet, Sandra told me to ask the King for a place to have church. She said that a prophet in the Bible named Nehemiah asked the King for help and he got it. I said, "Who is the King I need to ask for help?" Sandra replied, "The Mayor of Anaheim is the highest political figure in our world, so by faith, go ask him for his blessings." I wasn't sure if this is what God wanted me to do and it seemed a little foolish to me at the time to be asking the

Mayor of our city for help. When serving the Lord there are a lot of things that have made no sense to me, but later on I saw the hand of God all over it.

Next thing you know, I am making an appointment with the Mayor, sharing with him my vision to help the homeless and drug addicts in our town. His name was Mayor Don Roth, and he responded with much concern and was a major part of the foundation for Set Free Ministries in downtown Anaheim. Disneyland was growing leaps and bounds in our city, and they referred to themselves as "The happiest place on Earth," but I was determined to make Set Free Church the happiest place on earth. With the growth of Disneyland and all the new people moving here, old downtown was in need of a makeover. Old buildings were being renovated, and homes were being rehabbed all over downtown, I was at the right place at the right time when my wife sent me to Mayor Roth.

The Mayor hooked us up with an old bank building that had been closed down. We met there for about four months and used the building to house the homeless and to teach people how to clean up the gutters and walk ways of down town. I had men sleeping in the vault at night, counseling and giving food away in the daytime. One night an electrical fire started, and down came the building; fortunately, all of our men got out safely. Mayor Roth stepped right up to the plate when this happened, and offered us an empty carpet building to meet in before it was going to be demolished.

The carpet building is where we began to flourish with so many people coming to church that we were starting to establish ourselves as a church in downtown Anaheim. It was gang busters there as we began to grow in numbers and being a part of the baby boomer generation with many of our ladies having children.

It was nearing the time when we were ready to have our first baptism for all our new converts. Our men built our own version of a baptistery which looked like a gigantic bath tub. Upon completion we filled it up that Saturday night getting ready for our Sunday service. We had a big surprise when we arrived to church on Sunday morning. Sometime during the night, the baptismal exploded and flooded the main floor of the building. Set Free Church was once again homeless, and on the search for a place to lay our heads, trusting God all the way. Life is filled with so many growing situations and opportunities to push forward or quit. We had now been through the fire and the floods of life while we embraced the future with faithful eyes.

**Set Free in 1983. The beginning**

Downtown Anaheim had as many as fifty homes at a time that were boarded up until they were ready to be renovated, along with numerous buildings. I asked the Mayor about the possibility of renting the homes from the city until the time was ready for them to be newly constructed. He thought that would be a great idea because vagrants and drug addicts were starting to live in them, destroying the interior of homes with fires. We made a contractual agreement with the city of Anaheim to pay 50 dollars a month, with a 7 day move out clause. It sounded great to me and the Mayor was elated knowing we had the same goal in mind. We decided on five homes to begin with and we moved 50 people into those premises that needed rehab and a place for a new start. It was a great friendship helping clean up downtown Anaheim while God cleaned all of us up. I found out early in ministry, that if you take care of God's business he will take care of yours.

We were still homeless as far as a church facility was concerned. A friend of mine named Steve approached me about a building in downtown Anaheim that was for rent. It was a big store front building with lot's of space to grow as we saw the needs continue to increase. We had about 70 people in our church, most that were pretty broke and desperate for help. I had at least 10 people living in my own home right alongside all my children. People would often ask me if I felt safe with all those druggies living with me and fears of what they would do to my children.

I told them, "I'm a little afraid of what my kids might do to them." In the kind of ministry I do, you have to trust the Lord with all your heart and believe that God loves those that you minister to. The building Steve told me about was located in one of the worst gang areas in town—2 blocks from city hall and very close to the Anaheim police station. It was not exactly a place you would want to start a family church but where God guides, God provides. I decided to go with Steve and take a look at this property and pray over it in order to obtain God's leading

I fell in love with the place and as I viewed it from God's perspective; I could see a great future there. Some people would have just seen the negative things about this old building but I was a man on a mission and felt such a need in our midst. The owner of the property was a very cool guy named Bill Taormina who was a big player in the city of Anaheim and offered it to us for $2,500.00 a month. Our church had now been going for almost two years and we needed some roots to begin what we believed would be a great church. Steve and his wife Kathy were so very instrumental in the building of our church that I took their counsel on many things. I told Steve that it was just too much money for our Set Free family and I had some doubts come to mind that made me afraid. Steve told me that I needed to step out in faith and get the place, and that he believed our people would rise up to the task. I told him I didn't have the faith and he shot right back at me that he did and let's do it. Steve lifted my spirits and I trusted God once again for a mighty miracle.

Within a few weeks the miracle had come through and we now had a huge warehouse with absolutely nothing inside of it. I needed to remind myself to be careful for what I prayed for…I had now acquired an old dilapidated building with no light fixtures, no heating or air conditioning system, and it was way more than your average fixer upper. The hope that kept me going was seeing all the lives that were being changed. The building looked like most of the people I worked with who needed to be repaired from the inside out. In the Bible God says he reaches down into the dirty pits and pulls people like me out to give us purpose and meaning in our lives.

My family kept on growing with the birth of my newest son we named Hebrew Timothy Aguilar. I now had Matthew

John, Phillip Jr., Trina Joy, and my new baby boy, Hebrew. My wife came up with the name Hebrew after going to Israel and having a dream one night that we were the Hebrew nation. I decided at this time that I would change my views on birth control. I told my wife no more kids please. My assistant, Lois was having children right alongside of us, three beautiful daughters. I was so very happy to have my family, and an extended Christian family that I loved so very much. I became addicted to the ministry of the saints and my energy was without end.

# CHAPTER 13

# CHRIST'S SONS

The year was 1984 *(Ronald Regan is president and Michael Jackson wins the music awards)*, and we were now ready to lay down our roots with lots of room to grow and lots of energy to make it happen. Our strategy came from the Bible Acts: ch.2 where the early Christians met daily in the temple and from house-to- house to preach Jesus. We wanted to preach the love of Jesus to everyone in our city first, and then we wanted to reach America, and then the world. It seemed like a mighty task, but we were going for the gold. We had every type of four footed beast and creepy crawling thing coming to our church. Most of our people had no money, and lots of problems. A few of our people had good jobs and wanted to just help the less fortunate by mentoring them and showing them a better way. I started thinking about getting a Harley Davidson motorcycle again.

I made a promise to God that if he helped me get a motorcycle I would only ride it for him. Lois and Tim would accompany me to look at motorcycles quite often and dream about riding for Jesus on a new Harley Davidson. Tim didn't make a lot of money but he had a good job and best of all he had good credit. Tim decided to buy a Harley for both of us, so here we go down to the Harley shop and we're ready to ride for Jesus. Talk about answered prayer, Matthew 6:33 "Seek ye first the kingdom of God and all these things will be added unto you." God was adding a whole lot into my life. My ministerial look was changing from Baptist suit-wearing Pastor Aguilar, to the biker Pastor with boots and Levis. I was in second Heaven riding my new Harley down the streets of life. I started covering up some old tattoos and getting Jesus tattoos all over my body. I always have people asking me if God allows us to get tattoos. Most people have heard someone say that tattoos are not of God. The truth is that there is no place in God's word where he prohibits tattoos. I think it is a wonderful thing to decorate our temple for God.

We all rode in a pack for Jesus, laughing and praying as the wind hit our faces. The name of our first motorcycle ministry was Christ's Sons. It was a three piece patch for Jesus that we wore proudly representing our savior and all he had done for us. My blood brothers Bert, Mel, Billy and a guy named Biker James got it rolling and so many people hopped on board to make the biker ministry the backbone of our church. Our code was to always be the first ones to church, and the last ones to leave. I mean we rode all over the state of California telling people about Jesus as they looked at us like we were out of our minds. We broke the molds on how Christians look, along with our new music and the way we reached out to others. Lots of people loved our style, but the haters definitely out numbered the lovers of our ministry. Church people do not like change; they like to keep things like the good old days. My intentions have always been to give the same message, with a different method for the purpose of touching lives.

My daily schedule included an early morning wake up followed by a meeting with all the people who lived in our homes, giving them the good old beans and rice and Jesus Christ message. We would read the Bible and then clean our new building with mops and fresh paint, always seasoned with a lot of love and tenderness.

We bought used folding chairs and built a little stage. We used seeds and stems to build our little church and we knew better than to despise small beginnings. The church building was now being used for food ministry, church services, motorcycle ministry, clothing, and for anything else we had need for.

We enjoyed an array of activities at Set Free, like a basketball court inside the building, and with everything being portable we were able to have square dances, hockey games and anything else that came to our minds. We were open twenty-four hours a day, seven days a week. Set Free was the first church I knew of that never slept and always had someone on duty to minister to that lost soul that needed a touch from Jesus. God blessed us with a lot of people who could play instruments and sing like angels. Set Free Church was on fire for Jesus and we were ready to do our part to tell the world the good news.

My friends from the old Baptist days, Holly Palmer and her husband, Wayne (one of my dedicated soldiers) worked alongside me in the ministry. Lois and Holly were the most committed women I had ever met that served Jesus and remained loyal to the cause, utilizing all their talents to build a house of refuge. We had love from most of the leadership of the city of Anaheim and most of the churches were happy to send us their outcasts.

Local churches knew that if an outcast type of person ventured into their church, they would be able to send them to Set Free where they would be well received. Even the Anaheim Police Department was dropping off people at our doorstep day and night. It didn't matter where they came from, or what they were all about, we made room for them. God says there is treasure in earthen vessels, and I was ready to pan for gold as we kept filling up our city rented homes with hurting people. Pastors used to tell me I had a special gift for those types of people that didn't fit into their churches. I would tell them, "It's called the gift of inconvenience." I figured Jesus inconvenienced himself for me by leaving heaven and coming to Earth to pay for my sins. The least I thought I could do was take in people who had real needs and were willing to make a change. All those who thought their sins were just too big to be forgiven could come to Set Free and meet a whole lot of people just like them.

As I look back over the years, I can see the thread of God throughout my life making something beautiful out of the mess I created. I had made myself available to be used by God in any way He saw fit, knowing my life wasn't about me anymore, it was about Him. I told God to do whatever it took to draw me closer to Him, and boy, I sure didn't know what I was asking for!

Our church was growing and growing, and I was always surprised that people kept coming to hear me speak the word of the Lord. God gave me some sayings that have stuck with me throughout all my years of ministry. I always told people, "Satan Sucks; If you sleep with dogs you'll get fleas; If you're early you won't be late, It's either black or white; and you'd better be hot or cold." We had punk concerts, hip hop music, and the word was getting out quick that there was a church that you could be yourself at. People would often comment that Set Free is so real, which means a lot of different things to a lot of different people.

To me it means I don't care what you did last night, I don't care about your past, or what you look like, and you're welcomed at Set Free. Set Free people just try and love you right where you're at and we shoot straight with the truth, from the word of God--no sugar coating, no religious jargon, just the down and dirty truth.

I started hitting the streets, telling people that if God did it for me, he would do it for them. Many churches will tell you to come as you are, but as soon as you get there, they try to change the way you look and make a cookie cutter Christian out of you. I know there are exceptions to the rule, but overall, churches are very traditional and try to kill your buzz with some of their hang-ups. When you come wearing a hat, they say "take it off;" chewing gum, "throw it out;" under the influence, "come back when your sober." Set Free has always been a Holy Ghost hospital, ready to take care of the sick.

My assistant, Lois, told her husband, Tim, to give our phone number to the Trinity Broadcasting Network (TBN) as a resource for helping people. We had no idea how many people would call in and ask for help from all over America. Paul and Jan Crouch had a huge worldwide television ministry reaching the masses through their television network. In my Baptist days I wasn't allowed to watch Christian television, but now the sky was the limit and I could watch anything I wanted to. Now I had the freedom to praise Jesus in any way I saw fit and not care about the religious judgmental good old boys club. TBN started referring so many people our way that it seemed like we wouldn't have room for all of them. That did not bother us and we just kept on making room. Our living rooms turned into bedrooms; our feeding program was becoming overwhelming and the inmates were starting to outnumber the guards. We now had about a hundred people living in our five homes, so it was time to rent a few more from the city. Three meals a day, seven days a week, not including snacks ends up being a huge food bill.

**Set Free's 1<sup>st</sup> motorcycle ministry "Christ Son's"**

# CHAPTER 14

# SET FREE LOVES PAUL AND JAN

One day, Tim Trader informed me that Jan Crouch had asked her secretary, Joanie, "Where do we send people who are homeless?" Joanie told her, "To a man named Pastor Phil Aguilar from a church called Set Free. Joanie continued to state, "Pastor Phil takes them in to his own home." Tim notified me that Jan was amazed and so fascinated with the knowledge of a Pastor actually taking strangers into his own home. Jan questioned Joanie again and asked, "Is there really a Pastor who would take people into his own home? Joanie gave Jan the affirmative and reiterated, "We send lots of people to Set Free and Pastor Phil doesn't charge them a thing."

About a month later Paul and Jan Crouch made a personal visit to our church, and I was blown out of my mind. They were so nice and friendly and while my jaw dropped to the floor I let them know what a privilege it was to meet them. I just had to tell them before they left what a great blessing they had been in my life. I told them the new and improved Set Free was birthed from Trinity Broadcasting Network. Paul and Jan are unique looking on television, but even trippier looking when you are close and personal with them. I mean Paul has the biggest head of hair I have ever seen on a man, and Jan was wearing a pink wig that day and eye lashes to die for. It's good that I like unique looking folks, so they fit right into the Set Free crowd.

They asked what they could do for me and our Set Free Church.

From the beginning of Set Free ministries I always wanted to send the message that I was not in this for the money. So many people I had met over the years always talked about preachers wanting peoples' money, so I chose to take what was called a vow of poverty. That meant I could not own property nor own any other earthly possessions. I had never passed an offering plate at our church, and never asked anyone but God to provide for our needs. I told them our church always needed more housing for the homeless we take in. My own house at this time had 50 people living in it, and even my assistant, Lois, had left the good side of the tracks and moved into our ministry homes, and she now had people living with her family.

Our homes were never crash pads for Jesus or halfway homes. The Bible says that a man who doesn't work shouldn't eat. We ran our homes as discipleship homes, teaching everyone the value of hard work, and the disciplines of learning the word of God. From the time people get up in the morning, its Jesus, Jesus, Jesus.

Paul and Jan asked if they could buy a home for the Set Free Church. I shared with them that my lifestyle was to owe no man anything but love. I agreed to receive a home, but not own it and if they would just give it to us on loan. It was just a matter of weeks when Paul and Jan found us a home right down the block from our warehouse church. It was definitely a fixer upper home that reminded me of all the lives we were repairing in the name of Jesus. When you have so many people living with you, there is a lot of talent in your midst: painters, electricians, roofers and lots of laborers for Jesus.

Our people made that home look so very beautiful and we were counting our blessings. This was our first real home that we didn't have to worry about being kicked out of. It was all ours through the beautiful people at Trinity Broadcasting Network. Paul and Jan were so gracious to us, and I realized that God was moving upon our little ministry in a mighty way. Paul and Jan asked if they could come and dedicate the new home to the Lord on national television. I told them that would be such an honor and I praised God that he would send help from above like Paul and Jan. We named our new home the house of Paul, in honor of the apostle Paul in the Bible who God struck down on the road to Damascus. The apostle Paul spoke to me through God's word all the days of my incarceration in prison.

Upon completion of the home we moved in about fifty people: gang members, grandmas, and small children. Our homes were filled with drug addicts, and lots of angry violent people. God had used my past to allow me to handle my present, and comfort others with the comfort God had given me.

Two weeks after we moved in, Jan and Paul showed up at our new home with a whole camera crew. This was very different and a little bit strange to me. I didn't know much about the television ministry, but this was going to be a real learning experience. I would soon find out that with every blessing there is a price to be paid. When they informed me that they wanted to dedicate the home on national television, I was blessed beyond words and could hardly contain myself. So for the first time, here I am on National TV with Paul and Jan Crouch. I was just a loser from the wrong side of the tracks who God found at the bottom of the barrel. The Mayor and city council members showed up for this festive event, as did my dear friend, William

Taormina. They took pictures and did interviews with many of the people in our discipleship home. Next they had Paul interview me and share a little bit of my testimony of how I came to know the Lord Jesus Christ as Savior. It was a great day for the whole Set Free family as it made us a bigger believer in Gods word. The Bible says give and it shall be given unto you, pressed down, shaken together, running over, shall men give unto your bosom.

Shortly after this memorable occasion I received a call from a lady named Laura Massie who did the booking for Trinity Broadcasting Network. She notified me that Paul and Jan wanted me to appear on their television show. They wanted me to give my testimony to the whole world. I didn't think my testimony was that exciting considering that I was just another dirty down, depressed loser who God pulled out of a slimy pit. Little did I know that being on national television would mean millions would look and see this ex-con Biker Pastor. I was naïve when it came to the media—I did not realize that television can make you and break you. I had long left the suit and tie look and exchanged it for a pony tail, tattoos, and my trademark wrap around shades. Trinity Broadcasting Network's guests in those days were mainly conservative Pentecostal preachers. You could say I was definitely a new breed of preacher on that Network, with a whole new flavor and style.

Since I have always treated those that live with me like family, I showed up to the television studio that day with my family--100 people who lived in our discipleship homes accompanied me. When my name was announced to the national audience, the Set Free Gang let out with loud dog barks and all the street noise you could think of.

Set Free people are mostly raised in the streets and not aware of church protocol. (Paul Crouch way back in the day called us the Set Free Gang from looking at our outward appearance.)

It was a very exciting experience to be announced to the whole nation via television media airwaves. I was so very nervous, and my knees were knocking together. I knew the Lord wanted me to share my story, with the knowledge that it could be of help to so many hurting people. I started telling my testimony and I felt calmness come over me and I knew it was the Holy Ghost speaking through me. I was asked by Paul Crouch to end my story with a prayer for all the viewing audience to repeat with me. It was the sinner's prayer which goes like this. Dear father in Heaven please forgive me for my sins, I believe you died on the cross for me, and I ask you to come in to my heart and take over my life. I was done with the prayer and Paul told those who had prayed the prayer with me to call the television station and let the prayer partners know they had received Jesus. The phones lines lit up and I was told of the countless people who gave their lives to Jesus that night. I became a believer in the power of Christian television and the multitudes of people it could reach.

After my first appearance on television I started getting more phone calls than you could imagine. People who had seen me and heard my testimony felt like I could help their friends and family members. Every outcast, every tattooed person, and every radical black sheep from all backgrounds started calling Set Free for help. I had a church full of baby Christians and I needed help to raise them up in the nurture and admonition of the Lord. God heard my cry and started sending Set Free soldiers to lift up my hands as I was doing a good work for the Lord. I started seeing new people coming to church every Sunday morning with smiles on their faces ready to receive all God had for them. Before service every Sunday I would stay in my office and ask Lois if the people were showing up again for church. I just couldn't believe they would be coming to hear me preach God's Word.

**Our ministry home "God's Casa"**

We were becoming so busy that it became necessary for me to work 18 hours each day. Lois worked hard alongside me to manage the counseling and housing for so many new people at our church. Many of the new people we worked with had very hardcore self destructive personalities, and it was paramount that I keep watch on the men coming from different gangs, cities and neighborhoods. I was constantly searching for new ways to reach people for Jesus.

I was slowly becoming aware that Set Free Church was pioneering a new trail; therefore I needed to have every hand on deck, and get busy about the work of the Lord. I found that music could be very instrumental in reaching people, like little boy David in the Bible when he played before King Saul and calmed his tormented spirit.

The music we used to reach out to people was not your normal Christian flavor. By this time our music was so good that most people didn't realize it was Christian until they listened real close. I had one of the members of the band Sublime named Bud in our program that brought us some first class Christian Reggae. I also had a guitar player named Kid Ramos who was a world renowned Blues player who rocked our church with his guitar riffs and his rockabilly look.

There were two other large churches not far from us at that time named the Vineyard and Calvary Chapel where my assistant Lois came from. Her pastor was Chuck smith who was a major influence to pastors around the world. My assistant Lois also gave me a lot of history on Calvary Chapel seeing how her whole family came to the Lord there. Pastor Chuck Smith of Calvary Chapel would send a lot of needy people are way and our friendship with them was good. Calvary Chapel had flourished during the Jesus people days of the seventies, along with the Vineyard church (a break-off from Calvary Chapel that spread their wings worldwide in the eighties).

Set Free was preparing to enter the nineties with a new face on the culture of the inner cities of Southern California. I had no model church to look at for guidance with the type of people we were reaching and the culture they were living in. I was doing something I had never seen before. Our Noah's ark church was being filled up with every type of creature under heaven. Set Free definitely was attracting a rougher group of people that were not into your normal all American church. Our church had a dark gothic look, but our hearts were bright for Jesus. The number one t-shirt sported at Set Free was our trained to serve Jesus shirt.

I started getting called the Biker Pastor everywhere I went, and Jan and Paul kept calling me to make more live appearances on their popular television show. Our church kept on growing and growing and, growing. My wife stayed strong through it all, spending most of her time raising our four children and taking care of me. In the front of our warehouse was a designated motorcycle parking only with close to a 100 motorcycles on a given Sunday. The side streets were filled with our oldie but goodie cars that belonged to our low rider ministry. Pulling up to Set Free Church was like going to a car-and-bike show with the sound of hip hop and rock music in the air. Set Free became the happiest place on earth as people rolled in to be encouraged and to have a Jesus party.

Many preachers' kids grow up hating church, but I wanted my children to love church and enjoy being there. I had sports heroes like football Hall-of-Famer Isaiah Robertson enter our rehab program along with a lot of other professional athletes. God was bringing in talent from everywhere to help us build our little inner city church.

Lois had "hired" several assistant secretaries who worked directly under her, and she paid them plenty of Jesus Bucks(blessings) to work for her.

I discovered that the old Anaheim Baptist church I was a co-pastor of had sold their church facilities to the city of Anaheim. It was located directly across the street from City Hall so I asked the Mayor if we could rent the place. He got approval from the city council and it became the home of the Set Free junior church for children. By this time we had hundreds of our Set Free children in need of space to conduct church services that were especially geared to them. It was the same property and parsonage I lived in back in nineteen seventy nine and I could see the hand of God all over our work. My first project there was to build the first skate park in Orange County with huge half pipes that attacked another demographic of young people and their parents. God kept giving me ideas for reaching out to the masses and he sent the people to make it happen.

Within the discipleship homes we realized that there were over a hundred people that were drug addicts in need of detox. It became apparent that we needed to start a ranch within a rural area that would help them kick their nasty habits. My friend, Steve once again came through with help, and we found a big piece of property with some old structures on it in good old Perris California. The property was a very run down place with a few old trailers on it which made it perfect for people coming down from drugs. Due to our policy of never charging people—freely we receive and freely we give--it didn't take very long and our ranch was overflowing with people. I kept my word when I said we don't have room, we make room for people. The ranch was a boot camp for all those serious about changing their lives for Jesus.

Back in Anaheim a movement for God was taking place and there was no denying it even if you looked Set Free right in the face. I promise you that it was all God because I just showed up, made myself available, and I had a right heart condition for this work.

# CHAPTER 15

## GERONIMO, I LOVE YOU

As I had mentioned before, the Mayor of our town, Don Roth, was a very wonderful friend to all of us at Set Free, and we had favor with most of the city leadership. We spent thousands of hours volunteering for work projects in the city of Anaheim. Paul and Jan heard nothing but praise from Mayor Roth about our work, and Trinity Broadcasting loved us so much that they purchased another two-story home for our ministry.

We named it the house of Timothy after the young man Timothy who the apostle Paul mentored. We kept our homes and buildings groomed for excellence, winning the *Anaheim Beautiful* award numerous times because our homes looked so lovely. I was into doing make over's on our homes and our people lives. The police chief at the time, Chief Malloy, also commended us as we worked to clean up our beautiful city. The Chief said the crime rate went down in our city when Set Free moved in. We also won the coveted *Disneyland Community Service* award and it doesn't get any better or bigger than that. I mean Disneyland is the engine that runs Anaheim so by awarding Set Free the award it made a definite statement to our city. I was blessed that my landlord and friend, William Taormina, who was always in mix of the City of Anaheim happenings stuck to my side through thick and thin.

I also had the privilege of having Mayor Roth accompany me to Trinity Broadcasting Network to share his testimony about Jesus. Mayor Roth bragged to the national viewing audience about all the wonderful work Set Free had accomplished in our city. He challenged mayors to hook up with a local church and do what Set Free was doing. The police Chief loved our work; on the other hand, as Set Free grew bigger and bigger, the police Chief got a little nervous about the large crowds of scandalous looking people. He told me one day that he had some concerns about me going back to my old evil ways and if people would follow me. He was skeptical about the type of people I helped and questioned their change of heart. I assured the chief that I loved Jesus and my family and city too much for that to happen.

Mayor Roth went on to bigger and better things, as he was appointed an Orange County Supervisor. Our next Mayor was a man named Ben Bay who helped us in the same way that Mayor Roth did; he was a great friend and supporter of ours. Set Free could do no wrong at this time and best of all lives were being changed every single day. Gang members were making peace treaties and drug addicts were becoming addicted to Jesus. I became part of the Gang Council of Orange County with our focus to stop drive-by shootings. We made some good headway in helping our troubled youth.

Although I was blessed by what God was doing in our church, I was still missing my first born son, Geronimo. I thought about him often and prayed for his life to be blessed in spite of all the drama I put him through. I continued to wrestle with the guilt of having left him; nevertheless, somehow I knew he would grow up and have a good life.

The everyday life at Set Free church was consuming all of my time. Lois and I were constantly doing ministry work.

* * *

I was on a mission and nothing else seemed to matter. There were no time-outs for me, as I continued steadfastly doing a work for God.

As I look back on my time, I realize that I neglected time with my beautiful wife. Sandra was the greatest mother and she was the rock in our home. Sandra was an example of the virtuous woman God speaks of in Proverbs 31. Unfortunately, I became a Martha doing busy work, instead of a Mary sitting at the feet of Jesus. I definitely had evolved into an overachiever, and at times anal about it. The road to hell is paved with good intentions.

One day, my assistant Lois sent her husband, Tim, and I to help someone at the courthouse. While we were there we ran into an old friend of my ex-wife Karen, he was the attorney who handled our divorce. I was surprised to see him, and inquired about Karen and my son Geronimo. He looked at me with a very strange look and said "didn't you hear about her death?" I had no idea what he was talking about and asked him to tell me what happened to her. He softly recounted that Karen was remarried a few years back, and her new husband shot and killed her in front of my son Geronimo, and then killed himself.

Geronimo was 8 years old when it happened and I felt terrible inside and knew life could have been better for my son. I was heartbroken over the news and I asked the attorney where my son was living and how he was doing. He said Geronimo moved into his grandparents' home in Anaheim, which just happened to be right down the block from my church. I felt terrible about the things that transpired, and blamed myself.

I thought back to the first time meeting with Karen's Jewish parents and hearing them tell her that Mexicans are wife beaters. It all started off so wrong, and I was just so messed up trying to be a husband and a father to Geronimo. Karen was one of the most wonderful ladies this world could ever find and there were so many whys in my life. Karen loved me in high school, she loved me in jail, she loved me just the way my wife Sandra loves me now. She definitely didn't deserve to be married to a jerk like me. To top things off, I knew her parents would tell Geronimo nothing but bad things about me so once again a dammed if I do, and dammed if I don't situation had come into my being.

I couldn't blame anybody but myself for the hole that I had dug due to my past negative choices. When I got back to the church office I immediately hit up Lois and told her the good and bad news. Remember, Lois is my Jewish, Pro Israel, Zionist personal assistant. She always had me praying for the return of my son Geronimo and she is the one who told me Jewishness comes through the mother's side of the family. So my little Jewish Geronimo was living right down the street from where I lived and did ministry.

Lois put on her private eye hat and immediately found out where Geronimo lived. She paid a visit to his Jewish grandparents without speaking a word about it to me. Lois never asked me for permission to do anything-this girl was an all systems go ahead type of lady. They didn't receive the visit well as she tried to convince them to let me visit Geronimo. My Lois never gave up and was even more determined to find a way for me to see my son and declare my love for him.

Geronimo was about seventeen years old now and I'm sure he didn't want to see me after hearing about the tragedy of his mom being killed. Lois found out that he went to

Katella High School in Anaheim, and that he was a member of the high school soccer team. One afternoon Lois decided we were going to the high school soccer field and catch a glimpse of him as he practiced soccer. We drove over to the school and parked our car by the soccer field and as I looked out of the front window onto the field I saw this long lanky brown kid running up a storm. I told Lois "that's my little boy, I know it's him." I was so excited, scared, shaky and teared up by his presence. It was my son who I had not seen for close to 14 years and I didn't dare approach him for fear of rejection. What would he say to me? What would I do if he said this or that? I was in total confusion about my life and how things turned out. I had to drive away from the school because it is way too emotional for me. After all those years of praying for Geronimo, there he was, right in front of me. Geronimo knows absolutely nothing about me watching him from afar till this day.

Lois was determined not to give up on this son of mine and continued her quest to get me a chance to reunite with him. One week later I get a phone call from one of Karen's best friends from high school, her name was Yolanda and she was a blast from the past. She called to tell me that my son Geronimo was dating her daughter Summer, and that Geronimo was having drug problems and needed help. From the first day I gave my life to Jesus back in Chino Prison I have seen God work so many miracles in my life and here was answered prayer, and I didn't know what to do with it.

It wasn't more than two weeks later that I received a visit from a young man that wanted to talk to the Pastor. I was in my office and when my receptionist informed me that a fellow named Geronimo wanted to see the Pastor of Set Free. When I heard those words I hit the ceiling with joy and pain. My son Geronimo was just twenty feet away from me and I was panicking, praying and praising Jesus with all my heart for another miracle in my life. Life is so full of drama, heartache, and happiness with the seasons changing all the time. It seemed like a eternity before Geronimo entered my office as I thought back to the last time I held him in my arms. I said please bring Geronimo to my office as I was preparing for the counseling session of my life. I sat in my office chair calmly, still wondering if I was going to get yelled at for abandoning him and his mom. He slowly walked into my office appearing very humble from his body posture, as I asked him to please sit down so I could speak to him and find out how I could be of help. I wanted to hug and kiss him so badly after waiting and praying for him for all these years. I was aching inside from all the pain and suffering I allowed to happen in his life as God was purging me from my old wicked lifestyle .. I wanted to reach out and touch him, but I knew I had to take things slowly as baggage from the past doesn't get cleaned up over night. What was most important now is how my son was doing and how God can use me to offer help.

We were both in amazement as we looked at each other very intensely across my desk. We stared at each other and could tell we were definitely father and son. There was no doubt he was my son, and I was his dad. I could tell he was hurting and needed help in a bad way, his body looked frail and his eyes were dull ,you could see a black cloud over his head. He was definitely hooked on drugs and living a very dangerous lifestyle that I knew all too well. I didn't want to shove Jesus down his throat and I knew he had heard nothing but trash about me from his grandparents who had every right to hate me.

I did know that it took guts for Geronimo to walk in my church not really knowing what to expect. I started the conversation by telling him how I use to be a drug addict and how violent my life once was. I began to explain to him how Jesus changed my life and I am a new creation free of all my past addictions. I knew it was now time to show him a picture of the two of us when he was just a young child to prove I was truly his father. He was skeptical, but gave me an opportunity to speak into his life and the opportunity to sit in his presence. It was still so mind boggling sitting across from my son right here in my office after all those years I had prayed for this day. We spent about an hour talking, me doing most of it. It was a little uncomfortable at times, yet refreshing and I knew in my heart that this was just the beginning of a long and wonderful relationship.

I asked him if I could pray for him as we ended our first time of fellowship together and he agreed. It was obvious he was so broken and ready to receive Christ so I then asked him if he would like to ask Jesus to be his savior. I knew this was a bold move, but I wasn't sure if I would ever see him again so I went for the knockout. He shocked me and said, "Yes I would." We prayed the sinner's prayer together, and my son Geronimo gave his life to Jesus that day. I hugged him so hard and I thanked God for another mighty miracle from above. I asked Geronimo if he would come visit me soon so that he could meet his brothers and sister. He agreed to visit me in the near future and gave me his word that he wanted to rekindle our relationship. So out of the office and out the front door walks my son Geronimo, the love of my life. I was in third Heaven, and thanking God for the privilege of seeing my son, my first born coming home to me. I thought back again on the first scripture verse I learned in prison. "Delight thyself in the lord, and he will give you the desires of your heart." I had the most beautiful wife, great kids, great church, and now my son that was lost was back at home with his dad. I had the desires of my heart filled that day.

**Our 1ˢᵗ family Christmas with my son Geronimo**

# CHAPTER 16

## MUSIC TO MY EARS

Our church was growing and glowing for Jesus. Now I am happier than ever, and so in love with Jesus. One thing I had learned by this time in my Christian walk was to trust the Lord through the good, bad and ugly. When I first fell in love with Jesus I had to put my girlfriend Sandra on the altar and learn that God is the giver of gifts. Now with my son back I had to be careful to trust that Jesus would heal our relationship, not to lean on my own understanding, but acknowledge Him in everything. I was the biggest loser in the Aguilar family and now I got to be part of my whole family coming to Christ.

My sister was first when she came to my prison wedding then one at a time all of my family including my Mom and Dad came to know Jesus. Next, all of Sandra's family came to know Jesus, and Sandra's dad even became a Set Free pastor before going to heaven. The entire Aguilar family helped build Set Free Church. It's a real peaceful feeling knowing your whole family will be on their way to Heaven one day. It goes to show you that God will take the foolish things of the world to confound the wise.

Through the power of television, and most importantly through the power of God, people were hearing about the Set Free message of hope and a second chance at life. People were calling from all over the world to know more about Set Free Church and how they could start one in their town.

We were in the late eighties and my Jewish friends from the local Orange county Temples and a friend named Frank Eiklor updated me on some hate groups. There was a group of anti-semantic skin heads who were painting ugly things on the temple walls, and the local temples asked for our help. God called the Christ Son's motorcycle ministry to stand by our Jewish brother's through their time of persecution. We did paint clean up, and let it be known that we stood shoulder-to-shoulder with our Jewish brother's everywhere. Rabbi Haim Asa from Temple Beth Tikvah in Fullerton California became a dear friend to us along with Frank Eiklor, who headed up Shalom Ministries. They led us as we joined forces to wipe out the hate.

Set Free was on fire for Jesus as we sought to do all the Bible instructed us to do. Our homes were filled over capacity with people that had all kind of needs. Our rehab ranch was raising up soldiers for Jesus and it was time to go into the highways and byways of every city we had enough gas for. One of my fun filled visions as a young Christian man was to make life a big slumber party for Jesus. The next vision was to have my own Barnum and Bailey circus reality show to bring people into the kingdom.

My son Geronimo was now visiting my home regularly and getting close to his brothers and sister. He was starting to mature with his relationship with Jesus and I asked him to get involved in our concerts at church.

He was a DJ and knew how to do this rap thing real good. I told him to take the music of the world, change the lyrics and rap for Jesus so young people could have their own church music. The hottest music for kids at that time was a guy called MC Hammer, and a white rapper named Vanilla Ice. Geronimo started bringing his hip hop music full bore to our church and not only the young people loved it, but so did everyone else. It brought a whole new youthful spirit in our church and the whole place was on their feet and dancing to the music.

We started a hip hop dance crew doing popping and locking and all kinds of other crazy dances, the youth loved it and it attracted the attention of churches and street people everywhere to this church that was helping so many hurting folks. I had all the religious people upset with me again for doing rap music that they believed was not of God. They said it was of the devil and should not be allowed in church and that it would corrupt our children. Christians are always trying to blame music for the way our kids misbehave in life. I told them that there were two brothers in the bible named Cain and Abel who never listened to rap or hard rock, yet they had evil hearts. I was always way ahead of my time by bringing new ideas to the church world and getting a lot of criticism for it. I was just becoming all things to all people so that I might lead some to Christ. My intentions were pure, but the religious crowd is a rough group of people that can be judgmental at times.

Pastors just didn't understand that young people love music and they love to dance. I decided that I would rather have them dance in Church than in the night clubs. Due to the type of the music we used, instantly a multitude of young people started coming to Jesus and loving all the good music at our church and spreading the word everywhere. Geronimo became my pride and joy and motivated me to work harder for the cause of Christ... He was my prodigal son who was lost and now found. We were a team, like David and Jonathan, or maybe more like Al Capone and the Godfather. Whatever, we were jamming big time for Jesus and multitudes were coming to the Lord everywhere we went.

**Set Free Posse 1988**

Churches everywhere across the nation were inviting us to come and reach out to their young people and they always requested our Biker ministry and our Dance crew to be featured at their events. They never asked for my deacons or theologians from Set Free to come and teach the youngsters. They saw the success we were having in reaching the toughest of them all—the teens who would become the leaders of tomorrow. They knew young people liked to see cool looking people who loved Jesus and rocked their lifestyle. The look of hardcore bikers rolling into their town, with all these cool young people was a very effective tool in the hands of God. We named the rap and dance crew the Set Free Posse. We were out to round up sinners up for Jesus.

My haters have always given me the motivation to touch lives in spite of the criticism I have received. It continued to be part of my cross I had to bear. My philosophy is whatever it takes to bring people to Jesus was what I was all about. The crowds at church were growing bigger and bigger, it was a colorful group coming to hear God's word in an unusual setting. We bought hundreds of used chairs and started building two-by-four bleachers for the large attendance growing at our church. Every service was spirit-filled with an invitation for people to come to Christ. The music was loud, and the dress standards were "come as you are," and believe me, they wore some far out clothing and had some crazy hairdos.

I knew that I wasn't the greatest teacher, or preacher, but I loved people. The Bible says that if you are forgiven much, you will love much. I knew I had been forgiven for so many ugly things that I had done. I now had a heart full of love and concern for a dying world that I wanted to give the good news to. I called our church "ghetto fabulous" as we witnessed at least one or two of our used chairs break at each service. We all had a good laugh knowing that people weren't coming to our church because of some fancy facility. To the contrary, our building was cold in winter and hot in summer and you had to be high on Jesus to handle the conditions. There was definitely a revival happening at Set Free and there was no avoiding that it had to be God. It was way beyond my control as I just went along for the ride and didn't have any idea of when it was going to end.

A new couple came to our church and brought with them three beautiful daughters, the youngest was named Stacie; she was one of the most wonderful young ladies I had ever met. Her parents related to me that she had some depression problems going on in her life and hoped Set Free might be the cure. The parents were very wonderful Bible-believing Christians who wanted to join in the wonderful work our church was doing. By this time, Geronimo and I were inseparable. This was partly because of my guilty past, and partly because we worked so well sharing the good news of Jesus. He was definitely my son and his DNA was showing it in everything he did. The apple definitely does not fall far from the tree as I watched his charismatic behavior come alive.

Geronimo knew there were a lot of girls that liked him, so he had to make a decision to fall into sin, or to get married and do things right. Over the next few months Geronimo developed a strong attraction to this new girl Stacie and one day asked her to marry him—she said yes. She was only 17 so she had to get her parents approval which they totally agreed to with great joy. Geronimo and Stacie were a very happy couple and now I was planning a wedding for my oldest son. Her parents had become a very integral part of the church in a short time with the dad getting himself a motorcycle to ride with our club.

**Father and Son**

As the date of the wedding drew close, I could tell there was a control issue going on in Stacie's family's life. Her family was very closely knit, as was ours. Stacie would spend less and less time with her family and more time with the Aguilar's. I had hoped and prayed we would all be one, but that was not gonna happen. The wedding was getting ready to take place soon, and feelings were starting to show everywhere. Stacie's family was a strong Christian family, but we differed in some ways on how life should be run. Her family was not thrilled anymore about their daughter becoming an Aguilar. As I look back I am sure I could have been more gracious and not so hard headed about a lot of things.

We were now in the last years of the 80's at Set Free church. Seven years had passed and the Set Free was now on the map. People from other states and countries made their first stop to Disneyland, then Knott's Berry Farm and then to Set Free Church. Our church had a solid group of leaders, and a strong group of followers who loved Jesus with a passion. The marriage was now ready to happen and Stacie's family was a huge part of the ceremony. I felt so good and happy for my boy Geronimo knowing that he would have a helpmeet to help him along life's way. We had their wedding at a local community center through the help of my friend, Gilbert Melendez, a very dear friend to Set Free the honeymoon was planned and the future of this new marriage was about to begin.

I remember administering very strong vows in their marriage ceremony. I believe in short engagements and long marriages. The whole church showed up for the wedding, and I still can remember pronouncing them husband and wife. They seemed very happy as they took off for their honeymoon and even made it back in time for Sunday morning church.

# CHAPTER 17

# ODEN DID IT

My life was full time ministry with my wife, five children, and now a new daughter-in-law. Over 2,000 plus people were now coming to church. My long time friend and landlord William Taormina was still hanging tight as a friend and partner in our ministry. A new election was being held for the Mayoral position in Anaheim. The major candidate was a man named Fred Hunter, who was a narcotics officer for the city of Anaheim; he had spent a lot of time chasing me down back in my bad boy days. He got elected and was ready to take Anaheim to new heights, and he just happened to want to help me.

We became friends and he helped me reach the troubled people of southern California. By 1990 *(Iraq invades Kuwait and Bush issues troops in Saudi Arabia)*. Set Free was no longer a small church in Anaheim, but it became a movement in Orange County, California. People everywhere knew about us from watching television or seeing our motorcycle crew riding down the highways in huge packs. We decided to change the name of our Motorcycle ministry to Servants for Christ and chose the colors of black and white to be our new look. The motorcycle ministry of Set Free had continued to be the back bone of Set Free ministries, no longer was Disneyland the happiest place on earth. It was now Set Free, the biker church, the church with "those kind of people" that became the happiest place on earth.

Jealousy I found out is a very real emotion even in the Christian world. Christians are by no means perfect; they are just forgiven people because of what Christ has done for all of us. I can remember going to a prayer unity meeting at the Calvary Chapel church in Costa Mesa one night. I brought over a thousand people to pray with many other churches who attended a special event they were throwing. Most of our people were brand new Christians with a lot of wild fire in them. They did not know church protocol very well so they were experiencing new waters. All they knew was the Set Free way of life with our guidelines and standards for behavior. '

Everywhere we went our people passed out literature about Set Free Church for those who might know someone that would like our flavor. Well on this special prayer night an assistant pastor from Calvary named Bill Walden ask me to step into a back room at the church. He told me we had no right passing out Set Free material on their campus. I had no idea at the time what he was even talking about. He said we were proselytizing people to join our church and that it was wrong for our people to be acting that way. I am sure most of our people had no idea what that word even meant. I told him to get a life and that we were there to praise Jesus and nothing else. I have not always been the best communicator but I had no idea how upset this fellow was.

Sometime later in the year in I found out that he spoke to his boss, Pastor Oden Fong, who was a shot caller at Calvary, and they didn't seem to like me, or the Set Free style. Up till this time Calvary Chapel would send all of their rejects to us. None of that night bothered me at the time. I was too concerned about doing God's work. I use to be a dope dealer, and now I had become a hope dealer. We were in a war with drugs, crime, anti-Semitism and poverty. We were doing television specials, and getting national attention from the media. The word was out on the streets that there was a place for the black sheep of society.

Christian radio had just begun to flourish in Orange County so we jumped on the bandwagon. I was given a two hour spot every Sunday night with ten phone lines open during the program for people to call in. It was one of the most listened to programs going at that time as we kept finding new avenues to share the good news.

We were now leasing 20 homes from the city of Anaheim and they were packed with lots of beautiful people who needed our help. Trinity Broadcasting bought us another home we called Grandma Lois, named after the disciple Timothy's grandmother. TBN and Set Free had become a close knit family as we co-labored together for the glory of God. The crowds just kept on coming and we had close to 3,000 people attending services now. The old Baptist building we were leasing had nearly a thousand children every Sunday. There were over 300 people living in our discipleship homes. Our ranch was overflowing, and I was holding on for dear life as I began pasturing my first church. Paul and Jan Crouch had become the best friends ever to Set Free and to my personal family. The natural by product from a healthy church is to send out Pastors to start new churches and that we did first in California and then across the USA and into the foreign fields around the world.

This was all happening right before my eyes and yet I found it so hard to believe that God would be so hard up that he would use even me. God said if we are faithful in little things, he will give us bigger things. We were what I describe as a White Rhino church. A very unique, never seen before oddity that was definitely something new in our religious circles. The Bible says Jesus is a friend to Sinners and I knew we were a bunch of sinners who He loved very much. I believe that God called me in to this unique type of ministry. I had just enough faith to believe God would protect all my children and teach them to love the least of humanity as I sought to be an example to them.

My kids grew up never having their own room throughout their youth and shared all they had with others. I was reminded in my marriage vows that I was to forsake all comforts and pleasures for the sake of the ministry of reconciliation. Those words rung in my head year after year as myself and Sandra stayed faithful to our call. My children have learned so many valuable lessons from living the way we do, not being intimidated by people's looks, or where they came from, or what brought them to Set Free.

Churches, courts, and police all sent their troubled people to Set Free Church and yes it was hard at times dealing with all these needy people. We exercised the gift of inconvenience in our lives over and over again and God blessed us for it. My son, Geronimo, and my daughter-in-law Stacie moved into our home, along with about 35 other people. Sure enough Stacie got pregnant within a short period of time and I thought it was wonderful, but feelings weren't the same on the other side of the family.

Stacie's parents believed she was too young to be raising a family in the conditions we lived in. Maybe they were right? I guess I will never know for sure. I do know this that all things work together for good for those who love God. Stacie's family was feeling the withdrawals from not being around their little baby girl like before. Her family ran a candle shop where the whole family worked and now their baby girl was missing. I didn't want to get in the middle of a family feud, but Geronimo and Stacie said they wanted to work full time with me in the ministry. I kept my son Geronimo so busy doing ministry and Stacie was so involved that it was hard to fit in family time for either side. I was a driven man, and a definite workaholic for Jesus. It was just about Stacie's due date and the scene was set for a new baby Aguilar to enter our family.

Stacie gave birth to a beautiful baby girl they named Ashaya, which meant beautiful woman of God. It was my first grandchild and as usual I over did everything. Watching her take her first steps and having her in my arms at every concert we did, I fell so in love with her and didn't want to share her with anyone in the world. Only grandparents could ever understand what I am saying when it comes to grandkids. I just wanted to show this beautiful child to the whole world and tell them how proud I was of Geronimo and Stacie. Stacie didn't have much time for her parents before the baby, and now it would even be more difficult to visit with them.

I knew her family was dealing with separation anxiety more than ever now as Stacie's dad and I started bumping heads about a lot of things. I respected him a lot and his wonderful family, but I was a man on a mission. I wasn't about to let anyone slow down the progress that our church was making. Another blessing would soon be coming down the pike. Yes, Stacie was pregnant again with a little boy on the way this time; they named him Moshe Dyan after the great prime minister and military leader of Israel. Children are a blessing from the Lord and he who has his quiver full is blessed. Young Stacie becoming pregnant again at such a young age was another nail in the coffin to the relationship I had with Stacie's parents.

Stacie's family was at this time downright upset with what their daughter was up to at Set Free. I have always seemed to get the credit for what others do in our ministry. My life has been a series of events with others blaming me for their bad situation. I believe everyone has inherited blame shifting from our brother and sister, Adam and Eve. Adam blamed God for the woman he gave him and Eve blamed the serpent and the story goes on. Now it was all my fault that Geronimo and Stacie are having all these kids. It was my fault that she couldn't see her parents as often as they would like. It's lonely at the top; nevertheless, that's just part of the job description. I believe I tried to work things out, but maybe I should have tried harder. Life is definitely a growing experience till you die. I know this for sure, that I loved my grandkids more than life it self. The separation of Stacie and her family grew wider and wider and Geronimo and myself got busier and busier doing ministry.

Trinity Broadcasting Network had all our discipleship people become prayer counselors. Our people would answer live calls for Paul and Jan every night on their *Praise the Lord* show. Set Free became accustomed to counseling America. We felt so special knowing we could help people who called in with every type of need. Jan and Paul loved our Set Free family so much and they saw firsthand all the great work Jesus did through our crew. TBN had television stations across America, so Paul had a plan to help us set up detox ranches everywhere a television tower was located. We opened a new ranch in Chicago, Florida, Texas, Arizona and had plans for many more. As our ministry continued to grow I should have recalled Jesus saying, "beware when all men speak good about you, "because little did I realize how true that was. !

I have learned that there is always a little trouble in paradise. Life is filled with a little taste of Heaven here and there and God promised not to give us more than we can handle. Set Free is the first and only church I have ever had the privilege to pastor. It wasn't even my idea to be a pastor, but God called me and I resisted as long as I could. I realized I had no choice but to surrender to Gods will for me. I had no thoughts of becoming a public figure, I didn't plan on being on television, and speaking to millions of people, it was all God's plan for my life. I have seen many of my heroes fall in the heat of the spiritual battles of life.

I have witnessed church movements turn into monuments. I have seen pastors and evangelists get caught with their hands in the cookie jar over and over. It isn't how you start the race its how you finish. The great faith healer Benny Hinn has ridden on the back of my Harley. Evangelist James Robison has hit the streets of Skid row in Los Angeles with me. I have been on the frontlines of ministry with the wonderful lady Preacher Paula White and the list goes on with those who I have served with. I have often said "wise men learn from their mistakes" and wiser men learn from the mistakes of others." I believe my life has been more of the prior saying.

The trouble with my in laws escalated as they felt like they were loosing control of their daughter. I guess they forgot why she was brought to our church in the first place; nevertheless, I got the blame for it all—maybe I deserved it and maybe I didn't. Stacie and her family will always go down in my books as wonderful people. The final days of 1990 I was preparing for the greatest Christmas and New Years ever. I had a small part in over 50 new Set Free church's being planted Worldwide. I knew that Set Free Church was cutting edge, but I didn't realize that it was tearing some people up. I was blessed with the most wonderful wife a man could have. She was on this roller coaster ride to heaven and holding on tightly. My children have always been there for me, loving me and helping their dad do ministry to the not so lovely people of this world.

During this part of my ministry I was able to say with great enthusiasm that every day with Jesus is sweeter than the day before.

As I sat at my desk December 22nd in 1990 I opened a letter from Pastor Oden Fong. He was the overseer of over 390 Calvary Chapel Church's worldwide; he was also the right hand man to Pastor Chuck Smith, founder of Calvary Chapels worldwide. I read this letter with amazement and sorrow. Stacie's family had gone directly to Pastor Oden to spread rumors and lies. I immediately called Oden, and he seemed very understanding and believed the best in me, so I thought. He assured me that we would soon meet in person and work things out. I believed the best in him as a pastor from a great church. The Bible says if you have ought against someone to go to them and them alone first. The next step is to bring a witness and get their view on the situation. I was waiting for the first step when all hell broke loose. I never received the accusation list from Oden, or any attempts by him to mediate a meeting with those who had ought against me.

# CALVARY CHAPEL OUTREACH FELLOWSHIP

3800 Fairview Road, Santa Ana, CA 92704

Pastor Phil Aguilar                                     Dec. 19, 1990
Set Free Christian Fellowship
320 N. Anaheim Blvd.
Anaheim, CA 92805

Pastor Phil,

I am certain that by now rumors are flying everywhere that there is a united front led by Calvary Chapel coming against you and Set Free. This is not true. It is true that some very serious complaints have reached us and that we are concerned not only for the sake of the Body Of Christ, but also for your sake if these allegations are true.

If they are not true, then you truly have a conspiracy planned against you and many people are lying, trying to destroy your reputation. If they are true, then you are heading down the same pathway of Jim Jones, the Children Of God, Tony and Susan Alamo Foundation, and other shepherding cults built around a super-egotistical dictator and not the Lord Jesus Christ.

Everyone of these fellowships started right and ended up wrong...isolating themselves from the rest of Body Of Christ and thinking that they were the only ones doing the real work of God. Each of these leaders gained large followings but in the end were cast down by God. These were men of self-deceit. They had become gods to themselves yet did not realize it. I spoke with one of our associate pastors who left the Baptist Church with you to start Set Free. He said that you discipled him in Christ and that you were the most humble, loving brother that he had ever met. He said that you were the kind of man who would lay his life down for others.

It sounded like we are describing two totally different people here. My question is: What is the truth about you? I'd would like to talk to you an find out for myself. Would you be willing to meet with me? I'll meet you anytime, anyplace, anywhere. You name it. It might serve to clear everything up.

My bottom line is that I believe in Set Free. We need a Set Free ministry. We need a ministry that is reaching the street level people (something that much of the church is failing in). If Set Free is truly setting people free I would personally back you 100% and support and defend you myself. If Set Free is freeing captives from drugs and alcohol and but bringing them into another bondage, then the whole Church of Jesus Christ has a problem.

I have enclosed a list of the complaints and testimonies that have been directed at you so that you will know what is being said about you. Please let me know what you decide.

In Christ,

Oden/CCOF

**A letter from my "Biggest Fan", Oden Fong.**

# CHAPTER 18

# SAVE ME CHUCK

I now had this new situation to work out in my life. I didn't relish the thought of someone taking my business to the streets. I trusted in Oden Fong because of the great reputation Pastor Chuck had worldwide. The next chapter in my ministry was a regular television show every Friday night on Trinity Broadcasting which meant there would be more and more people coming our way.

I was super stoked at the privilege of sharing our Set Free Ministry to the whole world and having my friend, Tim Trader, produce it meant it would be our real story. Tim was also given the green light to do a one hour special on Set Free Ministries. The one hour special opened up with a drunk fellow sitting in an alley with no hope in his eyes and then you see this biker fellow with a menacing look on his face approach the drunk. It appears if the biker may want to do harm to the poor guy, but the biker is Pastor Phil who reaches down and grabs his hand and helps him up. Our ministry has always looked like the bad guys, yet we are sheep in wolves clothing.

We used that shot in the alley to be the opening of our Friday night shows on Trinity; we would then have our rap and dance crew doing Christian music followed by my sharing of the word, Pastor Phil style. Just the look of me and our team was so different in appearance than most of the shows on that network. Paul and Jan never judged us, but supported us winning souls and let us tell our story on television every single Friday night everywhere.

* * *

The exposure on Friday night television was out of this world. Some people came because they were just curious, some were fans, some were hungry for God, and some were just haters. The church exploded even more now with the constant media attention we were having. I was still having house meetings every morning with all of the people in the discipleship homes as they were the heart of my ministry.

My brother Billy was heading up our motorcycle ministry with about 100 bikers riding for Jesus with us. My brothers Bert and Mel were two on fire servants who helped me minister to the great crowds that kept on coming. I had to keep pinching myself from my disbelief that God was bringing all these people to my church. I would challenge all the street gangs in town to a football game and if they won I would give them money to buy a keg of beer. If they lost they would have to come to church. We never lost a game, thank you Jesus and sometimes we would have at least seven rival gangs in our church at the same time. Paul and Jan Crouch came over to my house and they watched us minister on the streets in the roughest gang neighborhoods. We had over a hundred hip hop dancers involved in our ministry, along with our skate park, surfers and our youth were bringing their parents to church.

I was getting older, but my spirit was excited about all the wonderful young people that had found a home. Their parents were often curious as to what consumed their children's time that they followed them to Set Free. I kept my young spirit to reach this new generation. Six months later with our television show taking off, the church had over three thousand adults and a thousand children regularly attending... I got hit with some more good news.

Paul Crouch asked me to be a member of the Trinity Broadcasting Network Board. I believe it was at this time in my life that I was way over my head in responsibility. I had no idea what I was getting myself into but I would do anything for Paul and Jan to show my appreciation for the way that they loved me.

**Me & the Set Free Posse at the L.A. Gospel Fest, 1989**

The board was comprised of Paul and Jan Crouch, Terry Hickey, Lori Duff and I. They shared with me that having a minority on the board would give them access to two more full power television stations.

I couldn't believe the honor I was given to be on the board of the largest Ministry in the world. People always questioned me about Jan's personal life and if she was a "for real" person.

To this very day I tell you Jan is more than the real deal and loved me at times when I didn't even love myself. Jan has been through so many hardships and struggles without ever losing sight of others. She is one of the funniest people I have ever hung out with in my life. We have watched movies like *Airplane* together, and I introduced her to a gangster movie called *American Me*... Jan has ridden on the back of my Harley Davidson motorcycle and traveled with me to Tijuana, Mexico. She loves souls, and just has a heart for ministry like no other woman I have ever met.

I called Jan one day and told her about the letter from Pastor Oden Fong and I asked for personal advice on the matter. She took the time to give me her input from the word of God and believed the best in me. Jan told me that she believed I was more like Jesus than anyone she had ever met—I knew I couldn't live up to that, but I was blessed that she would even say such a thing.

My assistant, Lois, now had nine volunteer assistants helping her with a mailing list of over 70,000 people. Set Free was a real threat to the devil's work on earth; we were truly one of the devil's worst nightmares. I had a mid week church service that I held on Thursday nights with thousands coming. I was unaware that half of the pastoral staff of Calvary Chapel in Costa Mesa was sneaking in to our studies. I didn't think Pastor Chuck would relish the idea of his leadership coming to Set Free. I am sure they were there to see the wonderful works the Lord was doing in our midst.

One of their pastors, Ray Snook told me that Set Free church resembled Calvary Chapel when they met in a big giant circus tent in the seventies. He told me we had the same revival spirit that was going on during the Jesus movement days. I was told that same story over and over as I met these new Calvary Chapel visitors who had a real desire to see God bring revival to His people. They were excited for Set Free and encouraged us to keep on keeping on.

After receiving Oden Fong's letter, and after talking to Jan Crouch, I asked Lois to set up a meeting with me and Pastor Chuck. I recently had a new fellow join our church by the name of Lonnie Frisbee, he just happened to be the first young hippie that went to Calvary Chapel and assisted Pastor Chuck with the Jesus people movement. The Jesus people movement attracted people from all over the world. The story of Pastor Chuck and Lonnie Frisbee was on the cover of the 1971 issue of *Time Magazine,* this young, long-haired preacher was instrumental in the whole Jesus people movement that made worldwide headlines. He was featured in *Time Magazine* with Pastor Chuck baptizing thousands at Corona Del Mar Beach. Lonnie was hooked up with all the big wigs in Christianity in those days. -

Lonnie recounted his testimony and told me that Set Free was the new Calvary for the 90's. I could tell that Lonnie was hurt and bitter about his experiences with the pastors of his past. I was told that Lonnie Frisbee had led the famous pastor Greg Laurie to Jesus. Lonnie was also instrumental in the great Vineyard Church movement with Pastor John Wimber.

Lonnie was obviously broken down when he came to Set Free, along with a small group of loyal friends who cared for his every need. I knew he was sick in mind and body when I discovered that he had contracted AIDS. It was around this time that people who had the disease were looked upon as lepers. Lonnie was being shunned by so many people who he had helped in the past; he had a case of Christian cooties. Set Free Church has always been a last stop ministry. I tell people if you can't make it anywhere else, give Set Free a try. I moved Lonnie into one of our homes and we began to care for his spiritual and physical needs. I recognized a huge spirit of bitterness was consuming him. Lonnie asked me if he could preach at Set Free one Sunday and I told him, after you spend a year being healed of your past hurts I will consider it." He then asked me if I could be a mediator between him and Pastor Chuck reconciling. Here I am having my own problems with Pastor Chuck's church and Lonnie wants me to work out a peace treaty with them. Well I gave it a shot and drove him to see Chuck, but Chuck made it real clear that it wasn't gonna happen.

The good part of the story about Lonnie Frisbee is that he got a lot of healing at Set Free church. As Lonnie's physical body continued to break down, he was being accused of being a homosexual who somehow deserved the AIDS virus. Christians are definitely some of the meanest people I have ever met. Lonnie needed love and the Set Free family and some of his dear friends loved him all the way to Heaven. I had made numerous attempts to hook Lonnie up with Pastor Chuck. He also needed a healing with Pastor John Wimber. Lonnie seemed to think that he needed these two pastors' approval to go on with his life. All Lonnie wanted was Pastor Chuck and Pastor Wimber's blessings to continue to preach Gods Word. He felt that he wouldn't be allowed to preach if they didn't give him the okay.

I took Lonnie to see Pastor John Wimber and the results were negative. Pastor Chuck and Pastor John both rejected Lonnie's request to continuing doing ministry I felt led by the Lord at that time to intervene on Lonnie's behalf so I told Lonnie I will put my blessing on him doing ministry if he would forgive Pastor Chuck and Pastor John. I started out by allowing him to preach a Sunday morning service to thousands of people at Set Free. He shared with me that his whole blood family had never heard him preach before Well they all showed up for that Sunday and listened to Lonnie fire up a message like a prophet from the Bible days. That was one of Lonnie's happiest days at Set Free. Lonnie's whole family gave their lives to Jesus that day. He related to me that during the fifteen years he preached at Calvary and the Vineyard his family was not there even once to hear him preach. Now here at Set Free they came and got touched by Jesus. I was so very happy for Lonnie.

I found out that Pastor Oden Fong was having private meetings with Stacie's family, and a group of about twenty other haters joined the "beat Pastor Phil down program." They had compiled an accusation list of things that I allegedly did or was doing that were wrong in their eyes. They made silly allegations like I treat my wife like a dog because I whistle to get her attention, along with a whole list of other horrible accusations that weren't silly at all. The biggest allegation I had to deal with was Fong's view of me as a cult leader. That list has followed me to this very day as I have continued for 30 years now to preach God's word. People still get a chance to read it on paper, or on the internet, its everywhere. Most of the list was just plain lies and a witch hunt from some very unhappy people. There was some truth to certain accusations about me, and I hope to be able to disclose them in a tasteful way. Why was this Oden Fong guy getting his nose in the middle of my family situation? He didn't know me, and had never been to Set Free Church. I received one letter where he said we would have a sit down together, and another letter from him where he tells me we will get together and talk. That never happened and now he was having exclusive meetings about me in which I did not receive an invitation.

In his meetings with my haters club his secretary Tracie typed up the minutes, and put it in a packet for safe keeping. Here my family was so happy serving Jesus and then some guy I don't even know is setting me up to be known as a cult leader. It's like I was a heart surgeon and some guy makes up stories of how I was loaded on drugs while performing surgeries. There are always some people who love to believe the worst. When you have over three hundred people living in your discipleship homes it is necessary to have rules, you must exhibit tough love. Most people have no idea what it is like to run a ministry like Set Free. The people I work with are armed and dangerous with lifestyles that are difficult to control. Now some hearsay from a family that is not happy about their daughter's life wants to cause trouble.

Pastor Fong didn't follow any Bible steps to try and resolve this family matter. These meetings went on for the better part of the year. Fong not only compiled a list of horrible accusations, but then his secretary sent them out worldwide to all their Calvary Chapel churches. I am sure that those wonderful Christian Pastors didn't spread the gossip, and rumors. Oh wait a minute, yes they did, and they told everyone that would listen. Gossip and sowing discord is something God hates, yet the juicy stories about me were too good to turn an ear from.

The ministry God had raised up at Set Free was under attack and a black cloud was over my head, and I was supposed to defend myself. I learned that if you can't get the enemy in the ring, there is no way you can defend yourself. I was being portrayed as a Jim Jones or David Koresh by Pastor Oden Fong. Jones and Koresh had led their followers to a death by suicide and that was just plain wrong to compare me with these cult leaders; furthermore, it was ugly for Fong to say such things.

I only became of aware of all these rumors when I started receiving cancellations to some of my speaking engagements across the USA. I called many of the pastors that cancelled my engagements and they told me that could not have me at their church until all these rumors were settled. All of the stories about me were on Calvary Chapel's Costa Mesa letterhead. Pastor Chuck had the greatest reputation as being a man of God, if it would have been on Pastor Fong's letterhead I don't think anyone would have even listened to the garbage.

Next, Fong turned the allegation list over to a ministry call Christian Research Institute in California. The man in charge of that ministry is a man named Hank Hanegraaff, who was a friend of mine and had never spoken evil of me. Hank was known for being able to identify cults and was a Bible scholar, to top it off, up to this day Hank Hanegraaff has never written or spoke negatively of Set Free Ministries. Hank was known to be the one who would give the thumbs up or down on someone being labeled a cult.

My assistant Lois was angered by the way Fong was dealing with all of this trash talking. Lois called a group called Christian Conciliation and asked them to arbitrate our problem with Pastor Oden. They wouldn't touch it with a ten feet pole. It seemed like nobody wanted to get involved with the beef between me and Pastor Fong. Pastor Chuck is a much respected leader in Christian circles and I was this new up and coming radical biker pastor that looked like one of the bad guys to many. Fong used Pastor Chuck Smith as his covering to get away with all the outlandish charges. I had highly respected men like Warren Duffy and others who stood up for me and tried to get Oden to have a prayer meeting with me; nevertheless, Fong would not budge from his belief that I was a cult leader. I questioned God about all this and He said just keep on winning souls for Jesus.

I started to learn some things about Oden Fong and I saw that his testimony and his life were very similar to mine. I wondered if maybe it was jealousy that he was feeling toward me. I know many of his parishioners spoke highly of me to him. All I could conclude was that he wanted to do what I was doing and wasn't able to for whatever reason. I tell people all the time that Set Free is a God thing--Pastor Phil had nothing to do with it. God blessed me in that season to be used by him, for his purpose.

### THE GOD FATHER SHOWS UP
Pastor Chuck during this whole mess finally sent a type of apology letter, but it never put a stop to the madness. Jan and Paul Crouch stood by my side all the way through my attacks from Pastor Fong and his friends. Thousands were coming to church, so many were getting saved, the television ministry was booming, the posse was pumping out new songs. I had so many pastors that wanted to start their very own Set Free Church during this holy war. Lot's of people seem to love you when you're on top, and there are those who want to see you go down for the count. I was leasing the whole block now where we had our church services. My assistants Pastor Wayne and Holly Palmer continued to be faithful servants, lifting up my hands and keeping me in prayer.

I must admit once again that the Set Free family is quite intimidating looking and I want to also remind you once again that "God looks on the heart, and man looks on the outside" . God was using me to get drug addicts, thieves, and gang members serving Him. Lois had asked Pastor

Chuck several times for a meeting so we could shut Fong's mouth.

Pastor Chuck finally gave the okay for me to have a meeting with him. Jan Crouch had revealed to me some information about Pastor Chuck's personal life  Jan shared about Smith's business in Hawaii and lots of incidentals about Chuck's life. I didn't want to go into this meeting without some type of artillery.  I had been a pastor for almost 10 years now, but I was just beginning to learn protocol in the big leagues of Christianity.  My past showed that I didn't do anything nice and easy, I did everything nice and hard.  The Bible says that all have sinned and fallen short of the glory of God.  That meant to me Pastor Chuck was a sinner too and that I could talk to him man-to-man.  My sincere intentions going into that meeting was for Pastor Chuck to shut the mouth of Pastor Oden Fong forever.  From everything I had learned from people who knew him, I was convinced that Smith had the power to tell Oden to shut his big mouth. I wanted Pastor Oden to stop stumbling little children in the Lord.  It was so wrong to tell someone that their pastor is a cult leader like Jim Jones or David Koresh.

Although some people think I rode my Harley everywhere, that day I drove to Pastor Chuck's church in our church van.  Upon entering the premises of Calvary Chapel we were greeted by the security team that were very cordial, and escorted us into a large office.  I brought my wife Sandra, assistant Lois, and my son Geronimo to get all of our cards on the table. Chuck is an older, robust, grandfatherly looking fellow who is very personable, and it almost sounds like a voice from heaven when he speaks. On the other hand I am a tall dark, tattooed, somewhat scary looking figure of a man that speaks the truth in love in a forceful way.

* * *

Pastor Chuck opened up the meeting by challenging me about the accusations I had been charged with. I was deeply hurt by his opening comments that he delivered in a way that made him rush to judgment about me. I should have just shut my mouth and sucked it up, but I didn't, and replied back with some real serious rumor's I had heard about him. I made the wrong move, and believe me I paid for it dearly. Pastor Chuck isn't perfect by any means, and I will always believe Pastor Chuck should have shut Fong's mouth. The wrong I did was not showing respect for a man of God and I should have given it to the Lord and just moved on.

The meeting ended up on a sour note, and things just got worse. It became increasing difficult to run a large ministry like Set Free when you feel that you have to defend yourself all the time. The prophet Nehemiah in the Bible had a hater's club also. God told Nehemiah to build a wall for his people and when Nehemiah began building, the naysayers of life came along and threatened him. They made ugly comments about him and called him a betrayer to the king. Nehemiah would then come down off the wall and try to please everyone by telling them what a good guy he was.

God told Nehemiah don't waste your time coming off the wall and leaving your work, just do what I told you and forget what anyone has to say. I figured my best defense was to go on the offense winning more souls to Jesus. One year after Oden's attack Set Free was still going strong in the midst of all the storms of life that had come my way.

# CALVARY CHAPEL OF COSTA MESA

3800 FAIRVIEW ROAD, SANTA ANA, CALIFORNIA 92704 (714) 979-4422

February 6, 1991

Set Free Christian Fellowship
320 N. Anaheim Blvd.
Anaheim, CA 92805

To Whom It May Concern,

Several months ago one of our pastors received complaints concerning Set Free Christian Fellowship. Not wanting to believe hearsay, the pastor asked for proof and received numerous testimonies and signed statements. He proposed to send a letter and a list of the compiled allegations to our affiliate churches. He decided to contact the pastor of Set Free first with the allegations before sending the letter to our churches.

Upon contacting Pastor Phil Aguilar he received testimonies to the contrary of the allegations. My suggestion was that we just put a lid on it and to let the Lord take care of whatever problems that might exist. Therefore we did not send the letter.

Previous to contacting Pastor Phil Aguilar, copies were given by the pastor who was first contacted to the other staff pastors and to the originators of the complaints. He did not send out any other letters of the allegations. We have heard that some copies have gotten around and it was not our intent to have that happen.

Paul in his Roman epistle rebuked them for judging another man's servant. Paul said before his own master he either stands or falls and God is able to make him stand. Pastor Aguilar is not our servant thus he is not responsible nor does he have to answer to us. But the ultimate responsibility is to the Lord and it is before the Lord that he stands or falls and we pray that God will enable him to stand.

Sincerely In Christ,

Chuck Smith/Senior Pastor CCCM

**Chuck Smith trying to stop his boy, Oden Fongs actions,
but it was too late**

# CHAPTER 19

# THE LONE RANGER

What a trip it was to see all the wonderful things going on in our ministry in spite of my hater club. I thought snake handlers and lion tamers had a rough job, but there is no job as dangerous and tough as working with people and all their deadly venom. I believe that your attitude determines your altitude. My attitude was coming from the Bible. Acts 20:24 says, "But none of these thing's move me, neither do I count my life dear to myself, I am going to finish my course, and I am going to finish it with joy, to testify about Jesus." I knew that no weapon formed against me could prosper.

The Gulf War was on in the Middle East and Set Free continued to visit Israel on a yearly basis. When I made a commitment to stand with Israel, I meant in the *good* and the *bad* times. The war had caused every Christian or religious group in the world to cancel their tours to the Holy Land. Only one group of Christians flew in while the Katusha rockets were landing in Tel Aviv Israel. Yes, it was the Set Free Soldiers for Jesus who kept their word and even wanted to be there more than ever knowing our friends were in harm's way. You know who your real friends are when the times get tough and there's a chance of danger to come your way. I have learned that over and over again in the ministry.

I believe there were 45 of us men and women who flew into Tel Aviv airport while the war was still heated up. Upon arriving at the airport we were given gas masks and medicine in case the gases from the explosions started affecting us. We then went to our hotel rooms and within 24hours of our arrival, there was a cease fire. The nation was at peace, and we were free to travel length and breathe of Israel without fear. God blessed us for being courageous and keeping the faith. During the next 10 days we had the red carpet rolled out for us as we enjoyed all the beautiful sites of Israel. We also made the front page headlines in Israel's number one paper the *Maarive*.

The headlines read like this I quote: "This was without a doubt the strangest visiting delegation in the history of the state of Israel. This was a group of American motorcycle riders whose average weight is about 220 pounds, with their sunglasses, black leather jackets and all the other paraphernalia of motorcycle riders. The aura of the group would cause the Iraqi Republican Guard to look like a bunch of nuns in a convent. We sat down with them at the feet of the Warsaw Memorial at the Yad V'Shem Museum in Jerusalem. It didn't take long for us to understand that they were courageous friends of the nation of Israel!" The Set Free crew had the greatest time of our life enjoying all the love from the people who are the apple of Gods eye.

When we got home from Israel I was totally refreshed once again. Our television program was still on every Friday night with millions of viewers. I was still on the Trinity Broadcasting Network board making million dollar decisions with Paul and Jan. The publicity from the television network made Set Free a household name.

Our local newspaper called to do a story on Set Free Ministries once again. Our press had been good for so long, that I expected it to be another positive article. It turned out to be on the front page, and it was no article, it was a six page section.

Set Free has always been able to sell a lot of papers with the headlines reading "biker pastor does this or that". Stacie's family and Oden Fong had gone to the press and they posted pictures of our scariest looking guys and they labeled us a cult and spoke about the thousands coming to church. It was incredibly ironic that we were so loved by some, and so hated by others. Lois was adamant about me fighting back, but I just didn't believe God wanted me to do that. Not defending myself made me guilty to some, but I was more concerned with how God felt. I just really believed at that time, that it took two to fight. How wrong I was, and how blind could I be, but I still I kept on keeping on winning souls for Jesus.

The honest to God truth is that every time I got up to preach, so many people gave their lives to Jesus that I just couldn't stop. It was all the Lord and it had nothing to do with me. I had made myself available to be used by the Lord in any way He saw fit. Paul and Jan Crouch would not waver in our friendship during these trials.

Jan loved our people from the discipleship homes and wanted us to have one birthed at their new property in Colleyville, Texas. I had started several ranches by now on TBN properties across the USA. Starting a ranch on Paul and Jan's personal property was going to be a first for me. I had always defined a ranch as a piece of land in the middle of nowhere with some old used trailers on it where people would call on Jesus for help. No animals, no ponderosa, no frills, just beans and rice and Jesus Christ. The important part of any Set Free Ranch program was the Word of God as I had learned long ago that the renewing of the mind was done by God's Word alone.

Jan's definition of a ranch was somewhat different than mine. Jan thought of a ranch as a place for the drug addicts and gang members to feed the animals and enjoy the nature that God had provided for them. She was such a cool lady that I decided to help her with her vision and pioneer a ranch of her own. Paul and Jan purchased a 61 acre piece of property in upscale Colleyville Texas. The property had several homes, a swimming pool, and its own manmade lake on it. It was so beautiful there, and I enjoyed visiting it occasionally with a whole team from California. I sent 15 of our best people from the discipleship homes in California to make sure things would go as planned.

I sent a good leader, a man I trusted very much, who had spent seven years training with us in Anaheim, California. The ranch started up with Jan and Paul making an announcement on nationwide TV with a picture of all the Set Free family at their ranch posing by a couple of horses. They asked for donations of horses and other farm animals and it was a hit right off the bat. My overseer was doing a great job tending to all the properties and taking care of all the horses that were being donated. Jan and Paul loved to go visit there and spend time with the Set Free crew and they treated them like their own. Paul and Jan believed that Jesus, along with some good country living and honest hard work would heal these kids.

Our people fed and took great care of the horses and did all the landscaping on this monstrosity of a place. Life seemed to be good at Colleyville Ranch. I had all of our people in Texas go to the local Baptist church down the street and be a blessing in the community. I know it must have been an eye opener to see fifteen Set Free people walk into their church that first Sunday morning. I sent a guy named Ace to the ranch who was a former white power guy with a big Mohawk and another fellow, Santiago, who was a rock 'n roll crazy man, along with quite a few other wild looking characters. The ranch people helped keep the city streets clean and performed other various duties to bless the town.

Back at home in California we were still busting our butts for Jesus. I just kept on doing the best I could under the attacks from old friends and enemies. I was fashioning my life after one of my heroes on television named the Lone Ranger who had an Indian friend named Tonto. He was a cowboy who wore a mask and rode a white horse alongside his Indian buddy. The Lone Ranger and Tonto would pull into different towns and by the way they dressed, there presence alone would make a scene. Everyone would wonder why the Lone Ranger would wear a mask, seeing how only bad guys wore a mask in those days. By the end of the day people would see all the good the Lone Ranger and Tonto did. As the Lone Ranger rode out of town everyone would say what a good man he was.

I knew when we pulled up on our Harleys and had all these different looking types of people hanging together that it would blow peoples minds. I taught our people that because we looked scary to people, we needed to act completely different to them from the way we look. I have always stretched out my hand, or given a hug to strangers with the love of Jesus. I knew the media was painting me as some kind of cult leader and trying to villanize me. I understood only to well that it is all about making headlines for print. I was also quite aware that I loved pushing the envelope to the max to give the public something to talk about. Finally, I knew that all thing's work together for good, for those that are called into God's ministry. I kept telling myself it can't end this way. I fought hard to keep the faith and not to fold under all the pressures of life.

I questioned God at times and said "Lord are you sure I can handle this?" It was now time for another bomb to drop on the Set Free family. I felt so dedicated to helping others and tribulation was just part of the package I had to deal with. The Colleyville ranch did great for about 6 months then I got a personal phone call from Paul Crouch and he told me that my overseer at the Colleyville ranch had allowed a minor of seventeen-years-old to live there which was against our Set Free policies. I had a rule about teenagers living there, but the rules were not followed. My overseer, without my blessing, took in a young man in that was a friend of another leader of mine. Paul told me my overseer had been accused of offering drugs for sex to this 17-year-old juvenile. I questioned Paul as to whether this was just a made up story by this youth or not. He would not talk about the matter and had me deal with the TBN lawyers to see how we would handle the situation. I stood by our Set Free overseer and believed the best in him.

Sure enough, the allegation of inappropriate behavior by a Set Free Pastor would hit the front pages nationwide. It read Pastor Phil Aguilar of Set Free ministries and Paul and Jan Crouch from Trinity Broadcasting Network were being charged with child molestation.

This season of my life I thought about the apostle Paul as he prayed to God three times to have a thorn removed from his flesh, and God said no. God told the apostle Paul "my grace is sufficient for you my son." I have stated many time's that I was fighting an enemy that I couldn't get to come in the ring with me . I was ready to fight the charges against my overseer, I have found it a lot easier to fight for my friends than to fight for myself. My overseer told me he was innocent, and the police said they were not going to file any charges against him. The press went crazy on the story, and even Christian smut magazines followed their lead. I was getting calls and letters from Pastors who believed the worst in me once again. I was 1,500 miles away, yet the blame fell on me. I had gotten the terrible disease of victimitis during this episode of my ministry. Poor me, why me, life ain't fair, and I was ready to throw a big pity party. I would learn later on in my life that life is fair. We are a sum total of all the decisions we have made in the past.

Paul and Jan's lawyer's told me we had to make a quick settlement with the family suing us. I had done some research and found out that this young man and his mother had filed other lawsuits against ministries in the past. I told the lawyers that we needed to fight this thing to the end. The lawyers for Paul and Jan explained to me the necessity of making a deal with the family. They told me that TBN was such a huge ministry, and having a big stigma like this would put TBN under a huge cloud of doubt. They also added that it would save a lot of money in the long run making a quick deal. The only thing they told me that convinced me to settle with the family was how Jan felt about it. They told me Jan would never be able to stand the pressure under the type of negative sexual questions she would be asked. I loved Paul and Jan too much to go against anything that would hurt them. The lawsuit was handled by the Trinity Broadcasting network lawyers. Trinity's insurance company paid two hundred thousand dollars to this family and my insurance company had to pay three hundred thousand bucks. It was a nasty lawsuit, and I looked guilty as hell. What a nightmare I was experiencing, along with all my other drama. I look back now and know that Jesus can bring you through anything if we put our trust in him.

**Taking Jan Crouch for the ride of her life!**

# CHAPTER 20

# NOT MY GERONIMO

If all this drama wasn't enough, the heat was just about to be turned up in the kitchen. Lois notified me that my boy Geronimo had secretly confessed to her about a girl he had been attracted to and she loved the attention and was playing on it. I refused to believe anything negative anyone would say about my Geronimo. I knew Geronimo trusted Lois and loved her very much as a dear friend who he could confide in. I also was aware that he would not want to relay any news like that to me. I had fought alongside of him for a long time now with his in-law stuff and this could not be true, or it would kill both of us. Love is so very blind, and according to Lois, the woman he allegedly had "been" with was out to get me. Lois told me that the pressures of Geronimo's in-laws were too much for him to bear, and he knew it was his own wife's family that was making our lives so miserable. Lois said he was to afraid to bring it out in the open, so he secretly asked for forgiveness, and just kept on as though nothing had happened. Lois saw this girl being used in the front lines of our ministry and Lois was trying to warn me about the temptations that lied ahead for me.

The accusation packets that Fong compiled were showing up on pastors' doorsteps everywhere and the hot water was starting to choke me. I always published a newsletter of the churches we would be performing at next. My enemies used this to launch hate campaigns at my next stops along the way. Our church attendance was still very high, our homes still over crowded, and lives were still being changed for the good. In the midst of all my darkness the light of God still shined brightly. I started Set Free Church with the vision of reaching those like myself, who didn't fit into the regular pattern of church. I wanted a place where you could just be you. I didn't want a church that was out for anything but helping people. In my Baptist Bible College days I would hear pastors ask three questions when meeting other pastors. How many you running, what is your offering like, and what are your land holdings? I wanted the gospel of Jesus to be free for everyone. When the ministry started to explode from the hundreds, to the thousands, I was certain it was God above doing the work. I had pastors from everywhere who kept on asking me how to build a church like Set Free.

Let me take you through a journey of Set Free Anaheim church in the early nineties. Picture in your mind if you will, Noah's ark. It was just like the Set Free warehouse. As the ark was filled with every kind of animal, Set Free was filled with every type of human being on the earth. It was a church where the cookies were placed where the kids could reach them. In other words I preached a very simple message for all to understand. Set Free let anyone in the doors and treated them with love. The Bible says that the only gift that never ever fails is love. I explained to people that Set Free is like a little café. We may not have the best food around. We may not be the fanciest place in town. But we know how to greet and seat people in a first class way. I encouraged people to remember names, and to spend time with first time visitors.

We had a Mexican deli across the street from our church. They had the best breakfast burritos in town. I never had carpet put on our warehouse floors so people could eat their burritos during church services. I never wanted anyone to get upset for dropping or spilling something on the floor.

Set Free has always believed that church is the people and not the building. I have always wanted people to feel at home. I don't care if you have a hat on, or if your chewing gum, or if you smell like booze, smoke or anything else. I am just glad you're at church and have never cared about what you did the night before; just glad you're at church Sunday morning.

Set Free Church in the nineties can only be understood as a period of time that God reached way down to the bottom of the barrel and used a motley crew to do a mighty work for him. Every Pastor or person that asked how I built Set Free, I told them it was all Jesus. They never bought that story and wanted me to write a syllabus or a study for them to learn how to fish the streets of life. Remember if you're forgiven much, you love much. The whole world is looking for love in all the wrong places. I was ignorant enough to trust Jesus to build this house. People all over the world are looking for a place that they can be accepted. I don't believe they need someone to tell them how bad they are. I think people beat themselves up enough.

Lastly Set Free Church in Anaheim in the nineties was way beyond cutting edge. It was way beyond radical; we were not trying to be first at this or that, God was just making it happen. Set Free was not copying any other type of ministry. It was God built and God sustained. In this story God is the only one who will be given the hero of life award. For all have sinned and fallen short of the glory of God. There is none righteous no not one. For the wages of sin is death, but the gift of God is eternal life. For whosoever calleth upon the name of the lord shall be saved. Set Free Anaheim was all about winning souls for Jesus. We were a Holy Ghost Hospital for the Lord opened twenty-four hours a day, seven days a week"24-7"..

I can remember back when I was 18 years old, high on some good drugs. I wanted God and I went looking for him at the Catholic Church I was baptized at. The door was locked and nobody was there to meet my needs and I remember saying that if I ever had a church it would never be closed. When I started Set Free I was able to fulfill my dream of a church that never sleeps and is always open.

Set Free was an emergency room for jacked up people with no insurance plan and was built for people starving for the bread of life. It got so crazy for Jesus at Set Free in 1992 that if you wanted a seat for Sunday morning service you would have to save it on Friday night. On Sunday mornings you would have to park blocks away and walk a long distance to get inside the church. Many times you would have to bring your own chairs because we would run out of seating room. Quite often you might be one of many that would watch from the streets. We didn't have big screen TVs or anything like that in those days. Down every block and every street you would run into greeters giving you a good morning hug. Greeter's in most churches have a little tag on their sport's coat and sometimes offer a handshake. Yet our Set Free greeters were mostly our motorcycle ministry men wearing their leather jackets. ,Many people would love to come to church just to get hugged by a biker.

Once you made your way in the warehouse building you would be listening to church music like no other church in town. Contemporary was not a word I would use to describe our music. It was way beyond contemporary, Set Free had rock bands, reggae bands, rap groups, punk groups, and low rider group's and on the list goes. You would notice in our building two by four bleachers that looked very uncomfortable, and very ghetto looking and if you looked up to the ceiling there was no air conditioning system or heating system to speak of. The floors were industrial beat up floors with no paint on them; our stage was huge, but portable so they could easily move them for our outdoor concerts.

You would have seen lots of young people with every color of skin and with every hair style imaginable, people with some money and people with no money. Only at the Set Free Noah's Ark church would you have seen bikers, bakers, butchers, businessmen and bums all seated together. I have always taught people if you're early you won't be late. I tell people that church starts when you get there because Jesus said wherever two or three are gathered in my name I am there in their midst. The intro music would be jamming at 9 a.m. and the crowds always came early to get their spots.

People were trained to serve Jesus, by being friendly to everyone. The Bible says to have friends, you must be friendly. We insisted on being the happiest place on earth, hundreds of our people were soul winners. A soul winner to me is someone who is always on a fishing expedition looking to see what they can catch. Jesus, in Matthew 4:19 said "follow me and I will make you to become fisher's of men." I have always taken that to mean if you're following Jesus you will be fishing for the souls of men and women.

At the end of every service I would invite people to come forward so I could pray with them for their salvation through Jesus. Soul winners all over our church would lean over to the person next to them and invite them to walk forward for prayer. Lots of people nowadays don't want to offend someone.by asking them to go forward. I would tell them if the person goes to hell, they will be offended by you for eternity. The warehouse had two gigantic garage doors where trucks could drive through and people could view. All of our windows were taken out so we could build bleachers outside for people to see in. The air was always filled with the excitement of coming to a super bowl playoff game. Set Free people were trained to work in the harvest fields of life all week long and on Sunday's our super bowl finale was praying for people to come to Jesus.

The Bible says when one sinner comes home, that all the angels in heaven have a party, every Sunday prodigal sons and daughters would pray their way back home to the heavenly Father. Each service we had people dancing in the isles when my son Geronimo and his brothers Chill and MJ did their rapping and dancing. Young and old alike loved the rap music, the lyrics were all about God, but the beat was all about dancing for the Lord. I remember rapping to a song that said "here we go everybody, gonna throw a righteous party, no drugs, no booze and no sex, this party is filled with respect for God the righteous one, Jesus Christ, God's only son. " It was so cool to see people dancing from sixteen to sixty. Everyone was loving life, and the crowds were sitting on the seat of expectation awaiting the message from the word of God.

Lois believed that God was using this Geronimo-Pastor Phil team in a dynamic way. She also told me it was a little too much Geronimo and me. Lois always had a powerful affect on me when it came to doing ministry. I trusted her as my most loyal friend, next to my wife. I understood what she was saying, but the crowds kept coming and asking for more. It has been said that pastors are just frustrated comedians and actors. At times I did feel like some kind of rock star and as a matter of fact more than once felt that I was a legend in my own mind. Power corrupts and no one can hear someone tell you how great you are over and over without starting to believe it.

**Set Free Church at its peak. Many people came to the Lord in this warehouse**

Sunday Service's ended after about two hours of songs, testimonies, and the preaching of God's word. Every service over a 100 new people would give their lives to Christ. In one way I knew that it was all God's work, and on the other hand I felt I was gifted during those 15 minutes in the spotlight. When church was over people hung out for hours just talking and enjoying the time together. I always spent at least 4 hours after church speaking to those who felt a need to have a one-on-one with me.

I remember hearing someone say that sometimes you can't see the forest amongst all the trees. I knew from God's Word that the enemy will first attack the leaders of any church trying to follow the Lord. I was also aware from watching so many other men of God quit the race, or be side tracked because of sin. I was now being set up for another downfall in my life. I can see now that I set the trap in motion all by myself. Every fighter who goes into the ring knows he will be hit or may be knocked down. I knew with Jesus I would never be knocked out. I built our ministry on God's Word and not on sinking sand. It was there that I learned about taking in the homeless, and fellowshipping, and breaking bread together and having a Christian family.

My focus started to change, and now it was all about Pastor Phil, Geronimo, the bikers and the Set Free Posse dance team. There was no denying all the great things that we accomplished in our ministry I was allowing all the demands of people from all over the world to get my attention. I hadn't taken my wife out on a date for years now. I hadn't spent one-on-one time with my children. It was all about winning souls for Jesus. Good intentions have paved the road to hell for many. I read God's Word over and over and saw greater men than I had fallen. I felt like I might be the exception to the rule and felt at times that God left me here on this earth to win the whole world.

I was winning the world while at the same time losing my family. Yes, I took my children with me on the bus, and planes everywhere I went but they weren't really with me. I was more into the performance of people, than the personalities of those in the ministry. Every time someone would call and say, "We need a Set Free in our town." I felt I had to be the answer to their prayers. I believed there was a need, but I failed to see that it was Jesus not me that they needed. I had one of those Elijah complexes where Elijah told the Lord there is none left but me to serve you. Lois definitely wasn't into traveling around the world with me so she stayed home and literally ran the administration of Set Frees Worldwide. Talk about a multitasking woman, Lois also didn't want to be near all the girls that traveled with my outreach team.

From my early years in life I realized I have always been a slow learner, or maybe there were some things I didn't want to learn. One new truth I was learning is the difference between fans and friends. The words "I love you" are so very easy to say. There are a million love songs, and a million ways to sing them. Through my many growing pains and struggles I was learning fast who was really on my team. I had been told by so many over the years, "I love you Pastor Phil." I often responded with "until I tell you something you don't want to hear". I was now living under the pressure of having to meet everyone's needs. I felt I had to keep everyone happy, and I became an enabler to many.

My son Geronimo who I loved with all my heart was the one I enabled the most. We were definitely a dream team for Jesus. Somewhere on the journey I put Jesus in the back seat and I decided to drive us into a ditch. I lived under the illusion that I had to run this black and white Set Free machine day and night. I took great pride in always being the first one there and the last one to leave at every event. I believed that the party didn't start until I walked in. I found out you have to be careful when you surround yourself with people that say so many wonderful thing's about you. You just might begin to believe it.

It seemed like everywhere I went people would stop and say hello, and tell me how much they loved me and my television show. They would give me testimonies of how I helped change their life. It was a blessing but, it started turning me into a different person. I started living my life like I was in a parade and had to keep on waving to the crowds. I was sending Set Free teams to Australia, Philippines, Spain, South Africa, China, Russia, Germany and everywhere else we got invited to go. Television appearances became the normal part of my life. When I showed up at events I was received with hand claps and shouts of praise. I felt like I was some type of hero or something. I needed to remember who I am, and who I belonged to. It had been a long time since the prison cell, where I referred to myself as a prisoner of the Lord.

Geronimo and I were living the life of two great friends enjoying the admiration and praise of people for our ministry. The things I despised in other preachers I was starting to become. My son Geronimo and I both had cool cars, Harley Davidson motorcycles and some cool looking clothes. We sure were looking fine from the outside. but the one thing we didn't have was a real relationship with our wives. .I was so consumed with ministry that my family had to wait in to line to even have a conversation with me. I would brag about not having any sleeping problems. I let people know that I didn't go to sleep, I passed out. .I used all the dumb sayings like I would rather burn out, than rust out.. I would tell people the Bible says we need to labor into his rest.. These sayings are all in the Bible but I used them for my own methods of madness at times.

I knew I had a real martyr complex when. I was invited to Hawaii to do ministry. .A dear Pastor and man who I admire very much asked me to bring a team of young people over to his church in Honolulu. .Geronimo and I and about 30 other team members flew to Hawaii to spend two weeks doing ministry. .Pastor Art Sepulveda hooked us up with housing and food. He was one of the coolest pastors I had ever met.

The people from his church were wonderful to us. .Most of my team was young and were thrilled about going to Hawaii for their very first time. Upon our arrival at the Word of Life church in Honolulu they brought us in as their very own. .We were set up to perform at their church and at a number of schools and clubs.

Pastor Art had set it up for us to have a lot of fun while we were there also. I was the workaholic who gave very little time for our team to go down to the beach. I was always under some dumb pressure that there was no time for silly fun. I didn't make time to smell the roses. I became like a truck driver who just needs to pull over and take a nap... The ministry is wonderful, but when you try to do it on your own strength you're finished.

When I got back to California all I could think about was lawsuits, accusation packets, and the people who were starting to jump ship from Set Free. Stacie's family got a hold of the *Inside Edition* television program that aired a show about me being a cult leader. They had shots of me pulling up on my motorcycle giving mad dog looks to the world. Once again the *Jaws* music was playing in the background. In spite of all of these slams by the media, Set Free remained afloat. By now our television show was receiving countless letters requesting help from the infamous Pastor Phil. In many ways I was starting to feel like I was just about done with ministry. In March 1992 I would print out our last news letter about Set Free Ministries.

A short time after printing my final newsletter, I received some more bad news; Stacie had found out about Geronimo's unfaithfulness and was leaving him. That meant I was losing her and my two grandkids that I adored more than my life. I was in mourning for Stacie, Ashaya, and Moshe. I was so pissed off at Geronimo for not being able to handle his business. I also thought it was wrong for Stacie to leave Geronimo. I was, and still am a strong believer in once married always married. My being upset with Geronimo was just my needing to blame someone. It is so easy to blame others when the times get tough. I started to become more jacked up in my thinking as the days went by.

# CHAPTER 21

# TROUBLE IN PARADISE

In the latter part of 1992 our wonderful friend and landlord William Taormina informed us our church warehouse was being condemned. There was also a news article in our local newspaper that quoted Anaheim council man Irv Pickler saying "Downtown Anaheim doesn't warm up to the look of bikers in leather jackets at Set Free church." We had been established now for ten years in the heart of downtown Anaheim. We were leasing a city block of buildings for all of our ministries. We were leasing the old Baptist church building for all of our youth. We had a full scale skate park built. We were leasing 30 homes that were the most beautifully landscaped homes around the city. I was on several leadership boards. We had opened up a pizza parlor and a Mexican eatery across from our church. This was our home and we were meant to be in downtown Anaheim.

Mr. Taormina told us our facility had failed the earthquake tests. I don't recall ever seeing anyone at our facility conducting any type of tests. It all seemed a little fishy to me. Mr. Taormina said he was concerned for the safety of our people and needed Set Free to relocate as soon as possible. I was aware that Mr. Taormina had many contracts with the city of Anaheim. He headed up a huge disposal plant that we helped him with. I just couldn't believe that this was some type of plot to get rid of us. I had many of our people approach me and tell me that Mr. Taormina is in bed with city hall.

During the exact same time we were being asked to relocate to a new place, there was a new election coming up for mayor of Anaheim. I started getting information about the new man running for Mayor of Anaheim whose name was Tom Daly, a young local fellow. Part of his platform was to cleanup downtown Anaheim. Set Free Church just happened to be right in the middle of downtown Anaheim. Tom Daly was hooked up with Disneyland who pays most of the bills in Anaheim. I had spent the last ten years in downtown working hand-in-hand with a man named John Poole who headed up the code enforcement department of Anaheim. Set Free had been the tool that cleaned up all the graffiti and made all our homes look so beautiful. What they now wanted to do was get Set Free out of downtown; I could see the handwriting on the wall. There is an old saying "you can't beat city hall" and they were right.

Since I was a young teenager in Anaheim I had dealt with profiling and prejudice. I was a dirty hippie who didn't fit into the mainstream world. When I changed my life for good after meeting Jesus, I still didn't fit into the mainline crew. I have always been a square peg trying to fit in a round hole. I purposed in my heart that I would try to please God and not men. I have fallen short many times, but always got back into the race. Disneyland was trying to get its foot in downtown Anaheim and all the politicians were on their leg. I totally agree that Set Free has always looked like the bad guys.

We have divulged in our own mission statement that we are too good for the bad and too bad for the good. I understand by choosing the path of nonconformity that I have taken the rougher road in life. It's all about who I am, and what I am all about. I love being true to myself and I will finish the course I believe God has put me on. Our landlord William

Taormina had to do what he had to do. He helped me along life's path when others refused to talk to me. He always had a heart after God and never wanted to be known as the man with the money. He wanted to be known as a man who loved God. I can remember a time when he shared a personal story with me. He told me that at the church he was a member of that he was invited by the pastor for a private meeting. He said he was so excited that he might be asked to teach a Bible study or do some type of leadership seminar for the church. The meeting turned out to be about him loaning money to the church and nothing about his spiritualness. He wanted so badly to just help people and please God. I would do anything for him and he treated me the same way. I lived in his homes and he gave me vehicles to drive. I got to know his beautiful wife and family and I was excited about his growth in the Lord. When he was having trouble at his company he would call me up for help and I looked for opportunities to be a blessing in his life.

Mr. Taormina convinced us that moving to a building on the outskirts of Anaheim would be a great benefit for us. I remember the day he walked into my office and said "I have this huge platter in front of you, just pick and eat." He was talking about a building he found for us that he believed would be just perfect. Mr. Taormina wanted to get a building so bad for us, so he took me to the location where he had found some huge warehouses that would accommodate thousands. He then showed me another property where we could set up junior church and build classrooms for all the children. He was truly excited about helping Set Free and we trusted Mr. Taormina, and knew he would be there for us. The buildings he showed me were huge and very modern looking warehouses and though they weren't in the neighborhood I wanted to be in, I understood beggars can't be choosey.

I had about 90 days to get it ready for the move. I didn't want to move out of downtown Anaheim because I loved being in the epicenter of all the action at city hall and the local police department. We had our own Cops for Christ ministry, and the blessings of the police chief were upon us at the time however it seemed like this was our destiny so we got on with the program. Our crew got to work getting this new warehouse ready for the Set Free church services. We had about four thousand adults and a thousand children coming to Set Free. The Set Free family worked day and night preparing the place for our first church meeting. We had lost some of our wonderful leadership in part to all the controversy about Set Free and me.

My lead guitar player Kid Ramos packed his bags, along with some of my dearest friends. It took the whole three months to get the place fixed up. We built a huge stage, and bought a ton of chairs to fill the place. We were now ready to open the doors of the new and improved Set Free. We still had our building for our children in downtown Anaheim at the old Baptist property. I figured we could legally fit four thousand adults in our new building with no code problems. The Mayoral election was just around the corner once again. At our grand opening service our friend and Mayor, Fred Hunter, was one of our special guests. Paul and Jan crouch were there to honor us with their presence along with Vern Jackson my favorite country singer from TBN.

Also In attendance was police officer Lou Lopez who headed up the police union for Anaheim. People just kept rolling in as we got ready for our dedication service in our new building. William Taormina our dear friend and landlord was right in the midst of it all.

The place was packed and overflowing with way more people than we expected. I was told over six thousand people showed up that day. The TV crew from Trinity Broadcasting Network was there filming the whole thing. I got up and shouted, "Let's praise the Lord," as the music began with our oldie but goodies for Jesus. Then Mayor Fred Hunter got up and preached a mini sermon as he mentioned the election was just a few days away and we were of course hoping for Mayor Hunter to win. November of 1992 was a month I will never forget. The church service was so cool, and everyone there was blessed beyond description. Over a hundred and fifty people gave their lives to Christ that morning. There was one person who gave their life to Christ that morning I will never forget, it was William Taormina himself that came forward that day. I still watch the video in amazement of all the people that got saved. Seeing my dear friend Mr. Taormina bowing his head and saying the sinners prayer was the cherry on top. I was full of tears of joy for my friend Bill and all the others that dedicated their lives to Jesus. It was worth the whole move and all the drama that went along with it to see my friend William Taormina pray to Jesus. I thank God that all of our service's have been video recorded to re live those wonderful day's. Oops did I tell you there is always trouble in Paradise?

I forgot to mention that we also had some uninvited guest's show up for our grand opening: the head of code enforcement, and the head of fire department and many other local officials. I was cited for having too many people in church and the same day as my grand opening I was informed that I would not be allowed to have church at that location any more. To top that off, the following week at the elections Mayor Fred Hunter was dethroned and Tom Daly was our new mayor.

**Grand Opening. Grand Closing**

# CHAPTER 22

# YOU CAN'T BEAT CITY HALL

Monday morning my trustworthy assistant, Lois, was on the phone to city hall. Over the last ten years she had developed a great rapport with all the leadership of Anaheim. They had her own personal phone number to call her in time of need. We had been faithful friends to the city of Anaheim. Every time they called us for help over the years, we were there at the drop of a hat. Lois knew them all by first name and we felt confident that we could work everything out and have a meeting place. Our friend, Bill Taormina, was not able to do anything to help us out on this one. All the doors were being shut in our face. This new mayor, according to many people in high places, had a secret agenda to get rid of Set Free and Pastor Phil.

Over the years I have been knocked down many time's but never knocked out. I was never a perfect Christian, but I have always had a heart after God. We only had one week to notify our congregation that we had no place to meet. The city finally broke down and let us rent the local football stadium to have church at. Lois told me that our friend Bill Taormina had many contracts with the city of Anaheim. She said they pressured him not rent to Set Free anymore. I don't know if that was the true situation at the time. I do know that we put over one hundred thousand dollars into fixing up our new warehouse. I do know that all the hard work we put in for the city was forgotten about. It was cut and dry situation with the new mayor that Set Free was on its way out.

I was personally cited by the code enforcer's for breaking the attendance law. I was given a $1,000 dollar fine; I didn't pay the fine and was arrested and put in the city jail. Bill Taormina did come and bail me out. Lois was on the hunt to find another place for thousands of people to meet at. This was not an easy task for a crowd of Set Free people. Our people were too strange looking for most churches to think about letting us meet there. Lois was so exhausted herself, trying to find a meeting place for our church. She felt betrayed when dealing with all these local officials that she used to be tight with.

Our elders and deacons were absolutely lovely people making the best of the situation. They tried to help Lois out but the problem was just too out of hand. I was pissed off, butt hurt, mad, sad—about a hundred other emotions came into play. My wife and family were so strong for me through all these trying times. I took full responsibility for the situation we were in. I never broke the law, but I did know how to irritate people with a bunch of radical Jesus freaks. Lois was always pulling off miracles for me so I thought maybe this might be another one. Lois will never cease to be one of the greatest heroes of my life.

The stress Lois was going through affected her health in a bad way and she became deathly ill with Hepatitis C, but used the last of her strength to finding our people a place to meet. We were still leasing the big old Baptist church building where our kids would meet. We had been utilizing this property for about four years now.

The city owned it, but I knew they had no use for the property and my prayers were that they would let us keep renting the discipleship homes. Our options to find a place for thousands to meet seemed to become a dead-end street. I asked many pastors with big facilities if we could lease space from them and they all answered with a hearty hell to the no. We had no other choice than to meet at our Junior Church building and do multiple services.

Lois called city hall and let them know our plans. They told us we would need to pull permits and upgrade the place for the large crowds that would be attending. We got right on it and fixed wiring, made new exit and entry ways, and got everything up to code. We had just finished changing all of our phone lines and stationary from the warehouse we had one service in. Now we needed to do the same thing at the old Baptist church building so there would be no problems. We just wanted the city of Anaheim to be happy so we could have church and continue our ministry of helping the needy.

We relocated to our old Baptist Church building in January of 1993, and all systems were go all adjustments had been made, secretaries were in place. Mail was being delivered to our third change of address. One day after moving into our junior church facility, the city delivered a 90-day notice to move out. I am not the smartest guy in town, but I can tell when someone wants me out of their hair. The building we now had moved into was being scheduled for demolition along with all the homes we were renting from the city. What a coincidence?

Lois believed that there was no way the city would be able to get away with this type of injustice. In her sickness she was still the Golda Meir *(Prime Minister of Israel in 1969-74, she was described as the "Iron Lady" of Israeli politics years before the epithet became associated with British prime minister Margaret Thatcher. Former Prime Minister David Ben-Gurion used to call Meir "the best man in the government"; she was often portrayed as the "strong-willed, straight-talking, grey-bunned grandmother of the*

*Jewish people")* of Anaheim. Lois was the toughest person I had ever met in my life. To her, the word "no" meant that in a little while the no would turn to "yes". She seemed to believe that the community would not let this happen to us. She believed all the thousands of people we had helped through the years would stand by us. Lois believed the Set Free families were loyal people to God and all of the people in leadership positions at Set Free were real servants for Jesus. They took their work for Jesus very serious. I take my hat off to all those who stood in there with me during those tough times. I knew that I was getting burnt out, so our people had to be feeling the pain as well.

# CHAPTER 23

## DAVID STAYS HOME

One thing for sure is when you're on top you have got the whole world at your feet. People love to be on the winning team, but when the poop starts to happen, the rats run for the hills. I was finding out very fast who was down for Set Free and who wasn't. I reflected back over the last 10 years about the people who loved me and helped build our ministry. I knew I was getting ready to say goodbye to my home and family and Set Free.

Of all the people that stood by me, number one of course was my wife who never ever stopped believing in me and has never left my side. She was strong in spirit, and her forgiveness of all my sins kept me in the race. There was Holly Palmer, my faithful friend from the beginning and her husband, Pastor Wayne my trustworthy assistant who rode with me and ministered along side of me for so very long.

Lois was my right arm, giving her last breath trying to help my family and I survive all the attacks coming our way. My brothers Bert, Mel, Billy loved me when I was doing ugly things. There were so many wonderful people that built this ministry. I was scheduled to take another team to Hawaii and hit all the islands with my friend Pastor Art Sepulveda. Art knew that I was going through some heavy struggles. He paved my way and opened many doors for our ministry to continue. To him I will be ever grateful. Everyone knew I needed a break from Anaheim but I don't know if they understood I needed more than just a break.

Lois convinced her mom to buy a greyhound bus for us to continue road trips when I returned home from Hawaii. All who knew me well could see the possible spiritual death of me as I was not dealing with the onslaught of life very well. I had gotten myself involved in some deadly relationships during those times and I didn't always heed my friend Lois's advice. My close friends were doing all they could to keep me from committing spiritual suicide. Lois always took things into her own hands when possible and she knew I would be out of town for at least two weeks on my Hawaii tour.

She scheduled a protest at city hall in Anaheim in an attempt to save our properties. She knew if I was there I would mess it up because I had a reputation of giving the farm away. It was best that I was gone because I don't really think I cared any more if we won or lost. I was pretty much a walking dead man at this time. I knew I had committed some ugly sins, and that I wasn't the Pastor I had been in years past. Lois enlisted Set Free Church's from everywhere to attend the rally and a protest march around city hall.

Lois invited all my supporters who had stuck in there with me, from Rabbi Haim Asa from the local Temple, Frank Eiklor the head of Shalom Ministries, Pastor Wiley Drake, ex-mayor Fred Hunter and a huge host of others were there to speak on my behalf. Lois made sure all the major news stations were on hand.

Our former mayor, Fred Hunter, stood up and questioned why the new mayor, Tom Daly, had to have our property, when there were so many other empty buildings in town. Mayor Hunter said he believed that city hall and the new Mayor had a hidden agenda. I knew in my heart that I was finished at least for now in beautiful downtown Anaheim. I felt like I was going to be tiered and feathered next. Lois had a great event and our Set Free people were so very supportive.

While in Hawaii I went through the motions, but my heart wasn't there. Pastor Art did all he could to help me through this hurricane of a storm. When I arrived home from our trip to Hawaii I checked in with Lois. She told me how great everything went, but it just wasn't going to work. I made an appearance at the next city hall meeting and we filled the place with Set Free family. We were there to make our last and final plea for help. The new Mayor wouldn't budge and the rest of my world started to fall down on me. My final words to the new Mayor at city hall that night were, "Mayor, I might just be moving right next door to you".

Paul Crouch was the man I trusted more than anyone on this planet. He called me up for a one-on-one. He asked me about a specific sin in my life and I spoke the truth to him and believed he had my best interests at heart. God knows my angel Lois had dedicated her life to serve the Set Free ministries and she was now sicker than ever. We sent her to Set Free Hawaii for a much needed rest.

A couple weeks later when Lois came back home the Orange County Register newspaper came knocking on my door asking me about my financial connections to the Trinity Broadcasting Network. I told them that I was just a figure head and no compensation was given to me. The news people turned that statement into me saying I was a puppet for Paul Crouch. A Calvary Chapel pastor from the east coast jumped on it and tried to get TBN kicked off the air. Trinity Broadcasting Network now came under investigation from the FCC. Paul Crouch got me a lawyer and I had to give testimony that I was a real board member and made real decisions. Next Paul Crouch called Lois to tell us that they were removing our television show and I also was removed from my position on the board at Trinity Broadcasting Network. I went from champ to chump in a hot second. I know God used me to help restore all of TBN stations by the testimony I gave to the FCC. Paul said I would be back on the air one day, and I have never stopped believing in Paul Crouch and his ministry.

Paul Crouch is a wonderful man, but it's hard to stand next to a fellow who has the whole world falling down on top of him. It was the beginning of 1993 and Set Free had booked another tour to Israel as we had made it a yearly ritual to visit the holy land. I remember going to the bus that was ready to take the Set Free family to the airport. I went to say goodbye to everyone, they had no idea I was not getting on the plane with them. I had been the leader of every tour and the one who got them excited about this trip. Now I was a broken down preacher who just needed a place to lie down and spiritually die. I should have been on that bus and headed out to Israel.

In the Bible there is a story about King David sharing about kings going to war, but at this particular time, King David decided to stay home. It was a big mistake for King David because his staying home resulted in his adulterous affair with Bathsheba. King David went down the tubes for a good period after that sin. I should have got on that bus because I too went down the tubes for a good period of time. Now Lois knew I needed to get out of town on the tour bus her mom bought us. I needed the fresh air of just telling people about Jesus with no politics involved. I handpicked a crew of about 60 young people and a driver we called Broski to drive us on a soul winning tour.

Paul Crouch called me and told me when all the dust settles that Set Free would be back on the air. By the way things were looking; the dust was not going to settle any time soon. My own congregation needed to have some answers from me about possible acts of sin in my life. They wanted to know exactly what was true about the allegations against me and what was not. I didn't feel it would benefit them or me if I told them the truth. I finally wrote a letter explaining that my personal life had gone off track and I didn't blame anyone or anything but it was all personal to me. I know people love to hear juicy gossip, but I wasn't gonna be the one to give it to them. I figured they could believe the best or the worst in their Pastor.

A block-long parade of Set Free Church supporters group for speeches in front of a former Baptist church at 305 E. Broadway, following the church's eviction from the building by the city. Below, Mario Martinez (center) protests eviction.

Jack Hancock
North County News

DEMONSTRATION

# Set Free members condemn eviction

## Crowd of 500 rally in front of City Hall

By Tenny Tatusian
North County News

Pointing the finger of racism and prejudice at the Anaheim City Council, hundreds of members of a religious organization Monday protested their pending eviction with a rally and a march that landed them in front of city hall buildings.

Set Free Christian Fellowship, a controversial organization made up of former drug and alcohol abusers and known for its black leather jackets and motorcycles, were told last month that they had to move out of a city-owned building on Broadway that used to be a Baptist church.

"We're saddened by what Anaheim's priorities seem to be," Set Free Executive Director Lois Trader said, adding that the orga-

nization has spent $16,000 removing the building.

The rally began at noon in front of the Set Free Palace. After listening to four speakers, including a city councilor, the 500-strong crowd marched west on Broadway and turned north onto Anaheim Boulevard to the front of the city government building.

"When I was mayor you didn't have this problem," Councilman and former Mayor Fred Hunter said. "We have an agenda in this city and I'm sorry to say it's of racism and bigotry."

Set Free member and rallier Shellie Najava said the city is discriminating against the organization. "No one is doing anything wrong. People who otherwise

Please see PROTEST/6

Article of the protest led by my good friend Lois Trader, to save our church.

• • •

FORGIVE ME FATHER FOR I HAVE SINNED

# CHAPTER 24

# GOOD BYE ANAHEIM

I was preparing to go on the road for an extended period of time. One of our elders had found a small meeting place for the remnant that still held on to the Set free vision in Anaheim, California. I knew I was ready to give my last hurrah in the city of Anaheim. In April of 1993 I scheduled an Easter Service at the Anaheim Glover Football stadium for my farewell message. It was a great service and close to seven thousand people showed up that day.

I was ready to turn over the church to one of our good men Pastor Bob Nixon. Lois came back from Hawaii, somewhat refreshed, but still not feeling good like the old days. I approached this farewell as a man who was dying and didn't want to be a burden to anyone. All the history of Set Free up to this time was me carrying the ball, and the final buck stopping with me. More than 80% of all the monies raised to support our ministry came from my speaking engagements. Our people were financially poor, but Jesus rich.

I was not living the Christian life I should have been living and I truly felt heartbroken that last service and I was there to tell all our people that I was not worthy to be the Pastor of Set Free Anaheim anymore. The stadium was nearly filled with crying people, who had loved our ministry and who had loved me. Anaheim was my hometown, where multitudes of lives had been changed for the good. So many memories, and I was ready to leave it all. Deep in my heart I believed I was doing a favor to our church and I had no idea I was leaving people to fend for themselves, and leave them with abandonment issues.

It was hard on so many people because the Set Free style of church was all they knew. Many were upset with me and looked for ways to hurt me for leaving them. My final words were those of General Douglas Macarthur, "I shall return." Many hearts were broken and many felt betrayed, and I was responsible for all this chaos in so many people's lives. I never wanted it to end this way. The Bible say's you reap what you sow, I had sown in the wind, and reaped a whirlwind.

There was always a remnant that would not leave my side and I just couldn't shake a whole lot of people who loved me when I was very unlovable. I felt like King David as he was on the run from King Saul and David had a motley crew of distressed, hurting people who stayed at his side. I refer to King David a lot because I so relate to all of his sin, and all of his pain, and all of his tears he shed of remorse. I didn't always do right, but I knew I had a heart to do right. The small building we had rented was now taken over by my friend, Pastor Bob, who I had worked with for many years. I believed he would be a good pastor to those remaining in Set Free Anaheim. I believed my leaving would make it easier on the existing Set Free Church in Anaheim.

I had our tour bus painted black and white with the Set Free Posse painted on the side panels. The people traveling with me were mainly young people, full of zeal for Jesus and ready to hit the road. A lot of them had traveled with me all over the world. Lois wanted nothing to do with the new Set Free in Anaheim so she just stayed back and rested. She would stay in touch, and always prayed the best for me. We were being split up for the first time in 11 years and we both had separation anxiety.

**Set Free Posse on the road.**

My son Geronimo and a whole crew of our top rappers and dancers got on board. I was going to miss a lot of dear people that I loved so much. The tour bus was now full with the Set Free Posse, including three of my sons (Geronimo, Matthew and Phil Jr.)

My wife Sandra stayed back with my youngest son, Hebrew and my daughter, Trina joy, as they were waiting on us to get settled somewhere in northern California. There was a town called Visalia where I often visited some dear Christian friends. I called my pastor friend from there and told him I wanted to relocate there and help him with ministry in northern California. He was thrilled about the opportunity of working with Set Free, Geronimo and me. All the other young people felt like we were on an adventure ride at Disneyland feeling so very care free. Think about it for a second if you will, tour bus, all the food you want to eat, wonderful friends and doing nothing but sharing Jesus hip hop style? Life was going to get better from here on out. Goodbye Anaheim I will miss you.

With my daughter-in-law gone Geronimo was a single man again and I heard that he liked this one girl in our group named Samantha. By this time I wasn't quite sure about what I thought about anything anymore and I was still trying to work on me.

It seemed like city hall had won, my daughter-in-laws family had won, and the enemy was trying to wear me down. I believed Visalia would be a beautiful brand new start for me and my family to relax and start enjoying ministry again without the haters club.

Things were beginning to go well the minute we pulled into town. My son Matthew joined the Redwood High School football team, and I opened up a skateboard shop to use as an outreach to the youth of their city . I found a beautiful 9-bedroom house for my team to live in, and I set up meetings with the chief of police, and all the community leader's to inform them that I was in their city to be of help. Life looked very hopeful the first 6 weeks in Visalia. There is many little rural towns' surrounding Visalia so we kept a busy schedule on a daily basis ministering to the young people in the area. Every weekend we would do concerts at different churches and at football stadiums. Everyone seemed so excited about us relocating to Visalia and the benefit we would be to their city. I had people driving up every weekend from Anaheim to help me with my new life there. Pastor Ron Wheeler, Erik Bryant, my wonderful friend Teri Gallegos and her family and a lot of other wonderful Set Free family loved me when I didn't even love myself.

I was having fun once again doing what I do best, sharing the good news about Jesus. I was starting to feel alive again without all the haters breathing down my neck. We were back in the schools speaking to the gang kids, and helping people get off drugs. The city of Visalia was ripe for the pickings and hundreds of people young and old were coming to Christ during our first weeks there.

One night we were doing a big concert at a high school stadium. There was a huge crowd that came to hear the music and the preaching. The rain started to come down hard all over the city. It rained everywhere in town but on the football field where we were performing at. It was a miracle right in front of thousands of people.

I knew Jesus was blessing our move up north and I would call Lois and let her know all the great things happening to us. She was so happy for me and my family. My ex-daughter-in-law's family kept calling Lois leaving her terrible messages of how Pastor Phil had left her behind and Pastor Phil doesn't care about her life at all. People are vicious and I had no idea what I was getting into when I surrendered to the call of Jesus.

It was too late now because I was too deep in to get out. Things were going so very good and I was actually feeling very happy again. Once again one of my favorite teachings was coming back to haunt me. I always told people the only problem about going someplace new to start fresh is you have to take yourself with you. I hope you're enjoying this roller coaster ride with me and my life that keeps taking those twists and turns. In the Bible, Jesus teaches us what is referred to as the Lord's Prayer, He starts off by saying "Our father which art in heaven, hallowed be the name, thy kingdom come thy will be done, on earth as it is in heaven. Give us this day our daily bread." Let me point out that he said "Give us this day" not a bunch of days or weeks or months, but this one day that we are living now. He tells us in His Word that today's problems are enough for us to handle. If I would have known what I would be facing in life, I don't know what I would have done.

I wanted to get back in the spiritual condition I once was and I wanted to be able to say without reservation, that every day with Jesus is sweeter than the day before. Every time I made a decision that I was going to go 100% for Jesus again all the demons of hell came after me.

I received a 911 call from Lois who gave me a head's up that there was a Calvary Chapel in Visalia out gunning for me. She said the pastor there called her and said he and a number of other pastors were going to the press about me and Set Free ministries. The Calvary Chapel pastor told her they wanted me to address the allegation list publicly in front of them on their local news station. It had been almost three years and that list was still being circulated. I told Lois that I would never sit at a table with those calvary-ites. I believed they were a bunch of headhunters out to kill me.

The Calvary pastor in Visalia must not have read the "I am sorry letter" Pastor Chuck had sent to me. I had already dealt with Pastor Chuck and Oden Fong and saw no reason to speak to these pastors I didn't even know. I shared with your readers before that I had this weird philosophy back in the days. I told people I would not argue with them, because I believed it took two to fight. I wasn't going to be one of the two. I was quickly finding out again that it only take's one to fight because you can be begging them to stop as they are beating you down, or you can be unconscious, knocked out on the ground, and they will still keep pounding you.

I had dealt with the toughest gangs throughout my ministry and I learned that there is no gang tougher that the Christian Mafia. For some reason these pastors who don't even work with the type of people I, do felt they had a say so in my life. Lois was right about this Calvary Visalia pastor and sure enough the television cameras were at my house knocking on the door. The paparazzi had found me and wanted to sell some juicy news about me and the Set Free crew. I have found that what some people don't like in others is what they don't like in themselves. Pastor Oden Fong would become living proof to that when he was caught with his hands in the cookie jar years later.

I called Lois and told her about my visitors and asked her advice. She stayed consistent about telling me I needed to fight back. I kept quoting scriptures to Lois that said vengeance is the Lord's but she was a fighter all the way, and maybe I should have listened to her.

Sandra was in town during this episode from the news media so we took a long drive one night and I shared deeply about my life and all I was going through. I was learning that I had to get past the "why me Lord" and get to the "what are you trying to teach me Lord. " My wife and I talked about my unfaithfulness to her and about a lot of

* * *

issues I had going on. She assured me that she had forgiven me, but that her heart was broken.

A couple of days later I instructed our crew to pack their bags and I pulled my kid's out of school and headed out to Pismo beach. Pismo beach is a resort town where we had also done a lot of ministry and I had a friend there who offered me a place to stay. Sandra went back to Anaheim to rest from all this drama and about two thirds of our group said they were calling it quits. I was broken hearted once again about all the pain I put my wife and children through. Visalia was robed of a ministry that wanted to help all the gang kids out of their negative lifestyle.

I was definitely a vagabond on the run believing that it is harder to hit a moving target. My crew was leaving me at a pretty fast rate now and I couldn't blame them for leaving me and the mess I was in.

I got another bomb shell dropped on me during this time that rocked my whole world like never before. I had a sin catch up with me and I was definitely guilty of this one. I won't mention names because I don't want to hurt anyone's reputation as I figured my reputation was jacked up enough. I know you would like to hear the juicy details, but just let your imagination run wild, and you will hit the nail on the head. I lasted about a month in Pismo beach and my family weathered the storms with me. I had plenty of time in Pismo beach to make the decision to quit the ministry as I was done putting up with the Christian cut-throat people I had come into contact with. I asked the Lord to protect me from his followers. I was hoping at least one pastor would come by my side and help me back to the arms of my heavenly Father. God did answer my prayer and sent me Pastor Larry Huch who reached out to me, but I just wasn't ready for help yet.  When you think you've hit bottom, you're not even close.

At the Set Free Christian Fellowship's last service, Pastor Phil Aguilar gives his message to a crowd of more than 4,000.

# An Unorthodox Goodby-

## Anaheim Church Says Farewell to Premises With Rock 'n' Roll Celebration

By ERIC LICHTBLAU
TIMES STAFF WRITER

ANAHEIM—Evicted from their church by city officials, more than 4,000 members of the controversial Set Free Christian Fellowship said an emotional goodby to their place of worship Sunday with a raucous, rock 'n' roll Easter celebration.

"This is our last service," Pastor Phil Aguilar, 45, said as he surveyed the packed bleachers at the city's Glover Stadium, about a mile from the city-owned site that the church is vacating. "There will be a lot of sad farewells for a lot of people here."

Set Free, whose congregation includes ex-convicts, drug addicts, the homeless and others among the community's downtrodden, has made a home in Anaheim for the last decade, earning civic awards and praise for its community work along the way.

But officials will soon evict the church from a city-owned building at 935 E. Broadway because the city plans to build a Boys and Girls Club, a gymnasium and a community center there.

Several hundred church members protested the eviction in

Kim Winn of El Toro and fellow church member Joseph LoPresti of Whittier exchange hugs after service at Glover Stadium.

February, marching to the steps of City Hall with placards and six-foot crucifixes in a peaceful demonstration. Many maintained that the eviction amounted to anti-Christian "discrimination," but city officials say they are merely trying to move ahead with local redevelopment plans.

On Sunday, however, many church members struck a different chord, saying that they have become resigned to the eviction and hold no bitterness toward the city, even as they prepare to pack up and vacate the building for good in coming weeks.

"It's the way of the world," said Daniella Duncan, 20, of Downey. She has been a member of the church for 1½ years and attended services Sunday with 10 family members.

Added Patricia Bass, 34, of Santa Ana: "We just lost a building. We haven't lost anything important. We are the church, we are the building."

Set Free members said they now hope to find churches elsewhere in the area to attend. Aguilar, meanwhile, said he plans to travel the region to preach his message of Christianity and hopes to set up a new home for the church in Anaheim in

**Please see CHURCH, B5**

One of the saddest days of my life.
The article of our final service in Anaheim, CA. April of
1993

# CHAPTER 25

# NOMAD

There were still plenty of Set Frees rocking and rolling for Jesus. I called my friend, Pastor Eddie Banales, from Set Free Pomona and asked him to take over the leadership of all the Set Free churches until I was healed from all of my bitterness and pain. Many Set Free pastors hung in there with me throughout my turmoil: Pastor Willie from Set Free Yucaipa, Pastor Marcos from Set Free Gardena, Pastor Aurio from Set Free San Jose, Pastor Tim of Set Free Huntington beach, Pastor Mike of Set Free Bakersfield, Pastor Rob of Set Free Long beach, Pastor Cowboy from Set Free Phoenix, Pastor Jeff from Set Free Venice, and Pastor Chip from Set Free Fresno and many others.. They were the ones who stayed close and continued loving on me. I was done with ministry and I wanted to find a place to hide out. I always loved Venice Beach, and felt they were my kind of people, so my friend Pastor Jeff Seymour hooked me up with a place to live and I was ready to move to one of the most radical cities in the world.

Thousands of people are on the boardwalk of the beach everyday living in a carnival, circus type of atmosphere. The people are some of the strangest looking, unique, wonderful people I have ever met. You don't see any Calvary Chapels booming in those neighborhoods due to the presence of a unique element of people. This made me feel safe from that group of mean-spirited people. I moved into a part of town they called Oakwood, which was a rough neighborhood that had a gang war going on in the streets surrounding my new residence. The property I moved into had a two-story apartment and a three-bedroom house on it. I was down to about twenty people living with me and my family when we got there. I was down to seeds and stems financially speaking and I needed a hustle to earn money to support my family.

Pastor Jeff showed me how to make incense, and I opened up three incense and oil stands right on the beach at Venice. I had some wonderful ladies who had hung in there with me and they ran the ghetto enterprise. Jennifer, Goldie, and Kellie will forever go down as real friends in my history book. I remember my boys MJ and Chill (Phillip Jr.) putting an offering box out on the beach and rapping for money donations to buy things teenagers need, because we all had to fend for ourselves and that included my boys. My wife opened up a booth on the beach selling imported furniture from Bali, and she became quite an entrepreneur herself. My best friend Chip and my Servants for Christ motorcycle brothers were always lifting my spirits. Set Free has never shaken the biker image from people's heads. No matter where we have lived or worked, we always were considered the bikers for Jesus. Our Set Free men have always looked rugged and tough on the outside but they were full of Jesus in the inside.

At that time I was driving a 1993 white Astro van with some cool looking wheels on it. I was upset with God and I decided to take the big "Trained to Serve Jesus" sticker off my vehicle and replaced it with a sticker that read "shit faced and pissed off". To show off my anger, I took it a step further and removed my custom license plate that read BIKRPAS *(biker pastor)* and changed it to read "Chief" and underneath the license plate I hand painted "of sinners".

I was now officially being called "Chief" *(not just because of my Native American roots, but as in the Chief of sinners)*. I was doing anything I could to distance myself from being a pastor and even from God. Word went out that I was not doing Set Free anymore and I had three different outlaw clubs hit me up about joining them. I thought about it at great length seeing how I was being treated better by them than by most of my Christian so-called brothers.

Believing I could just change my name and blend in to Venice Beach was a joke. God does not change his mind when he calls someone into the ministry. Everywhere I walked on that beach people would recognize me and ask me for prayer. To the point where even in the filthy public restroom of Venice beach, I had someone knocking at my bathroom stall asking me "pastor Phil is that you in there, I need some prayer brother." During my most backslidden times people still wanted to know where I was having church. I hated it, but I loved it too. I was so broke in Venice that we had to trim down to just a small group. No longer could I afford to take everyone on trips to Hawaii or even the local hamburger stand. While living in Venice, I was mad at God, on the other hand, I kept searching for the road map to get back home to Him.

The most heartbreaking part of my time in Venice beach was the departure of my son, Geronimo. He left in the middle of the night without a word to me or the rest of our family. After the wonderful restoration of our relationship, it was now over. I had to take full responsibility for my bad decisions over the years and I was living the Bible stories first hand, one by one. I felt I had been wrongly accused like Joseph, I sinned like King David, and I was a deserter like Peter when he betrayed Jesus. I knew one thing for sure; God wasn't done with me yet. At my very worst in times of bitterness and being mad at God in Venice beach, all I could hear my heavenly father tell me was, "I love you son, I love you son, I love you son."

Its Gods love that leads us all to repentance and God loved me when I didn't even love myself. Everyone eventually left me at Venice, except for Sandra, my younger children, and a few others... I guess it was time for another chapter in my life and one thing for sure is I knew I had finally hit rock bottom. There was no way but up for me now. So much hard work and discipline is required to climb the spiritual mountain of Jesus. Coming down, back sliding is very easy and I didn't just hit bottom, I broke through the ground and ended up in the bowels of hell. I had people tell me to just get back in the race, but some people have no idea that when you hit bottom as hard as I did, you don't even know how to get back up. You need the Christian paramedics to get the defibulators out on you. You need mouth-to-mouth spiritual resuscitation.

I had a friend named Gilbert who told me he had 38 acres in Lake Elsinore California to use for ministry. I made a decision to give the ministry one more shot, and I sent out a newsletter to the few faithful friends that I was starting a training center in Lake Elsinore where we would just study the Bible together. In my newsletter I admitted to my backslidden state and believed God called me back to work for him. I was pretty beaten down and at a very humble place in my life where I knew I could relate to every kind of problem.

# CHAPTER 26

# SUE THE BASTARDS

Two weeks in to making another attempt at my new walk with Christ in Lake Elsinore I received a letter in my mail box. It was from Pastor John Duncan, Calvary Chapel of Lake Elsinore. I had never met or heard of him before but I guessed that the only way these pastors could be noticed in life was to jump on me while I was down. I told Lois I was going to write Pastor Duncan a letter and plead with him to leave me and my family alone. He had sent a horrible letter out to the whole community warning people about me and I soon had the police at my front door inquiring about this so called dangerous man.

I was definitely getting beat up again, from my head to my toes. I knew my life had changed or I would have made a personal call on this Duncan guy if you know what I mean. Paul and Jan didn't like what was going on with all the negative letters Calvary chapel was sending out. I had friends advising me to do some crazy things to these people, but I thought about King David when King Saul was trying to kill him. David humbled himself and would not hurt anyone. Through all of this madness I maintained my desire to please my heavenly father.

Paul Crouch personally called Pastor Chuck Smith and set up another private meeting with me. Paul told me to take a witness so words would not be distorted afterwards about what happened behind closed doors. I felt that God wanted me to go see Chuck all by myself and I didn't take the wise advice of my friend Paul. So here I go again trying to gain access in the Christian world and once again excited to be able to talk with Pastor Chuck. I was definitely now a broken man going to see Pastor Chuck with nothing but love and I only wanted peace and protection for my family. I showed up for my meeting with Pastor Chuck early that eventful morning. It had been three years now since we had our last meeting and three year's of torment, and pain from Calvary Chapel Church's all over the place. They had been stalking me like a head hunter looking for a new skull to hang up.

Pastor Chuck was very kind and hospitable as I entered his office, and I was eating humble pie on the way to our meeting so that God would bless our time together. There was a surprise guest at the meeting--Pastor Oden Fong. I asked myself what in the world is this clown doing here at my private meeting? I won't say what I'm thinking, but I know Pastor Chuck and Oden had a strange relationship of some sort. I acknowledged Pastor Oden and was very respectful and I got right to the point. I asked Pastor Chuck what it was that I needed to do to make things right so that I could just go on and do what God had called me too. I told him I was willing to do anything at this point to protect my family from anymore negativity coming our way.

In church I taught my congregation what I learned in elementary school that sticks and stones can break my bones but words can never hurt me. That was a lie, because words can hurt you and they can destroy your life worse that any other weapon.

Pastor Chuck had said three years prior in his apology letter that I was not accountable to him or the people of Calvary Chapel. But for some unknown reason Pastor Oden Fong and all of his Calvary friends didn't care what Chuck had to say and thought they could just gang bang me. In the world you can just crack someone in the head who you get pissed off at, but as a man that claims to love God the rules are different. I really wanted to know what I had to do to bring peace so I asked Chuck if he wanted me to start attending Pastor Oden's Bible studies. I was willing to go to any length to save my family from any more hurt. Pastor Chuck told me he had no problems with me, and mentioned he had problems with his own pastors. Pastor Chuck made me feel like the war was over and as I walked out of that meeting Pastor Chuck handed me his new book called Grace. He signed my copy, and we prayed and hugged and Oden also hugged me, and I gave thanks to God for the healing that was taking place. I walked out of that office with a big load off my chest and I convinced my biggest skeptic Lois that things were going to be alright now. During those times I felt that Pastor Chuck had the keys to life, and he opened the door to let me in.

I thought the meeting was a great success and I thanked God over and over again. I was now ready to get back on the frontlines for Jesus doing what I was called to do by God. Within 72 hours of my private meeting with Pastor Chuck and Oden Fong, I received a letter. Somehow the private meeting I had with Chuck and Oden got leaked. This wannabe of a man cowardly sends me a letter without ever giving me the opportunity to meet him. Lois called Pastor Duncan's office to try and arrange a meeting with me but just like Oden they were afraid of their own shadows. Lois was upset about him even getting his nose in the middle of this matter. She personally went over to Pastor Chuck's house to get this straightened out once and for all. Pastor Chuck was not there but his wife Kay was. Lois started venting and Kay said that Chuck was sick and tired of this Oden- Pastor Phil thing. Lois told her about her failing health, and said please have Chuck stop this because it is destroying lives.

Lois was now living at her brother's home in Newport Beach trying to convalesce. She not only had a bad liver, but a broken heart from all that happened to me and Set Free. I will never confess to the ridiculous accusations of being a cult leader. When you work with hundreds of drug addicts and gang member's you have to give tough love. Paul Crouch heard about my meeting with Pastor Chuck and Oden. He was sick of all this treatment from the so called Christians at Calvary Chapel. Paul and Jan called me and asked me to come on their television program and speak about all the hate Calvary was giving out. I left Lake Elsinore, and my friend, Pastor Eddie and I decided to co-pastor Set Free Pomona. I had to get out of Lake Elsinore before the head hunters shot me down. I started doing church with Pastor Eddie and tried to just move on once again.

The night arrived for me to go on the *Praise the Lord* show with Jan and Paul. I took Pastor Eddie and our whole Set Free crew from Pomona to watch the show. Paul opened up the show with a lot of scriptures about love and forgiveness. The Set Free crew in the audience packed the place out and gave loud praises to Jesus. I sat on the stage next to Jan and Paul looking out at the Set Free family. They had stuck in there for me through so many testing's and trials, and they never gave up on me.

Paul began to speak about the flyers that had been posted all over the place about me. Paul gave a description of what the flyers insinuated, and Paul made it very clear that he thought it was a terrible thing being done in the name of Jesus. It was hard to believe that grown up Christian people would go around slandering other Christians publicly.

As Paul's compassion and temper arose he looked smack dab into the cameras. Without hesitation he said "You Calvary Chapels better clean up your own act". I was stunned at what Paul was saying on national TV. Paul had remained such a wonderful loyal friend and I knew the haters club would come after him. Paul then looked at me and said, "The Bible says you're not to take a Christian brother to court. "Phil I don't know if these are real Christians by the way they are behaving", then he said "IF I WERE YOU PASTOR PHIL, I WOULD SUE THE BASTARDS." Then just to make things perfectly clear, He looked right in to the camera's eye one more time and said, "IF I WERE YOU PASTOR PHIL, I WOULD SUE THE BASTARDS."

I knew Paul was my friend and trying to help me, but I knew I was doomed now for sure. I knew that the entire klan of head hunters were loaded for bear now and ready to come get me good. I will forever love Paul and Jan for the stand they took for the Set Free family. That wasn't the first time Paul stood up for our church family. One night I was on TBN with Evangelist Nicky Cruz. Nicky and I came out on stage and the place was once again packed with the Set Free family. Our people were new Christians from off the streets and they weren't aware of how Christians express there selves with words like amen and Hallelujah all the time. The Set Free crew applauded with dog sound barks like people in the audience of late night TV show host Arsenio Hall. They meant no disrespect at all to anyone.

Nicky rebuked the Set Free family and told them to behave like real church people. Paul Crouch rebuked Nicky immediately and said these are new Christians and not aware of any so-called correct church behavior. Paul understood the Set Free family because he spent time with us. He knew our hearts were after God. Set Free Church never had any money scams. I owned no property due to my own choices and we never had any fancy facility, and never had a hidden agenda. As a matter of fact Set Free has never had an agenda. Set Free Church has always been a one-of-a-kind ministry, not better than any other, just a different flavor. I relate Set Free church in Anaheim to being part of the great salad God has set up on planet earth. Some churches are the lettuce, some the cucumbers, some the croutons, some tomatoes, some carrots, and Set Free is the *Tapitio* on top. Were a little bit spicy but we give the salad some flavor.

The cruel ruthless head hunters were shooting at Set Free from every side. We were wounded badly, but not dead yet. Many of the head hunters bragged about the disappearance of Set Free from Anaheim. Unexplainable sightings of the Set Free Church had been reported quite often to the head hunters. I guess I thought a moving target would be more difficult to hit and for many Set Free people they believed that Set Free Church in Anaheim would rise again. That night at TBN ended with mixed feelings for me. I knew Jan and Paul had their television network and millions of partners to stick behind them. I was very well aware that the battle would get heavier for me.

I received a call from Lois a few nights after our appearance on TBN with Paul and Jan. Lois told me about a major news station that wanted to do a show on Set Free that would reflect our good side. I had learned from the past that TV likes ratings and ratings come from juicy stories. Lois didn't trust anyone, but for some reason a man named Hal Eisner changed her mind. He somehow convinced Lois that he wanted to put a better face on Set Free. It might have had something to do with him being Jewish or maybe Lois just had a weak spot in her. He also said that we needed to put this Oden Fong on blast and let the world know who he is. . Oden Fong had been hiding behind Pastor Chuck for a long time now and I told Lois, "I guess things can't get any worse than they are now." I told Lois I would agree to the show and I said let the dice roll. The first part of the interview was conducted at my new apartment in Pomona near the Set Free Church. I couldn't believe I was actually doing an interview with a major news station because they always had a way of making me look bad. I know I don't have the look that makes you think about Jesus at first impression, but I have discovered that Jesus comes in many colors, and Jesus could very well come to your town on a Harley Davidson so be on the look out. The camera crew also went to one of our church services at Pomona Set Free and interviewed lots of people. The interviews seemed to go very well. I was trying to believe the best once more. I had forgotten about the part in the Bible that says test the spirits. Since then I have always tried to apply the trust God and test people theory. The Bible says we are all like sheep who wander around without a shepherd and what a dumb sheep I was, and not all that smart now.

It was now late September of 1994, and I went to Lois' house to watch the television program. Lois had just begun taking Interferon for her liver disease. Lois was so frail, brokenhearted and hurt from all this persecution from the Calvary Chapel churches. Before the program started I thought back to my beginnings at Set Free. It was Calvary Chapel Pastor, Raul Ruiz, who I first went to for advice. He sent me to Pastor Romaine, Pastor Chuck's assistant pastor and the rest is now history. The show was getting ready to be aired and I started to freeze up. I was nervous, scared, and apprehensive about viewing it. I didn't believe I could take another atom bomb on my life. Lois went upstairs and decided to watch the show by herself and then give me the run down. I was hanging out with her husband Tim and my family, trying to act like I didn't know what was going on upstairs with Lois. It was about 45 minute's later Lois walked down the stairs and looked at me with haunting eyes. I could tell by the look on her face that it was going to be terrible news. She told me that they showed very little of me talking, and then only in a sinister way.

What they showed very clearly was Pastor Oden Fong standing in front of Calvary Chapel Church in Costa Mesa. Oden Fong stood just a few feet away from Pastor Chuck's office along with some ex-Set Free members. Pastor Oden Fong clearly told the world that he believed I was a cultish in my leadership. That's like telling someone there not a crack head, just very crackish. The editing of the program was just so misleading to all the viewers and Pastor Oden said I was kind of like David Koresh from Waco, Texas. In the background you could clearly see the burning fires where whole families sacrificed their lives for their leader. He also said that I was a little like Jim Jones while the back drop was pictures of dead bodies in Guyana who had drank the deadly Kool Aid.

Then they showed a map of my journeys from town to town. They stated Pastor Phil had been run out of Anaheim, Visalia, Lake Elsinore, and Pismo beach. It was all mentioned with such gleeful smiles on their faces. I was a disease they were glad got kicked out of town. I thank God that he loves people right where there at. Lois said it was horrifying to watch . I asked Lois is there anyone who might have watched it, and gotten something good out of it. She quickly said, "not a chance" . She told me the only consolation prize was Oden's big face on national TV talking trash about Pastor Phil. I know now why the old hymns of the faith have words like "Onward Christian Soldier's, marching as to war." "Through many toils and tares, I have already come. ". The Christian walk is hardcore, and there is a hater's club that is always trying to take someone down. I just never thought when I started my service to the Lord there would be Christians trying to kill me. I was devastated once again with the results of trying to tell my side of the story. I called Pastor Eddie and thanked him for all of his help and allowing me to team up with him at Set Free Pomona, but I will be staying with Tim and Lois in Newport until further notice.

# CHAPTER 27

# WANTED

Tim Trader is a surfer and he decided to start a ministry at a coffee house called Java Jungle in Huntington Beach. Tim would do Bibles Studies at the beach every Sunday night. Tim's plan was to wait till I regroup our remnant of people and go for it again. Lois was upset that Tim wanted to keep sharing Jesus while she was dying of liver cancer. Four days after the television program with Oden calling Set Free a cult, I decided to attend Tim's Bible Study. Lois was lonely and she got off her sick bed and came down there with me. We were getting cabin fever and needed to get some fresh air. Lois was dying from Hepatitis C, and I was dying from a broken heart. Life was tearing me up and I kept asking my heavenly father if a brother could get a break.

When we arrived Tim was doing a bible study with quite a few people right across the street from the beach. Tim was a very devoted and loyal friend, and always believed the best in me and Set Free. Lois and I decided to walk down Main Street to get a bite to eat when another kick in the ding dong was going to come our way. Lois and I noticed these bright yellow posters everywhere as we strolled down the street. I picked one up and saw the faces of Lois, Tim and myself with some of the same old nasty things being said about the three of us. It was getting uglier as the days rolled by and this lynch mob was not only out to destroy my life, and my whole family, but they must have wanted me dead. I may not have been the person that would fight back for myself, but when they decided to mess with Lois and Tim the eye of the tiger came out in me. I was ready to lay the smack down on anyone who thought they had the right to mess with my people.

Lois had been my defender, my friend, my co partner in building Set Free Ministries worldwide. Now Lois had a different feeling seeing her own picture on those posters and she felt different knowing that her own children would see all this smut about their parents. I knew who the people were that were doing these terrible acts, and it hurts a little bit more when you know these are the same people you helped when they were knocked down in life. I have always preached that when you feed people you will get bit, but never did I think that the lion's mouth would be around my head.

Lois still looked to me as the strong man of God, but she had no idea how hurt I was inside. I felt so sad for my family having to go through all this bullshit, but when pushed into a corner my creative juices begin to flow. I am no different than little boy David when he saw Goliath bad talking God's people and he stood up and said, "is there not a cause?" It was time for me to stand up and say my peace. I was honest with all who needed to know that I had fallen and needed help getting up. I was clean with God when I asked for His forgiveness. I knew I was a man of peace when I didn't resort back to my old ways of hurting people. I didn't need to go to a confession booth and Calvary Chapel wasn't going to be the judge that would determine whether I loved Jesus or not.

I also knew that greater is He that is in me, than he that is in the world. I knew I could do all things through Christ which strengthened me. When I saw my dearest friend Lois's picture on that poster I made some strong decisions. It wasn't just about me that I was fighting for, but for my dear Lois and her wonderful family. I moved in to one of our Set Free Home's that my Christian brothers were still running in Anaheim and prepared for war.

# HAVE YOU SEEN
# THESE PEOPLE ?

## PHIL AGUILAR / TIM and LOIS TRADER
### OF
Set Free Tribe, Set Free Christian Fellowship, Set Free Church
### Beware of them!!
They will do and say anything in order to have people join their
### Cult like group!!
They speak about Jesus Christ and they claim to be Christians,
but be warned... THEY ARE NOT REAL CHRISTIANS
Phil Aguilar has been run out of every town he's gone to.
Yet, he continues to move from city to city.
He is now attempting to get a foothold in your city
Huntington Beach!!
Tim & Lois Trader hold what they call a "Bible Study.
You may also notice them walking around the pier area... trying
to get people to come.
The Traders are closely tied to Aguilar and have been
instrumental in hundreds of abuses committed against
hundreds of people. Lois Trader has and continues to make
serious threats against ex-Set Free members hoping to silence
us. Both Aguilar and Tim and Lois Trader are not normal people.
They are very dangerous. Please take this as a serious warning!

**The flyers that were publically posted by Oden
Fong & friends**

# CHAPTER 28

# THE VALLEY OF DEATH

I chose not to write this chapter because I don't want to go into details about people who made my life a living hell. I also refuse to defame anyone's character by giving you any juicy gossip.

# CHAPTER 29

# TOMMY TO THE RESCUE

Against my better judgment Lois had filed a lawsuit on Oden Fong and some of the culprits he was hanging out with. I was seeking God's wisdom on what step He wanted me to take next. I was pretty much done with my bitterness and realized that I would always meet Odens along my way in life. I knew I needed to get serving God again, but was wondering where I would be safe from my enemies. I turned on my television one night to Trinity Broadcasting Network. A preacher named Tommy Barnett, who I had gotten to know quite well from a distance, was speaking. I became acquainted with Pastor Barnett from a huge Pastors school that I attended from time to time. Pastor Tommy has always been a pastor's pastor and one of the leaders of a denomination called the Assemblies of God.

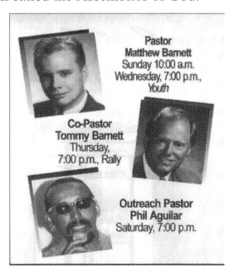

The first time I heard Pastor Tommy speak I became a fan of his. He was a real soul winner, and a valley walker, which meant he hung with people not only when they were on the mountain tops, but in the valleys of life as well. His pastor's school was located in Phoenix, Arizona and was a top notch place to learn more about building soul winning churches. When Pastor Tommy spoke, he would bring a lot of laughter to all with some of his jokes. The thing about his jokes is that I knew all of them because they came from a Preacher named Jack Hyles, who had the biggest church in America at that time. He was one of my heroes and I found out he was one of Pastor Tommy's also.

I would write or call Pastor Tommy on occasion and let him know about the good, bad and ugly of my life. When I was in great turmoil about the Calvary thing, he would console me and encourage me so very much. That night Pastor Tommy was speaking on the Trinity Broadcasting Network about a vision he had to reach Los Angeles, California with the good news of Jesus. He spoke about his 20-year-old son, Matthew Barnett who was on fire for Jesus and vicariously through his son he was going to live his vision out in Los Angeles. Pastor Tommy already had a mega church in Phoenix, Arizona and I mean this church of his was huge and located on a gigantic piece of property. He had one of the largest Christian bus ministries in America, headed up by my dear friend Pastor Jeff Alaway.

I was looking for a new place to continue ministry and I felt compelled by God to give Pastor Tommy a call. Lois of course did the calling for me and told Tommy that I would like to help him build a church in Los Angeles. Lois had sent Pastor Tommy newspaper articles about what Calvary Chapel was doing to me from time to time. Pastor Tommy always replied with nothing but good news, and with support from the heart.

Pastor Barnett had acquired a church named Bethel Temple in the heart of downtown Los Angeles that could seat a thousand people. He also acquired 14 homes located on the same block. The congregation at the church was a small Filipino family of wonderful people and Pastor Tommy would fly in every Thursday night to preach a message to the congregation. During the week his son, Pastor Matthew, would conduct Sunday services and Bible studies. Pastor Matthew was young, but he was a dedicated holy man of God. I showed up one Thursday night to greet people at the door with a warm welcome and to show Pastor Tommy I wanted to help. The first job I had in my prison church was to be a greeter and welcome sinners in. Here I was once again doing the job I loved best, loving people. Pastor Tommy and I talked about my history of building churches and being a soul winner. That is one great thing we had in common and it was enough for both of us to partner up. Tommy was willing to take me on as a project, and only a strong man of God like Tommy could handle me. He was pleased to have me on board and I was patiently waiting for orders from headquarters.

Pastor Matthew had a group from the Master's Commission, young people trained to hit the streets for Jesus, living in Los Angeles with him. They were part of Pastor Tommy's group in Phoenix, Arizona who volunteered to help build this new ministry. They were young and excited about being in the famous city of Los Angeles. There are a lot of mission minded people that want to go to New York, Miami, or some other big city for God. What most people don't understand are the difficulties they will come across when they enter into these cities controlled by so much violence.

Downtown Los Angeles is full of more gangs than any other place in America. I mean violent gangs that make a lot of preachers run for the hills. Pastor Matthew was bold as a lion, but all the Master's Commission kids were not of the same caliber. When the Masters Commission kids heard the gun shots and felt threatened, they packed their bags and ran home. Pastor Tommy had hired a music minister for the church who had no idea how to relate to the inner city folks and his heart just wasn't into it. Pastor Matthew was pretty much left alone there to fend for himself, so I believe Pastor Tommy was very happy that I could be there with his son. It was a win-win situation.

Pastor Matthew lived in a high rise apartment called Bethel Towers near the downtown Los Angeles Bonaventure Hotel. My style was different in that I would have preferred to live in the church building itself. Pastor Matthew and I would spend a lot of time together and developed a wonderful friendship. I was so broken, so hurt, and now I was offered an opportunity to get back in the mix for God with these wonderful men. The methods for reaching people in Phoenix, Arizona, and Orange County were somewhat different than what it would take to reach people in Los Angeles. Pastor Tommy told me he offered the job of helping his son to many first class pastors and they all turned it down.

Everyone was afraid of the danger it would bring to themselves and their families. I was still driving in from Orange County to help out with the new church when Tommy asked me to move to Los Angeles to assist full time in building this work of God. We both talked at length about this vision and agreed that Los Angeles was a different sort of cookie, and that we needed to do things in a different manner. We both put down our old ways and began to work together, in agreement that we would win this city to Jesus.

I told Pastor Tommy that I would need my right hand Lois to help me, and he agreed and rented a home for both of our families. I must tell you again that Phoenix and Orange County are a so very different than Los Angeles. I have always been just crazy enough to trust God and everything was definitely happening in Gods timing.

I had just received a letter from Paul Crouch saying it was time to take back the ministry homes he had purchased for Set Free. I asked Paul if I would be able to ever be a guest on TBN again and I could tell by his answer that my days were over with the TBN family. I was thankful that I had Pastor Tommy's help and I made my move to LA. Church services at the Bethel Temple Church were very low in attendance and the music sucked. Pastor Tommy asked me if I knew anyone who did music ministry, so I recruited a crew of my old Set Free people and we renamed our band the *Los Angeles International Band*. That was the name Tommy wanted our new ministry to be known as.

The Set Free band was use to doing a very different type of music than mainline churches play. I had to sell Pastor Tommy on my kind of church music and at first he wasn't ready to bite the apple, but when he saw the church people's reaction, he hopped on board full bore. Our band already had the street look to them and I knew that we could relate to the inner city very well. Set Free has always been on the cutting edge of ministry to the streets, so we got doing our thing right away.

I took songs like Smokey Robinson's "My Girl" and changed the lyrics to "My Lord" so un-churched people could pick up on the tunes quickly. I call it "getting the songs saved." Anyone who is un-churched can relate to classic songs they know and all you have to do is change a few words and the song is born again brand new. Before you knew it we had disposed with most of the old hymns and traded them in for new ones. The Bible teaches us to sing psalms, hymns, and spiritual songs to the Lord and that is exactly what we were doing. We were becoming all things to all people so we could win some to Jesus. Method's change, but the message of Jesus is still the same.

Presentation is everything when you want to reach people for God and Pastor Matthew was excited, I was excited, and most importantly, Pastor Tommy was excited. After three months of being a servant at the new church Pastor Tommy officially invited me to come on board as one of the three pastors. I was now assigned to be the outreach pastor in charge of reaping a new harvest for the lord. Pastor Matthew would preach on Sunday mornings, Pastor Tommy on Thursday nights, and I would speak on Saturday nights. The Bible says one can put a 1,000 demon's to flight, two can put 10,000 to flight, and three can turned the world upside down. It was an unbeatable team, the father, the son, and the Holy Ghost.

Pastor Tommy's wisdom and potential to raise funds, Pastor Matthew's Godliness, and my street smarts made for a winning team. Only God could have brought the three of us together, and I was once again thankful for the opportunity to just be on God's team.

Once it was confirmed that I was on staff, I invited my Servants for Christ Biker buddies to our new church. My biker ministry has always been the backbone of our churches as they were the ones who always did the dirty work. They greet and seat people, set up tables and chairs, and were in charge of all the clean up at all events. They were excited to see me happy serving Jesus again and willing to do whatever I needed.

Sheep beget sheep, so in order to reach young people I called on the assistance of my children who performed Christian Hip Hop. I informed Pastor Tommy that the kids would be rapping and dancing for Jesus at church. I can still remember Pastor Tommy asking me if I would call it choreography instead of dancing. I told Pastor Tommy that when the prodigal son came home from a life of sin, his heavenly Father threw him a party and there was lots of dancing going on. It's hard to teach old dogs new tricks, but Pastor Tommy allowed the hip hop dancing, rapping, R&B, and rock 'n roll music to go on. He knew it was reaching the people and that's what Jesus died for. Pastor Matthew and I would work hard all week doing ministry and on Thursdays Pastor Tommy showed up to encourage us all. I couldn't wait to give him a report every week of all the wonderful things God was doing.

There was an empty gravel lot at the end of our street the church owned so I asked for permission to put a basketball standard up. Inner city kids don't have any money and they are always looking for a place to hang out. If you reach the kids the parents will follow was a very important lesson I had learned at Set Free. Then I set up some weights and exercise bars for people to utilize. I put a few picnic benches together and we now had our own ghetto fabulous park. God had taught me to be thankful for what I had and to use it to the fullest. All of my sons were young and hung out with the neighborhood kids and we developed a real family atmosphere in what others called a gang neighborhood. Many pastors like to helicopter in and helicopter out but I love a hands-on ministry of being with the people to help meet their needs. In Bible College we were taught not to get to close to the people in your flock because they would see your weaknesses. I wanted people to love me where I was at, and if they didn't like me they could move on. Throughout my life, people have either really loved me or hated me.

# CHAPTER 30

# WE LOVE L.A.

The church was growing at an incredible rate now, and I never asked Pastor Tommy for money for anything. I was dedicated to serve the Lord under him and to help him with the vision that God gave him. I told Pastor Tommy about the discipleship homes we had at Set Free in Anaheim. He was unfamiliar with the concept, but open to any ideas to win more people for Christ. Pastor Tommy had 14 houses on the same block as the church building and I explained to him I never had a hired staff at Set Free to do the work of the ministry. I told him hirelings come and go, but dedicated servant's serve as unto the Lord. I told him that my kids have never had their own bedroom, and my wife and I have always had at least 30 people living in our own private home. I shared with him the discipleship homes aren't for everyone and the people who head them up have to have a real love for people. To live with someone is to know them very well. Sometimes it even means knowing things about them that you really didn't want to know.

I need to make this point clear one more time about my purpose in life. In my wedding vows my Pastor made it clear to me that he would not marry me and Sandra unless I was committed to my wife and full time ministry. In our vows the words, forsaking all comforts and pleasures for the sake of the ministry of reconciliation were loud and clear. Those words at my wedding have never left my mind and I made good on my word. I told Pastor Tommy, "If you let me, I will fill up all these homes with people from the streets who will be the best staff you ever had." It was a little freaky to him at first, but when he saw how it worked he was on board for the ride.

We brought in a full staff for our church that included our own clean-up crew, our own flier crew, and our own basketball team. We had lots of people ready to hit the streets and tell others about the saving grace of God. We were using our church facility 7 days a week just like in the good old days of Set Free. We started throwing hip hop concerts and filled the place with young people as well as the older crowd.

God caused a revival on that block in the beginning of 1995, and believe me I know what miracles look like because I saw it happen in Anaheim first hand. Now here I was witnessing it again, this time in Los Angeles, California, and we were looking for more room for all the people. God was using this raspy voiced preacher named Pastor Tommy Barnett to pioneer something bigger than all of us. It felt so good to know that God gave me another chance to serve Him, and I was happy to be a comeback kid one more time. Life ain't over till the fat lady sings, and there is no way but up when you have been knocked down.

By this time, Pastor Tommy, Matthew, and I had bonded like blood family during which time Pastor Tommy brought me out of my depression and became a true mentor to me. I didn't know it at the time, but Pastor Tommy had called Pastor Chuck Smith and told Chuck that I was teamed up with him and the Assembly of God denomination. Pastor Tommy secretly asked Lois to drop the lawsuit against Pastor Oden and the

Calvary Chapel crew. Lois was happy with our new situation and our lawyer had told Lois that Calvary said they would paperwork us to death. I knew Lois was just happy the lawsuit was served because now many of the head hunters backed off completely. Lois knew from the onset that there is no way to fight against a multimillion dollar organization like Calvary. The law suit was dropped and I didn't really care. I was now rebuilding my life with my future as a Pastor and servant of God.

# CHAPTER 31

# THE DREAM TEAM

We now had completely filled the old Bethel Temple Church with every kind of people under the sun, and our discipleship homes were full to capacity. We had trained our people to mow all our neighbors' lawns and to help people fix things that were broken and look for ways to meet any need we could. We had compassion to love our neighbor's right where they were at. It didn't matter if they knew Jesus or not. We were expressing the love of Jesus by our good works. "We are saved by grace, through faith, a gift from God."

I had the awesome privilege of now being part of Pastor Tommy's team to conduct our first inner city pastor's school. We had people come from just about every state in America. I was a special guest speaker now at Pastor Tommy's school in Phoenix and was going to be a main speaker at our own school in Los Angeles. The prodigal son or daughter story is true in so many people's lives and we can all be the comeback kid if we ask Jesus for help.

Pastor Tommy never thought small about anything, he was a dreamer, a worker and a thinker. Pastor Tommy was a very competitive man who wouldn't settle for a tie, he had to win in everything. The man truly did everything with all of his heart. He believes his dog can bark louder than all the other dogs on the block, and he applied that thinking to our ministry. Pastor Tommy and I were not in Los Angeles to compete, we were there to complete. We fed off each other's energy and the combination made sparks fly in the spirit. Pastor Matthew was another hot coal, keeping our fire for God stoked up. We had used up every square foot of the property at Bethel Temple which God had given us stewardship over. I was flying high and ready for the next big challenge in my life.

Pastor Tommy wanted to find the biggest building he could in the Los Angeles Hollywood area. He was a man of great vision, and addicted to the work of the ministry. He would bring his leadership from his Phoenix church to LA to support us in all our outreaches and to cause us to challenge each other. One night Pastor Tommy took me all alone up to this spot located on a hill overlooking downtown Los Angeles, and the famous Hollywood sign. It was the Queen of Angels Hospital of the greater Los Angeles metropolitan area.

It had been closed now for over five years and it was being used as a Hollywood location for movies to be filmed. Where we parked you could see a panoramic view of about 10 gigantic buildings with the Los Angeles smog in the background. It sat on approximately 9 acres of land and the buildings went as high as 15 stories. There were over 1400 hundred hospital rooms, a cafeteria, gymnasium, and lots of other facilities attached to it.

My eyes were fastened to this sight as a possible new location for the Los Angeles International Church and Dream Center. Pastor Tommy asked me to dream along with him as we prayed and planed for our future.

**The Los Angeles Dream Center, formerly The Queen of Angels Hospital**

I saw the possibility of having over 500 people living on campus in our discipleship program. I thought about starting a Set Free University urban training school for street ministers. Also a vision for a television studio, our own health spa, prayer rooms and so many other ideas came to my mind. Any facility God has allowed me to use I had filled up with people, and I knew this one would be better than all the rest. All of a sudden there was a great silence that came upon the two of us as we dreamed our dreams.

Pastor Tommy looked me in the eyes and asked me one of the most important questions of my life. He said that this project was too great for just him and Matthew to take on and he wanted a commitment from me that I would stay with him until it got going strong. He asked me if I would make a commitment to pioneer and build this place until it was filled up with people. Pastor Tommy told me he would not buy the property unless I would promise to help him build it. Just the thought that one of the greatest church builders in the world thought that he needed me was music to my ears.

I was speechless for a few minutes and thought about my new relationship with Pastor Tommy and Pastor Matthew. They had taken me in as one of their own and never brought up my past and never made me feel like an outsider. Pastor Tommy had taken me to his mega church in Phoenix and shown me off to his other pastors, to the point that some were jealous of mine and Pastor Tommy's love affair.

I am not kidding you, Pastor Tommy became my best friend and I would do anything for him, and I do mean anything. Through all of my years of ministry I was always a thorn in somebody's flesh. People had either loved or hated me. Now after all the bull s...I had been through, I have someone who believes the best in me and my family.

Lois had just finished her interferon treatments and was getting healthier as the days went by. I told Pastor Tommy that I was down for the cause and that he could count on me to be there for him. The facility would cost millions of dollars to purchase so Pastor Tommy had a lot of fundraising ahead of him. Pastor Matthew was so young, but energetic and full of faith and love. As for me, I was just a veteran street pastor with lots of years of experience dealing with the rugged people we would be taking in. I didn't need much to make me happy--put a roof over my head and a place for people to hang out and I'm in heaven. Shortly after that night in August of 1995 Pastor Matthew and I prepared for our new move and the grand opening of the Los Angeles International Church and Dream Center.

It took hours to walk through the whole facility. It had so much potential for being a city set on a hill just like the Holy Temple in downtown Jerusalem. So here we are with so many empty building's that needed more than just a little tender love and care. I was up for nights on end until it was time to set our moving strategy in motion. Pastor Tommy's job was to travel the world and talk to pastor friends and businesses to raise money to buy this enormous property and the money to make repairs. Pastor Tommy was dedicating his life to seeing this dream come true of producing an international church that spoke all languages and reached all cultures.

It was not going to be just a church, but a dream center—a place for people to learn how to dream and then help people fulfill their dreams. It was a place for people like me with broken dreams who needed help to restore their dreams. Pastor Tommy was also committed to bringing in the greatest Christian speakers to speak life into all our people. Pastor Tommy was definitely the fireball that made this all this happen. My history proved that I didn't know how to raise money but I was good at filling up a place with lots of people with problems. Pastor Tommy had already done so very much for me and my whole family. We were not only living again, but thriving in ministry. All the other Set Free churches were thrilled about the new ministry I was part of and joined in the fun.

Pastor Tommy had this financial burden that would cause him to be traveling the majority of the time selling his vision to others. Pastor Matthew was full of vim and vigor and was ready to work the streets of one of the most dangerous cities in America. My first job was to acquire some laborers to bring this huge facility up to code. I needed electricians, painters, carpenters, masons, cooks, maintenance people, and so many other skilled helpers to raise this place from the dead.

Once again it was time to recruit laborers to go into one of the greatest harvest fields ever. The Bible says the harvest is plenty but the laborers are few, so pray the Lord of the harvest sends forth laborers. Remember my philosophy of life is that I believe life should be one big slumber party. One big happy family serving Jesus is what I have always been about. At one time in my younger days I wanted to be in the circus.

I even tried to enroll in the Barnum & Bailey's Clown College. I was turned down because of my drug abuse. Now I had the opportunity to be in one of the biggest circus acts for Jesus ever. I can tell you from experience, living with people is better than watching any reality show. When you're dealing with drug addicts and all the games they play it can be downright funny, they have grown up bodies with a teenager's mentality. I was so ready for this new chapter in my life. I have always kept a young spirit in my thinking. I am an energizer bunny when it comes to the work of the ministry. I was truly addicted to the ministry of Jesus. I am part vampire because I don't sleep much and I love to squeeze every second out of every day.

I was the first person to move on to the new facility. Pastor Tommy gave me carte blanche to any room on the property in which to live. I chose the nuns' quarters because it was a self standing two-story building with 13 bedrooms and nine bathrooms. I moved my family in, along with another dozen people. Right next door to my place was a two-story house where Tim and Lois moved their family into. Moving Lois from Newport Beach to this gang-infested area was truly a miracle from above.

Our first night on the property I decided to walk the perimeter of this huge structure and pray for God's help in reaching our neighbors. The Queen of Angel's building was surrounded on every corner by what police referred to as local gangs in the Rampart district. The biggest so-called gang in the area was the Temple Street gang. In all actuality they were not really gangs to me; they were all the youth from the area that grew up together in that rough city. These were young people who were looking for love just like the rest of us. When times got hard they had to protect themselves from enemies. I needed to recruit an army to have any real impact in downtown Los Angeles. Moving my crew from Orange County to Bethel Temple wasn't easy, but moving them to the Rampart district was downright tough.

As I was doing my evening stroll around the neighborhood to feel it out, I saw a dark young man who gave me a look like "what are you doing here?" I have spent most of my ministry working with the hardcore, so I walked right towards him and introduced myself as Pastor Phil from the Los Angeles International Church. I told him I was there to help all the families in the neighborhood. I asked him if there was anything I could do for him. He said he needed a place to live, I told him that I had just moved in and that I would hook him up. He seemed shocked, and I've learned over the years that most people are surprised when you invite them into your own home. He responded with, "I will be over at about 11 p.m." I asked him his name, and he said, "Bird from Temple Street!" I told him I would see him later, and I was looking forward to getting to know more about him.

After walking around the neighborhood I went home and asked Sandra if she would like to take a cruise. We hopped in the car and rode up and down the streets of Westside Los

Angeles. It was now about 10 p.m. As we cruised up and down the streets praying for our new city I saw this fellow Bird walking down the streets by himself. I pulled the car over to the curb very quickly, and to my surprise Bird pulled a gun out on me. I was in shock and pretty frightened. I was now learning the ropes in the inner city of Los Angeles. You don't just roll up on someone down there.

I shouted, "Bird it's me Pastor Phil," Bird put the gun down. I said, "Are you ready to come to my house?" He said he was, he hopped in the car and we took him home. He was my first recruit at the new Los Angeles International Church and Dream Center, I showed him his room and we all went to bed. My first night at the new facility was already bearing fruit.

* * *

FAX (602) 493-9390

13613 North Cave Creek Road    Phoenix, Arizona 85022    (602) 867-7117

**TOMMY BARNETT,** *Pastor*

FAX TRANSMISSION TO:  PASTOR PHIL AGUILAR
                      213-250-2001

AUGUST 27, 1995

DEAR PHIL:

WE JUST FINISHED OUR SUNDAY EVENING SERVICE AND I'M WAITING TO
CATCH THE 12:30 AM ALL NIGHT FLIGHT TO TALK TO MY MILLIONAIRE
FRIEND ABOUT THE LA CHURCH.  MY THOUGHTS WENT TO YOU AND
MATTHEW AS YOU MAKE THE MOVE AND LEAD THE CHURCH TO THE
DREAM CENTER!

GREATER THINGS THAN EITHER ONE OF US CAN IMAGINE ARE AHEAD!  IT
TRULY IS EXCITING.

PHIL, I SURE LOVE YOU AND WANTED TO TELL YOU AGAIN HOW PROUD I
AM OF YOU, AND THE HONOR OF WORKING TOGETHER IN THE WORLD'S
GREATEST HARVEST FIELD.  YOU ARE AN AMAZING MAN AND I AM
HONORED TO CALL YOU MY FRIEND.

LOVE,
    YOUR FRIEND

TOMMY BARNETT

# CHAPTER 32

# BACK TO WORK

The building I lived in was the only one on the property that had running water. I knew I had to get this place fixed up in order to bring people in. I started asking people who had been dear friends of mine for many years to consider moving to Los Angeles and help me build the world's greatest ministry. God has given me the ability to get so excited about any new project I am into. In my drug days I would let people know about the best drugs available and now I am telling people where they can come and get their dreams back. My Holy Spirit fire was igniting the fire of others all around me. Remember one Christian on fire can put a thousand demons to flight. Two Christians on fire can put ten thousand to flight; three Christians on fire can put billions of demons to death. I was watching the Lord build an army for Him.

Before you know it my Set Free soldiers and soldierettes were coming out of the woodwork to help me. The buildings were a mess in every possible way imaginable. There was no electricity or water, and I had no budget to work with. On the other hand, I could offer people a place to live. Pastor Tommy had taught us that the miracle is always in the house. That meant to me that we had the riches in our own people to rebuild this Dream Center. I had a great band, a wonderful hip hop crew, and now I had some hard core laborers who knew how to mop, clean and build.

With those men and my wonderful family I knew we could turn this place into one awesome outreach center. The whole cast of characters were coming together just like a major movie. Lois orchestrated the administration of this new venture. Pastor Marcos from Set Free Gardena brought his whole crew to join in the fun. My friend Rob Sheltman from Long Beach Set Free got our band hooked up better than ever. My wonderful brother, Pastor Eddie, from Set Free Pomona was backing my play all the way. I had a whole crew of mighty men and women of God ready to do a good work. My dreams were coming true again, just give me a place to meet and I will fill it up with people. The weeks rolled by and the gymnasium was now all fixed up and ready for my sport's league.

I invited local neighborhoods to put basket ball teams together and come play in our league for free. Before you know it our schedule for Set Free basketball was ready to begin. We had our own Dream Center team headed up by Pastor Matthew. Within weeks, the cafeteria was up and running and serving hundreds of meals a day. Before you knew it I had over 100 Set Free Soldier's and soldierettes living at the dream center.

Pastor Tommy offered me any room on the property for my office. I looked at one room on the 15$^{th}$ floor over looking the Hollywood freeway where I could see the Hollywood sign. It was a beautiful view, but it wasn't for me. I love being right smack dab in the mix so I set up a folding table in the middle of the parking lot. I love hands-on ministry and now I had room for tons of people to come and get discipled.

The biggest event going on in Los Angeles at that time was the OJ Simpson trial. The media called OJs lawyer's the dream team. Pastor Tommy, Matthew and I decided to call ourselves the real dream team. We were on fire and people were coming from everywhere to watch us burn. I had Set Free volunteers everywhere on the campus building, cleaning, and repairing the facility for the great harvest that was about to come. We were having church in our fixed up gymnasium to begin with where we could seat close to a thousand people. Pastor Tommy was still doing Thursday night church for us and Pastor Matthew was doing his Sunday mornings while I continued the Saturday night services. Our music was fantastic and the church was growing at such a fast rate.

I spoke to Pastor Tommy about starting a *His Hand's Ministry*, which was a ministry devoted to clothing and feeding the poor, along with about 50 other ministry ideas. Pastor Tommy loved all my ideas and was always supportive and uplifting. Pastor Tommy would have us set up the gym with as many chairs as possible, he loved a packed house and we wasted no space when it came to making room for more people.

I spoke to Pastor Tommy about my television ministry I once had on Trinity Broadcasting Network. I told him that millions of people could get involved with the Dream Center if they saw it on TV. I got a hold of Paul and Jan Crouch, and knowing I was now with Pastor Tommy they allowed us to air our grand opening on national television.

We celebrated Thanksgiving of 1995 on TV; this was our new grand opening of the Los Angeles International Church and Dream Center. The show opened up with Pastor Tommy, Matthew, and I welcoming the TBN audience to our Thanksgiving grand opening of the Dream Center. Pastor Tommy let me set up the entire three-hour show that introduced the Dream Center to the world. Immediately after speaking, Pastor Tommy allowed me to take over the show. I had our band play some of my favorite oldie songs that we got saved. It was a first for Trinity television viewers to see this type of ministry and hear the kind of music we played.

I had my sons MJ and Chill's hip hop crew do a whole set of rap music with the dancers doing their thing. Pastor Tommy knew he could trust me to do the very best for him. Then I chose some wonderful people from our church to give testimonies of what the Dream Center had done for them. All in all it was a fantastic grand opening and a spectacular show. Life was so exciting, and Set Free ministries, along with Pastors Tommy and Matthew Barnett, were the foundation of this wonderful new ministry.

It was the thrill of my life picking Pastor Tommy up weekly at the airport and meeting all the preachers he brought in to speak. Tommy would have me give tours to all the visiting pastors and show them the people that the Dream Center was reaching out to.

The biggest highlight for me was when Pastor Tommy had the healing ministry of Benny Hinn come to the Dream Center. I got Pastor Benny on the back of my Harley and took him on a short thrill ride he will never forget. Pastor Matthew and I were making appearances on the Trinity Broadcasting Network, sharing our dream with everyone. I so loved being allowed once again to speak to the multitudes via satellite television.

Teaching Benny Hinn faith on the back of my Harley

Slim-Pastor Phil-Benny Hinn-Matthew and Tommy Barnett

New ministry doors were opening for the body of Christ to come and join us at the Dream Center. A ministry that comes to mind was Friendship ministry, headed up by a great man named Don Tipton. He had a large ship that delivered goods to the whole world and we were blessed with hundreds of neighbors that were Russian Jews and we were able to feed them all. The Dream Center now had about 400 people living on the campus and finally we had some running water. We had ministries for the Spanish, Filipino's, Russian and a Jewish ministry. We had prayer and healing ministry and services for the disabled, along with after-school programs and so many other wonderful ministries. I was allowed to invite anyone who had a viable work of God to join in the fun.

Matthew Crouch, the son of Jan and Paul Crouch who owned Trinity Broadcasting Network was looking for some help with his new production company. I set Matthew up with a huge area on the property to produce Christian television shows. Pastor Tommy wanted us to be like the Los Angeles International Airport with all the different airlines from all different countries. Pastor Tommy wanted our ministries to represent everyone. Matthew Crouch utilized a lot of the men in our discipleship program for the TV shows he was producing at the Dream Center. Matthew Crouch and Tommy worked out a deal for Matthew to produce a show telling the world all about the Dream Center and how it operates. I was being blessed by God to be privileged enough to be a charter member of the Los Angeles Dream Center and Church.

During this time period I was doing outreaches to all the middle schools and high schools in Los Angeles County. I was able to speak to anywhere from five to six thousand young people a week. My sons would do their hip hop to get the youngsters attention and then I would speak to them about making the right choices in life. My dear friend Lillian Zelmmer was my co-partner, mentoring young people across the city of Los Angeles. People love being part of something that is impacting the whole world and we were doing our best to be a blessing to all. We were running buses to skid row several nights a week and serving thousands of hot meals weekly. I was able to help start 60 different ministries in our first year of moving on the campus at the Dream Center. To this very day that fellow Bird who I met upon my arrival at the Dream Center continues to be a part of Set Free.

# CHAPTER 33

# CASE CLOSED!

I loved working alongside Pastor Tommy and Matthew very much. There was a new revival going on in downtown Los Angeles, California and it was moving so fast that I couldn't catch my breath. Pastor Tommy is known for having one of the greatest Pastors' schools on earth. It was now time for us to show off the Dream Center to pastors worldwide. We prepared for our first Pastors school at the Dream Center. The Assemblies of God denomination news had made mention that the Dream Center was now one of the fastest growing churches in America. Set Free had been on that list in the old days. I never get too impressed when I hear those statistics. Pride goeth before the fall, when you start counting how many people you reach, it may go to your head, at least it had for me.

Pastor Tommy noticed I had a large security team on hand for our Dream Center Pastors' School. He asked me if they were new converts. I told him they were the local Temple Street youngsters, and that they were not yet Christians. I said if anyone was going to steal or does damage around the Dream Center the Temple Street crew would protect it best. Pastor Tommy and I had a few different philosophies about working with people. He didn't understand why I would take people into my home who were not Christians. I told him I believed Jesus loves people right where they are at. Jesus speaks in the Bible about taking in strangers, so even though we had our minor differences of opinion, we moved on ahead with our plans. I was on fire for Jesus, and I was on top of the world doing ministry with the dream team, but in life I have found that most good things must come to an end.

I have done over a thousand weddings and have seen people so in love with each other but the old "no you hang up, no you hang up" la la land so in love type of story is not reality. People think they can live on love alone. People just don't connect that lust is different than love. I tell people that when you meet someone for the very first time, it's just their representative that your meeting. To live with someone is the beginning of knowing them. You can say I love you so sweetly, speak all the sweet vows, light candles and pour sand, but love is a commitment. I have had thousands of people over the years tell me they loved me. I warned them that they would only love me until I told them something they didn't want to hear or something that they didn't want to do. There truly is a thin line between love and hate. Real love is Jacob in the Bible working seven years for Rachael and it seemed like just a moment of time to him. Now that's at least a good beginning to real love.

The Dream Center was becoming a success. We now had an abundance of ministries happening on the campus. I was speaking to over 10,000 young people a week and it was making a difference in so many lives. Pastor Tommy continued to preach at the Thursday night services, and Pastor Matthew was packing out Sunday mornings.

Pastor Tommy brought in a new man from the Phoenix church to oversee things at the Dream Center. I had been the first one to move on campus, and I was the one who recruited the laborers and did all the dirty work and now this guy rolls into town giving orders? To put it simply, we bumped heads over and over again. I do not want to bore you with the details but suffice it say, it was time for the

Set Free crew to start looking for a new adventure. The Los Angeles International Church and Dream Center was born out of a dream of Pastor Tommy's many years ago. His son Matthew carried the dream to Los Angeles and put feet to his father's plans. I was a fallen, hurt, and wounded preacher who needed some love from above and Pastor Tommy instilled me with hope, love, and a place to find my first love again. I will forever be indebted to Pastors Tommy and Matthew for giving me another chance at ministry. The Dream Center is going stronger than ever today and I thank God for that. The Dream Center is a unique place and the Set Free family's fingerprints are all over the property. We will forever be connected to that wonderful work of God. I vowed to finish my commitment of two years at the Dream Center and move on.

Since God had placed me in charge, before leaving I ran our first Pastors school at the Dream Center. We had so many pastors from all over the world coming for instruction on how to hit the streets of the inner city for Jesus. There was just one major problem at the Pastors School. Many of the pastors started realizing Set Free and yours truly was pretty much in charge of the place. I think some jealousy got in the mix and for whatever reasons I could see once again the handwriting on the walls and I was not going to be able to hang on much longer. I was right about it being time to move on and was just being thankful for the love I was shown. Pastor Tommy and Matthew will forever be my dearest friends in Christ. My wife Sandras opinion of Pastor Tommy is a whole different story, but you will have to wait for her book to come out to hear about it.

I moved on with my family, some close friends, and of course with the Trader family. We opened up a youth program called Los Angeles for the Broken that was located off Hollywood and Vine in downtown Hollywood. We worked with troubled youth there for approximately one year and continued doing Set Free Church service and outreaches. Life was good and I was still loving Jesus and doing all I could to reach out and tell the world how good Jesus is.

We were now closing in on 1997 and we were ready to head back to Orange County. My golden boy son MJ who was now 19 years old gave me the great news that he was going to be a father. I was in shock, and I didn't gladly receive the news at first. I was still heart broken over the loss of my first two grandchildren. God reminded me that children are a blessing from the Lord and I needed to get over my hurt. The child was a little boy aptly named Matthew Junior. The baby's mama was struggling with a lot of problems in her life, so MJ got full custody of Lil Matthew. In the Greek that meant my wife and I got the privilege of helping raise our new grandson. We found a big home to live in and I was getting ready for yet another chapter in our lives. This chapter kept on growing as I became aware that my one and only daughter Trina Joy was using drugs. I would knock on her door in the morning and I would hear the voice of my sweet little girl. The next morning as I knocked I heard the voice of Satan coming from behind the walls. I lived in denial that my sweet little angel would ever even consider doing drugs. One day I decided to break the unwritten law of breaking in her bedroom. She was now 17 and should be entitled to her privacy I thought. Upon entering the premises of her holy of holies I saw a box of close to a hundred Bic lighters.

I mused in my mind that she must be a collector of them for some strange reason. I grabbed hold of one of the lighters and tried to ignite it, then another and then another, they all failed. Here I was now a drug counselor for over two decades and I wouldn't accept the fact that my daughter was a drug addict. When I confronted her she got angry and lashed out at me and threatening to move out when she was 18 years old. Neither of us could wait for that day to come. My wife Sandra begged me to let her continue on living in our home and just pray for her. Her eighteenth birthday arrived and I gave her a huge birthday party in the hopes of winning her over. When the party was over she took her gifts and moved out to some friend's house in Los Angeles County. My wife's heart was broken and I was ready to turn on my tough love towards the situation. We cleared out her room the next day and opened it up for someone in need of help with their life's issues.

I got a phone call from Trina telling me how I dare give her room away. She rebelled for a few weeks and then called me with a heart that was ready to make a change. I sent her to our Set Free ranch in San Diego County against my wife's wishes. Sandra said you can't send her to a place full of a bunch of drug addicts. I re-emphazied to my wife that our sweet little angel was now a full blown drug addict. Tough love worked for my daughter as she cleaned up from her addictions, and met her husband at the Set Free Ranch. I gave my daughter to the Lord and not only got her back, but a wonderful son in law. It was not over yet for my family problems as my youngest son Hebrew, aka Roc was a 9th grader full of a lot of testosterone and ready to rock n roll. Hebrew got into so much trouble that I put him on restriction for all 4 years of high school. It wouldn't be long before yet another situation come into my life to test me and see what I was made of. It was a beautiful sun shinny day in Anaheim when I got a surprise document delivered right to my front door. It was a lawsuit from three individuals who were former Set Free members from the early nineties. It was a big sock in the stomach once again and I fell to my knees. The charges were all stemming from the accusation that I was a cult leader. The allegation packet from Oden Fong would resurface and Oden's face would be right smack dab in the middle again.

My lawyers conducted a deposition on Pastor Oden Fong, and Fong once again brought up that I had the same similarities to David Koresh, and Jim Jones. I was charged with brainwashing my members, and causing separation anxiety for their children. There was a whole list of other accusations involved. Fortunately my church insurance from 1993 covered any lawsuits against me. I had a small group of angry Set Free people still spewing their venom about me. I don't know about the road you have traveled but I have seen the mountains and the seas, I have traveled the world and many have loved me and many quite the opposite. I knew all three women in the lawsuit very well as each of them had come to me as broken individuals needing help. One of my best friends was the man paying the attorney for their lawsuit. What could I do but fight it to the end because I was not going to run anymore.

I went to Lois about the lawsuit, but she was still dealing with her own issues and did not want any part of this battle. I knew I had to have my day in court and I was ready to give my side for the first time. I spent the next 18 months going through depositions, and supplying material to my lawyers in order to fight this ugly case. The news media was again excited about piling stuff on top of this biker pastor and trying to beat me to a pulp.

This time it wasn't going to be so easy for them. I put my spiritual fists up and said "bring it on."
Once again God was there to fight for me as I defended myself. My life has been one battle after another and I thank God it has been one victory after another. It took almost two full years before I was ready to appear in

Superior Court and face my accusers. During that same time I received a letter from my son Geronimo that spoke about his new marriage to one of our Set Free girls. Geronimo included some things he had been holding in his brain for quite a while. It was the kind of letter no father would ever want to receive from his child. He spoke about me in the most evil ways possible and indicated that he never wanted me around his new wife. I hated to hear all that he had to say and I did not agree with what he was saying. As a father I received the letter as a son that was just crying out for help. I forgave him and moved on with my life. I spent a lot of time with my lawyer working on the law suit and I could not wait to get in that courtroom. During that time one of the accusers had checked herself into a treatment center for drugs. Another one of the accusers called my lawyer and tried to get a ten thousand dollar personal pay off to get out of the lawsuit, the third girl ended up working at a strip club and back on drugs!

As a father I received the letter as a son that was just crying out for help. I forgave him and moved on with my life. I spent a lot of time with my lawyer working on the law suit and I could not wait to get in that courtroom. During that time one of the accusers had checked herself into a treatment center for drugs. Another one of the accusers called my lawyer and tried to get a ten thousand dollar personal pay off to get out of the lawsuit. The other girl ended up working at a strip club and back on drugs.

I was actually very excited about the whole ordeal. I had never defended myself publicly, and it was now time. The morning of court I walked into the courtroom by myself. I was so use to having Lois at my side and always felt more confident having a fighter like her next to me.

Before picking the jury, the judge asked the plaintiff's lawyer to read her opening statements. She spoke for about 45 minutes and then the judge stopped her. He asked her a few questions about Set Free ministries. "How much money does Pastor Phil charge for his detox program?" The answer was absolutely nothing at all. He then asked if there were locks on the doors keeping the addicts from leaving the facility. Once again the answer was no. The judge told her that he understood how the program at Set Free works. He said Pastor Phil is the king, and his wife Sandra is the queen and if anyone disobeys their orders they are banished to the Set Free Ranch in Perris, California.

The judge also asked the plaintiff's attorney what her reasoning was for assuming that I was causing separation anxiety to the children. The attorney replied that the children cried whenever the mother dropped them off at the Set Free nursery. The judge responded with the fact that lots of children across America cry when parents drop them off at day care centers. At that point, the judge threw everything out, right there on the spot! I left the courtroom that day completely innocent of all charges. I was upset that I never got to take the stand on my behalf; however, I thanked God for vindicating me.

# CHAPTER 34

## DON'T CALL IT A COMEBACK

It was finally time to move on with my new life. I had a friend who had a small office where I began Bible studies. I didn't know if I wanted to do a church again because I had been burned so many times and I was not sure if I wanted to do it all over again. Good friends kept telling me that I should stop helping people out who do not appreciate it. I knew in my heart how God helped me and I just could not stop helping others.

Moses missed his blessing by complaining about the people God had him lead through the wilderness. I had a prayer meeting one night at my home and a girl named Christina Seymour told me that I needed to get back to serving God hardcore again. It hit me like a ton of bricks and I gave my whole heart back to God again that night.

It was right around this time in 1998 that I purchased our first home ever and was ready to lay down some roots for the first time in quite a while. A dear friend bought the house right next door to my home to utilize for our discipleship home.

Its trippy how God uses people you would never imagine in your life. I then found a new friend named Don Overstreet who was a church planting strategist for the Southern Baptist denomination. He became a very dear friend to me and God used him to bring me back to my first love of ministering to people. He belonged to a very conservative group of Christians but he himself was as down home as you can get. He took me under his wing and found me a church building to meet in and I started going for it again.

I started up another band, and started taking people into my home, and here I go doing Set Free style preaching and teaching. Formerly, I was a drug addict that had to have his fix every single day of the week. Now I had become a hope addict who needed a Jesus fix every day of the week? Through all the pain that I allowed people to put me through, I just kept on with God's plan for my Life. It was the end of 1998 and many of our Set Free Churches were working with the southern Baptists and getting a lot of love from them.

My friend Pastor Willie from Set Free Yucaipa was doing great and I was proud of him for never giving up. I sent Pastor Willie some of my best men to help him build his church and he has continued in the ministry to this day.

Don Overstreet was totally into helping plant new churches and he saw that Set Free had a great disciple program where young preachers could be raised up. Don knew that with the help of the Southern Baptists, Set Free churches could pop up all over the country. I helped plant over a hundred and fifty Set Free churches by accident. Now the Southern Baptist came into the picture with a strategy and money to back them up. Don had me assist him as he traveled across the country planting churches and encouraging pastors.

By now I had worked with all the different denominations and clearly understood that Christians come in different flavors, but they all love the same Jesus. I loved working with Don and he encouraged my life so much. I told him I would love to be on full time staff with the Southern Baptists doing just what he does. He mentored me for almost two years and just when I thought I had a shot at working with them and actually getting paid for it, the bomb dropped. My reputation was that of a hot potato, too hot for some to handle. Don wanted me in, but the *good old boys* gave me the thumbs down. I must tell you I was a little butt hurt!

I had just sent one of my best Soldiers to start another Set Free church in San Diego California. His name was Pastor John Cabrera and he had been with me from the beginning of Set Free in 1982, a very loyal and highly respected man in the Set Free World. Pastor John was used by God to start Set Free Churches all over San Diego County. Pastor John asked me if I could send Bill Vanderford, one of our most trusted men to assist him. We needed a Set Free Ranch to house all the drug addicts that came to us in the San Diego area. The Southern Baptists purchased a large property and it soon became our Set Free ranch. Then a motel and homes were purchased to help Set Free spread the good news of Jesus Christ. My life was so good again doing what I did best, pastor, win souls, and just love my wife and all my Set Free Friends. Our Set Free Soldier's bike ministry was still riding hardcore for the Lord. I kept my friendships with a lot of the Southern Baptist, even though they were a little too judgmental for me. Set Free churches have continued to be birthed with the love and help from the Southern Baptist denomination. Who would have thought an old loser like me would be used by God to pioneer the very first Set Free Church.

Many of the Set Free churches had forsaken me for one reason or another, but in God's book I still had fruit that abounds to my account. I do want to thank the Southern Baptists for making it possible for me to get my Doctor of Divinity degree and for the help they have been to so many. I started the mother church for Set Frees which are now located all around the world. I pray before we go to Heaven that all my Set Free kids would come give their daddy some love. I might be a bad daddy sometimes, but I'm still their dad. The apostle Paul said you may have many instructors in Christ but only one spiritual father.

In 2001 we found a Baptist church in Buena Park, California where we could meet permanently; it was a good size church with lots of room to grow. The Pastor there was an old friend of mine who was part of my Set Free Board. His name was Pastor Wiley Drake. He was a very controversial figure himself. He helped me in so many ways and stood behind me through some of my biggest trials. No matter what size facility God provides me with, He helps me to fill it up with lost souls. The invisible sign on my forehead was now reading, "Haters, losers, abusers, and everyone else come unto me and I will point you to Jesus." The band was rocking, my kid's were still rapping for Jesus and our Bikers were still putting in their work. I had lots of outlaw club members come and give their lives to Jesus in our Buena Park church. The Set Free Soldiers motorcycle crew was instrumental in working with all the bike clubs around. In our area the biggest clubs were the Vagos, Mongols, and the Hells Angels. I did funerals, weddings and lots of counseling for bikers all over the state. My son MJ was still rocking his hip hop crew with songs about Jesus. My son Chill was singing the best worship song's ever. My daughter Trina was taking care of the nursery. My son Roc, a.k.a. Hebrew was out there getting the bikers rolling for Jesus.

My son Geronimo had me and my other sons Mj and Chill come out and do some concerts for him. We were getting along good again, and I was so happy to be back in his life. I went to Richmond Virginia to see him and share with a number of Pastors from there about building a new ministry for Geronimo. I encouraged Geronimo to build a ministry like the one I did in Los Angeles. I shared with him if he did an outreach on Saturday nights he wouldn't be competition for the other churches. My biker brother Bert had introduced him to some good Christian people in Virginia and the rest is history. Geronimo started having children and I was so blessed to know all my children were serving the Lord.

We stayed in Buena Park until about 2005, building a great ministry for Jesus and making our motorcycle ministry stronger than ever. One night the woman who headed up the law suit against me in 1998 came back to Set Free for a visit. It was an unbelievable sight as she walked forward during one of our worship songs with a bouquet of flowers in her hand asking for forgiveness. God had changed my heart so very much that I readily forgave her and asked her to hook up with the Set Free family again. She ended up going to our Set Free in Santa Maria started by a wonderful man of God named Don Gonzalez.

A wonderful couple in our church was celebrating their 50$^{th}$ wedding anniversary and asked me to oversee the event. Coincidentally their niece was another girl in the lawsuit and this person was also repentive about her behavior. She said they all needed money and I was the easy target. Well they found out wrong, but I thank God for revealing so much forgiveness in my life. The third girl is still spewing venom about me, but I pray for her all the time.

So many wonderful people came to Set Free church during that period of time to hear the word of God. I had a beautiful stripper that gave her life to Jesus named CC who became my faithful assistant. I had one of the biggest porn stars in the business named Sky Lopez who moved into our discipleship homes and caught on fire for Jesus. I had music celebrities like Sen Dog from the group Cypress Hill, Fieldy, and Head from the band KORN. Fieldy spent over a year with me and became one of our Set Free Soldiers. I went on tour with KORN from California to Florida. Fieldy caught fire for the Lord and never went back to his old ways. Everywhere we toured Fieldy shared Jesus with all of his fans. I got to share the love of Jesus with Jonathan and Monkey from the band back stage at every venue. Head and I got to hang out in Israel right after he gave his life to Christ and life just couldn't get any better. At least I had those feelings until my Hepatitis kicked in and I was ready to go be with Jesus forever. I lost 32 lbs within a 4 week period of time. I have never had health insurance so I was asking God for a healing. My friend Tracie from the Set Free Possee crew back in the old days was my helper in so many ways. She had to drive me to anyplace I needed to go, and with her hands on my arms was the only way I could walk. . My wife Sandra would have her head on my chest at night and listen to see if I was still breathing. I believe you have to have the will to live when your body seems to be shutting down. I knew that God still had work for me to do so I remembered the words of the Lord "when your body is broken down it is your spirit that sustains you". Sure enough God sent me someone who gave my wife some natural herbs that brought me back to a normal and healthy life with a few months.

The first 12 years Set Free Church was planted and rooted deeply in Anaheim California. The next 12 years Set Free was on tour through the wilderness of life. I truly believe that any soldier of the Lord that has a tale to tell must walk with a spiritual limp. The Christian warfare is so very dangerous with so much friendly fire going on. God taught me so much through my wilderness journeys and I was definitely a leader of a Nomadic tribe. Set Free churches were popping up again all across the country as we kept falling in love with Jesus over and over again. Many Set Free members came back after a long absence to rejoin me in serving the Lord together again!

Lois was being mellow during those days in Buena Park. She had a lifetime of ministry under her belt already and wasn't about to go on another roller coaster ride with me. She took a back seat and then faded into the sunset and started her own ministry. I will always love and respect her for all the years she dedicated to helping me speak to the whole wide world about Jesus.

We spent a good five years building our Saturday night church ministry in Buena Park, California. It was packed out and we were doing Bible studies all over Orange County.

# CHAPTER 35

## SOLDIERS FOREVER

Things were going so very well again in my life. The church was filled up and our Soldiers were riding the streets excited about Jesus. Our first biker ministry was called *Christ Sons*. Then we changed it to *Servants for Christ*. Now it was time to change things up a bit. The Bible says you cannot put new wine in old wine skins so we changed our name to *Set Free Soldiers*. I was looking for a few good men that wanted to make a commitment to reach beyond the front lines of war. I wanted soldiers that would not become intimidated as we worked in the outlaw biker world. The Set Free Soldiers kept their duties as the church greeters and would do all the set ups and tear downs at church and outreaches. These men and their families became the new behind the enemy lines Set Free Soldiers for Jesus.

I retired the Servants for Christ patch and kept our new men to a higher standard. I use to allow our Servants for Christ to wear our patch even if they didn't ride a bike but now I wanted riders for Jesus on Harleys heading up and down the streets of California. As I look back at the trail I have carved out in my life I see a lot of wonderful experiences I had because of great decisions I made, but also experienced a lot because of very poor decisions.

I started to realize that success is harder to handle than failure. Being a loser, quitter, and a blame shifter comes so natural to our lives. Every time things were going great I would put my finger in the pie and mess it up. Sometimes I was just plain bored and wanted to do something new and didn't care what the cost was. I have self destructed so many times in my life and I know how to tip the table of life over real good. Stinking thinking began to enter into my head at Buena Park and I wanted to cut down the troops to the mighty 300. I just couldn't stop the flow of people wanting to come to our Set Free Church. It was taking a toll on my marriage again, and I wanted to change things up. I was happy to see all the lives being changed, yet boredom set in my soul. Idle hands are the tools of the devil and I took my eyes off Jesus for just a minute and there I went sliding down the spiritual stairway of life. I gave a letter to my congregation that I was going to move on with some new ideas I had for ministry. A friend of mine opened up a night club for rock bands, so I asked him if I could have church there on Sunday mornings. That upset a lot of people in our ministry, just the idea of having church in a bar; I didn't last to long meeting there before I had another offer on the table.

A buddy of mine named Abraham reintroduced to me a Pastor friend named Mario. Pastor Mario was a God sent in my time of spiritual need and a true friend. He was a great guy who always believed the best in me and our ministry. Mario and his wife were so happy to offer their church facility for us to meet in. I took it as a sign from God that Pastor Mario really did want Set Free to share his church building. The thing I did different this time was to make it an invite only church; I wanted a small dedicated group that wanted to do deep intense bible studies and not just a bunch of baby Christians crying all the time.

Pastor Mario knew about my situation with Pastor Oden Fong and all the trouble he had caused me. He knew of his plot to try and destroy our church and myself with his lies about me being a cult leader. Vengeance is the Lord's and I do not find joy in others trials and faults ,so when Pastor Mario informed me that Pastor Oden divorced his wife and is remarried to a woman he now has children with. I truly felt sorry for him and I didn't care what had caused the divorce. The Bible says, "He without sin cast the first stone." I sure was in no position to be casting stones at anyone. I sent Pastor Oden a love note and told him I had forgiven him of all the hurt he had done to me.

**Me and my old "friend" Oden Fong at the O.C fair.**

I wished him the best in life with his new family. I have said it so many times, and here I go again, it's a small world. I had the privilege of seeing Oden a short time later with his new wife and two children at the Orange County Fair. Forgiveness is a wonderful thing, and I thank God for all the trials and testing that came from my friend Pastor

Oden Fong. I began to discipline our Soldiers and our other member's in a deeper way than ever before. I didn't want a large crowd of people anymore. I wanted a dedicated Bible study group that was sold out for Jesus. I wanted quality, not quantity.

One of my Soldier brothers I call Papa is an actor, writer, and movie producer in Hollywood. He asked me if I would like to do a reality show for television. I had a lot of experience over the years doing not only Christian television, but stuff for MTV and other cable networks. I said yes and Papa started getting the script together and started pitching ideas to different television networks. He hired one of the top management firms to sell our show. Papa is a dedicated long time friend who I have known and loved for years. He had an idea for a reality show that had us riding our Harleys to church, concerts, parties and helping out all those in need. He wanted to show the discipleship homes and how we helped people detox from drugs, and get their lives back together. He saw the value this could be to people everywhere and I knew we had a colorful community of people in our church. I was excited about all our future plans and I began to gear-up for what might be the best season ever. We came up with so many ideas for the show and new that it would be a hit around the world. Dog the Bounty Hunter show was just being put on the back burner so we figured we could fill his shoes and more. I figured we could do stories on all my children and everyone in our church, and pick the craziest people in our discipleship homes to do a story about.

The Set Free family has traveled everywhere and my sons MJ and Chill have taken their hip hop crew to entertain the troops in Bosnia, Iraq, Afghanistan and many other nations. I just knew with all my heart that our television show would be exciting, and teach people so much about real life.

During this period of time I found out that a group of my neighbors were having secret meetings about me and our people. I sometimes find it hard to believe that I am that interesting of a person that others would waste so much time on me. Why are people so afraid to confront the person they have a problem with face-to-face? I have always been easy to find and live in a fish bowl for all to see. I have lived in Anaheim all of my life except when I was trying to shake the Calvary characters. My mom and dad went to Anaheim high school, my brothers and sister went to Anaheim High school. I mean we have history in this town. I am an Anaheim Angel fan, and an Anaheim Duck fan. I love Anaheim.

# CHAPTER 36

## SAINT OR SINNER

Clave "Papa", my Soldier friend and producer landed a pilot deal for A&E television network. The program was entitled *Saint or Sinner,* allowing our television audience the weekly opportunity to be the judge of what we do. The plan was to watch the daily lives of all the people who lived in our Set Free discipleship homes. We named our street Hope Street and we were all about giving hope to others through sharing Jesus. We were no longer dope dealers but hope dealers.

A&E television network gave our producer a large sum of money to make a one hour pilot of our lives. I was so stoked and excited that a television network as big as theirs believed in our product. At this time we had about fifty people living in our homes with problems that ranged from drug addiction, alcoholism, violence, and a lot of abuse issues. The pilot took a lot of hard work to direct, film and edit as we rolled film day and night in order to condense what we do into a one hour pilot. This was not an easy job even for skilled producers or camera people.

It was now time to begin the filming of our reality show and guess what happens to me? Sure enough I thought I had the flu, but within 24 hrs I was bed ridden and in a Diabetic coma. I was rushed to the hospital and put on life support. The show had to go on without me with all the funds being allocated already. God miraculously healed me again and within two weeks I was ready to rock n roll for Jesus. I am not kidding you when I tell you that I should have died. I can't believe how much God loves me and wants to keep me here on planet Earth. We first filmed shots for the opening of the show with my son MJ rapping about how the Set Free Soldiers look hard, but how they love God. The thing that made our show different than any other intervention show was the Set Free Soldiers look like bad guys, but spend all their time helping others We wanted the television audience to judge us by our work and not by our looks as they saw me teaching, preaching, and riding with my motorcycle club.

The show has my sons riding their motorcycles along with me, and yes, we look like we would be heading out to an outlaw biker party. That was the whole twist for the show that we rode to church, prayer meetings, funerals and weddings. When we did ride to outlaw biker events it was for the purpose of spreading the good news that Jesus loved bikers too. The music and the look of all the main characters would cause the viewer to look forward to every new situation we came across. Our show would be the Christian version of the Sons of Anarchy program. All of our Harleys and clothes are black to give it that dark gothic stealth look. We are not part of or an extension of any motorcycle club on planet earth. We are a Christian club with Christian values but we have the look of a hardcore motorcycle crew so we can go behind enemy lines.

Everywhere we go people always ask what our club is about and that opens the door for us to share with them about Jesus. The show then shows shots of people who live in our discipleship homes doing odd jobs and keeping themselves busy when they are not in group therapy or having a bible study.

Over the last 30 years Set Free has taken in the homeless, dope fiends, losers and abusers of life. We were filming house meetings daily and nightly for the viewers to learn what we teach our people. Our show blows celebrity rehab and every other type of program out of the water. I wanted our viewers to decide if they believed we were SINNERS OR SAINTS.

Our pilot focused in on the lives of three people that had come to us for help. Our first character was a young man who wanted his dads love so much that he reached out for attention by stealing things. The second fellow was a drug addict who wanted to break the curse of constantly going back to prison. The third was a young beautiful preacher's kid that lost her son to the addiction of Methamphetamine. The first fellow we tried to reunite with his father, but it appeared his dad had moved on with his new life. Our second man got over his drug habit, went back to school and started a wonderful new career and never returning to prison. The third young lady became victorious over her drug addiction and got her 9 year old son back. To top things off she got hired working for a major hospital and gave her heart back to Jesus. This young lady ended up helping me to be the man of God I am today.

The whole pilot demonstrated the way in which many lives were changed at Set Free as we work with people 7 days a week 24 hours a day. The pilot showed our church services, outings with family and friends, and a myriad of other activities the Set Free Soldiers and their families were involved in.

**A&E filming my three son's four our reality show Saint or Sinner**

After shooting all the footage and editing took place it was late June 2008. I was so very excited that we had an opportunity to be on secular television network showing the world how a bunch of bad boys turned good now used their time helping others. The very thought about bikers spending their lives ministering to the lost strikes a strange chord in people's hearts. Like I have said so many times before Set Free isn't your typical biker club, we are a ministry first. My stand with all clubs is nothing but the most utmost respect for all. I have done ministry along side of every club in some way, shape or form.

The law has tried to label bike clubs as gangs, they are not gangs, but are brothers with common interests just like any other club someone might join. I will be doing a funeral for one club on a Monday, a wedding for another on a

Saturday, and a bike run with another on a Sunday. I refuse to prefer one club over another because I am a man of God who must love all.

Christian biker clubs are popping up everywhere around the world. In my area of southern California at least ten other Christian clubs have come out of the Set Free church movement. The first Christian club to branch off of Set Free is a club called the *Soldiers for Jesus* that my brother Bert Aguilar started many years ago.

My brother Bert headed up up *Gangster of Love Ministries* and preached Sturgis and Daytona bike events yearly. He has led more people to Jesus than anyone I know. I have another blood brother Billy who ran our *Servants for Christ* club for many years and since has started a club called the Prophets, very similar to the Set Free Soldiers in that they love Jesus first. Loyalty does not abound much within the Christian biker world as you see them hop from club to club.

The club that most everyone has taken some of their style or looks from is the best known motorcycle club in the world, the *Hells Angels*. Everyone in my biker world always thought of the *Hells Angels* first when it came to motorcycle clubs. I grew up with my brother Bert hanging out with them and bringing them to my home. I know there are alot of great clubs worldwide and I look forward to sharing Jesus with them all.

Set Free Soldiers are truly the originals when it comes to Christian clubs in our area. There was only one Christian club I was aware of when we started our first motorcycle ministry. Our club is dedicated first and foremost to the Lord Jesus. I have made it a policy for our members to never be involved with any type of drugs or violence.

On occasion I have had a few members of our club carry a weapon, being violent and getting arrested, in our club a member is thrown out for any actions like that. Just as we were getting ready for our A&E program to go on the air worldwide, trouble reared its ugly head.

# CHAPTER 37

# TIL DEATH DO US PART

On a sunny Saturday morning in late July 2008 the Set Free Soldiers headed out on a bike run to the beach areas of Orange County. The first stop was Aliso beach to watch one of our kids in a skim board contest. When the contest was over we cruised along the Pacific coast highway catching a beautiful view of the ocean. We were now enjoying a ten mile ride with the sun shining on our faces and the wind blowing in our hair.

One of our soldiers had recently purchased a home in Newport Beach right next to the pier. Newport is one of the most beautiful places on earth and visitors from all over the world travel to this vacation spot..It was the town where I grew up surfing and hanging with all my surf buddies.

It was a typical hot summer day with thousands of tourists enjoying the day in this very expensive part of Orange County. We headed first to our favorite hamburger stand that we frequented often. After filling our big order, we ate and I announced to the Soldiers they had 1 hour of free time to people watch, get some ice cream or just lay on the beach.

About five of us entered a sports bar named Blackies to play some pool and have a cool one. Blackies Sports Bar is a popular place to watch football games and listen to music. The other Soldiers were just milling around the shops enjoying the sea breeze and watching the surfers. I walked in the bar and went to the back near the pool tables. I took off my leather vest due to the extreme heat of the day. We ordered something to drink and proceeded to do what we do best, just hang out and enjoy the company of our Soldier brotherhood.

For you Christians that might be reading this, we were not there to get drunk. Blackies is a tourist place with no drama at all, until that day. Approximately five minutes after we went in, a group of fellows walked in and as they approached me I extended my hand to the first man nearest me. He started talking to me about something I did not quite understand and before you know it a bar fight was ensuing. God knows I tried to calm things down but it was too late to stop the winds of change that were about to take place. What would transpire in the next few minutes would change my life once again. A great misunderstanding took place and the Set Free Soldiers were defending themselves in a heated exchange!

It all happened so quickly and my Soldier brothers pushed me out of harm's way with lightning speed. I have never laid hands on any man since my conversion to Christ. My life is all about peace and I have done my best over my 30 years of ministry to love and be a friend to all.

Suddenly, I am up against a wall at Blackies telling my Soldiers to cease. I was able to stop the violence from continuing any further. There was no need for violence that day, and it could have turned out to be a great conversation with hands being shook. I instructed our Soldiers to stay put and felt that it was just a bar room fight.

Everyone left the bar except my fellow soldiers and a few other patrons in the place. We proceeded to leave Blackies and walk towards the beach when we were surrounded by the Newport police department. Within minutes we were handcuffed and thoroughly searched for any type of dope or weapons.

The cops asked us numerous questions about the incident, I told them it was just a bad misunderstanding and I didn't have a clue who the other guys were. After being detained for half an hour, we were released. I was upset about our incident with the other men but thanked God no one was seriously injured.

I noticed the only Set Free Soldier that was not with us was my dear friend Glenn. We were getting ready to head out to Huntington Beach next, but after the drama in Newport we decided to head home. I had a Soldier meeting a few days later and asked Glenn who had been my best friend for so many years, who I loved like one of my own brothers, what happened to him.? He gave me some kind of song and dance story, and I told him I do not believe in leaving a soldier behind. I then put the word out on the streets that I was ashamed of our involvement in the bar room fight.

After the meeting when we were alone Glen told me he was pulled over in his car as he left Newport Beach (he should have been on a bike) and a knife was found. He said the police gave him the knife back and was released. This was a real shocking surprise; I never saw anything but fists flying and definitely no weapon!

**Soldier ride to Newport Beach**

# CHAPTER 38

# IS THAT A TANK IN FRONT OF MY HOUSE?

Less than two weeks after the Blackies incident at approximately 5 a.m. in the morning on August 6 of 2008, my world came to a screeching halt. Without my knowledge the street I live on was surrounded with over 300 hundred Swat Team masked police officers. Two helicopters were flying above and a tank was parked in front of my home. Flash grenades were shot off to awaken us from our sleep. If you have never heard the sound of one of those bombs going off you have no idea how horrible it can feel. I have never been so frightened in my life. It sounded like the world was coming to an end. I looked out my window and I could see riot gear swat team members with M16s all aimed at my homes.

I have two homes located right on the corner of a busy intersection., the loud speaker was blaring for me and my family to come out. Five city police agencies were on hand to arrest my sons and me. The police came to my home expecting to find a large stockpile of weapons and ammunition, but what they found was lots of grandchildren, my sons, and my daughters-in-law.

As I walked out I was met by my wife in a police vehicle. I had no idea why they were arresting us, and I especially did not understand why they arrested Sandra. She was handcuffed and gave me a look I will never forget. They drove us around the block a couple of times and then they dropped off my wife. They then took me to the Anaheim Police Department and began questioning me. I have lived in Orange County all of my life and I have never seen or heard of a bigger raid than ours. "Why Lord?" was the biggest question running through my mind. The detective interviewing me was very cordial, but he was barking up the wrong tree.

Set Free may look like a bunch of bad boys, but in no way were we ever involved in anything illegal, he was looking at the video from our trouble with the *Hells Angels* at Blackies. After about three hours of interrogation, he asked me if I was going to stick to my story. I said, "Yes, because it is the God's honest truth."

The next thing you know I am locked up at the Anaheim City Jail and there I saw another seven of our Set Free Soldiers in various cells. I still was not aware of what we were being arrested for. Hours later I was finally given a piece of paper that listed my charges: Attempted murder, possession of firearms, brass knuckles, and street terrorism. The bail for me was set at one million dollars.

Seven Set Free Soldiers and I were then transported to the Orange County Jail. After we got to the jail we were taken to a section called the loop. And for the next 24 hours we would be questioned over and over again. Pictures were taken of all of our tattoos and the sheriffs at the jail were all watching the Set Free Soldiers videos we had posted on *You Tube*.

I was unaware that night and for the next week that we would be the major headline on news stations worldwide. The front page of every newspaper had a story about the Set Free Soldiers. We were villianized by the press and lies were spread across the internet.

While in jail our legs were put in shackles, handcuffs clasped to our wrists. Two days later we appeared in court for our arraignment, and on the third day we were bailed out. Our family picked us up and we rejoiced in the knowledge that we were back home with our wives and children who were left terrified. Once again I saw how the news reporters and law enforcement love to make up stories.

My family began to describe what happened to them while we were locked up for three days. They said the Anaheim Police stooped so low that they locked up our Dashound puppy, Scooby. I had no idea why they would do such a cruel thing like that; fortunately, I had a wonderful friend who bailed poor Scooby out.

I was told the police threatened my family and traumatized all twelve of my grandchildren who lived with us. My grandchildren who at that time ranged from one year to 15-years-old were questioned and harassed. They actually placed all five of MJ's kids in a paddy wagon with their dad handcuffed in the front seat. My family was put through hell for no reason at all. Only God gave me the peace of mind to not hate these terrible bigoted police. I knew a lot of them were just doing their job, but the leadership knew better and they did not do their homework well.

The policed claimed that they had an informant who divulged that we had automatic weapons and were ready for a stand-off with the police. Nothing but BS and harassment was going on with the Anaheim Police. They kept asking my family where all the money was, and where were we hiding my Mercedes Benz and Bentley automobiles they assumed were mine. I knew these guys were way off track.

They told my family that Set Free Ministries was over and that I was going to jail for life. Set Free Ministries was a stick in their eye and they were mad and wanted me gone, off the face of the earth. They asked where all the drugs were at and even insinuated that my daughters-in-law were running a prostitution ring. I knew right then that the police detectives must be out of their minds. They impounded all of our motorcycles and all of the vehicles my family owned. My whole family was left homeless. They had no money, no vehicles, car seats or baby food for the children.

The Police and the Drug Enforcement Agency dug up our gardens and tore down our homes looking for drugs. It was so shameful the way they treated my family. This was an injustice led by some hateful people who will ultimately have to deal with God. The Anaheim Police could have asked me for permission to search my home at any time, and I would have gladly said yes. Up to this day the police have never given a substantial reason for invading my home and scaring my family and my grandchildren to death.

Come on, we are a small group of Christian bikers with no arrests for violence at all. Why did they need 300 officers with M16s putting those laser red lights on all my family members? When my grandchildren see a police car now they don't think of them as our friends, they continue to live in fear even though almost two years have gone by.

Many people have encouraged my family to sue the police for the evil actions they committed. There was absolutely no reason for them ever to come and do and say the ugly things they did. For thirty years I have ministered within the city of Anaheim, helping thousands of drug addicts get off the dope. I have helped countless numbers to leave a violent lifestyle and become an asset to our community. It was just plain wrong to judge us because of the way we look.

It was also wrong that they thought we should not have protected ourselves in the dangerous situation at Blackies. We are law abiding Americans who have a track record of doing nothing but good. Do we look scary to some people? Yes. Do we look like bad guys to some? Yes. Do we ride loud Harley Davidson motorcycles? Yes. Do we have a patch we wear that says *Set Free Soldiers*? Yes.

We are guilty of nothing more than loving the brotherhood we belong to. We are the Set Free Soldiers 'till death. We are in the Lord's army, fighting the devil himself. The behavior of the leadership of the law enforcement agencies that day was wrong. I have forgiven them, but I will never accept what they did to be anything but injustice.

# 7 Christian bikers arrested in Orange County raid

**Los Angeles Times/August 7, 2008**

## By Tony Barboza and H.G. Reza

Long controversial for its aggressive evangelism aimed at those with a troubled past - ex-convicts and drug addicts among them - the Anaheim-based Christian motorcycle gang known as the Set Free Soldiers found itself in deeper trouble Wednesday when its leader and half a dozen members were arrested on suspicion of attempted murder.

The arrests, which followed a double stabbing in a brawl with the Hells Angels at a Newport Beach bar July 27, was the latest brush with the law for the group of black-leather-clad bikers, which has straddled the line between Christian outreach group and outlaw motorcycle gang.

By late Wednesday, authorities had arrested 10 members of the Set Free Soldiers and the Hells Angels during raids in Anaheim, Costa Mesa and Rancho Santa Margarita that started at 5 a.m., said Sgt. Evan Sailor of the Newport Beach Police Department.

The operation involved more than 150 officers, including SWAT teams and federal drug enforcement agents.

Seven members of the Set Free Soldiers, including leader Phil Aguilar, 60, have been charged with conspiracy to commit murder and are each being held on $1-million bail, police said.

Three members of the Hells Angels are also in custody, including John Phillip Lloyd, a 41-year-old Costa Mesa man charged with assault with a deadly weapon. The other two were arrested on drug charges.

Others are still being sought on arrest warrants.

The arrests stemmed from a 15-person brawl at the Newport Beach bar Blackie's by the Sea, where Set Free members allegedly stabbed two Hells Angels members.

During the brawl, the Hells Angels also allegedly struck one of the Set Free members in the head with a pool ball.

On its website, which appeared to have been taken down Wednesday evening, Set Free Soldiers call themselves "a group of men who love Jesus and love to ride hard."

"We are not your normal motorcycle club," the statement reads. "Some say we are too good for the bad guys, and too bad for the good guys."

Archive for Saturday, August 09, 2008

# 5 Christian bikers face gang counts

*Orange County prosecutors scale back charges against the Set Free Soldiers in a Newport Beach bar brawl with members of the Hells Angels, one of whom faces a weapons charge.*

By Tony Barboza
August 09, 2008 *in print edition B-3*

Five members of a Christian motorcycle gang were charged Friday with a variety of felony weapons and gang crimes after high-profile raids this week targeting the Anaheim-based group.

The charges marked a retreat from Wednesday, when authorities arrested seven members of the Set Free Soldiers, including founder and pastor Phillip Aguilar, on charges of conspiracy to commit murder. An eighth member was arrested on suspicion of attempted murder.

The charges were in connection with a double stabbing during a bar brawl with the Hells Angels late last month.

On Friday, the Orange County district attorney's office filed just one attempted murder charge, against Jose Quinones, 42, and charged Glenn Schoeman, 56, with being an accessory after the fact. They were being held on $1-million and $100,000 bail, respectively.

Aguilar, 60, the group's leader and pastor; his 29-year-old son, Matthew Aguilar; and Michael Timanus Jr., 29, face felony charges of illegal weapons possession. They were expected to post bail, which was set at $50,000 each, according to their attorneys.

Phillip and Matthew Aguilar also were charged with possessing brass knuckles.

All five were accused of street terrorism for being part of a criminal street gang.

One Hells Angel member, John Lloyd, 41, also was charged with having a loaded firearm in a vehicle.

Additional charges may be filed, said Deputy Dist. Atty. Erik Petersen, adding that the Set Free Soldiers are a violent street gang because "they carry on a pattern of criminal gang activity."

Set Free members say they are a Christian ministry that helps rehabilitate ex-convicts and recovering drug addicts. But authorities maintain that they are an outlaw motorcycle gang.

In Wednesday's raids in Anaheim, Costa Mesa, Rancho Santa Margarita and Norco, more than 150 police, SWAT teams and federal agents arrested eight Set Free Soldiers and three Hells Angels.

The raids included four homes that Aguilar owns in the 300 block of South Archer Street in Anaheim, where authorities found multiple firearms.

The arrests followed a July 27 fight between Set Free members and Hells Angels at a Newport Beach bar.

Police said Set Free members stabbed two Hells Angels and one Hells Angel struck a Set Free member in the head with a pool ball.

Attorneys on both sides said the case will hinge on a surveillance video taken of the brawl.

Sandra Aguilar, Phillip Aguilar's wife, said after the court hearing that the group had been unfairly targeted by police, who she said terrorized the group's children and grandchildren during the raids and "turned our homes upside down."

"They cannot believe that we're Christians because we have tattoos and ride motorcycles," she said. "It's sheep in wolf's clothing."

THE ORANGE COUNTY
**REGISTER**
ocregister.com

Sunday, August 10, 2008

# Christian bikers glad pastor is out of jail

## Motorcycle ministry Pastor Phillip Aguilar speaks about his experience.

**By SERENA MARIA DANIELS**

The Orange County Register

ANAHEIM – The pastor of the Set Free motorcycle ministry, out of jail on $50,000 bail, spoke about his arrest to more than 100 of his parishioners over the weekend.

Pastor Phillip Aguilar, 60, founder of the Set Free church, told the congregation he was not angry about 150 police officers raiding his properties on Wednesday. Officers from police departments throughout Orange County got warrants to search and seize properties from several Set Free homes.

He said he knows the image his organization portrays – one of heavily tattooed motorcyclists who drive fancy bikes and cars – played a role in how officers reacted to the barroom brawl in which he and six other members of the church were arrested on attempted murder charges.

"The people I work with are a rugged-looking crew," Aguilar said.

A crew of the Set Free Soldiers is accused of fighting with members of the Hells Angels at Blackies by the Sea in Newport Beach late last month. The attempted murder charge against Aguilar was dropped, and prosecutors have charged him and two other members with weapons violations and street terrorism.

One Set Free member, Jeremy Gaither, 28, was reportedly hit in the head with a pool ball. Two Hells Angels members were stabbed, authorities said.

To help change the church's image, often referred to as a Christian biker gang by authorities, Aguilar told parishioners to stop loitering outside the Archer Street properties, and for his friends to stop parking their Bentleys and Mercedes Benzes in front of his home.

"When people go by and they see these cars, there's this perception about who you are," Aguilar said. "Even the mail man comes by and says, 'Hey, what's up, Trump?'"

Parishioners say the Set Free family is

Published Thursday, September 25, 2008 8:19 PM PDT

Topstory

# Pastor pleads not guilty

**Prosecutors say he leads a criminal motorcycle gang whose members were arrested during a fracas in a Newport Beach bar.**

By Brianna Bailey

The pastor of the Anaheim-based motorcycle club the Set Free Soldiers pleaded not guilty Thursday in Orange County Superior Court to weapon and gang charges stemming from a bar brawl with Hells Angels in Newport Beach in July.

Phillip Russel Aguilar, 61, of Anaheim is charged with felony counts of street terrorism, being a felon in possession of a firearm, and possession of a deadly weapon.

The pastor's son, Matthew John Aguilar, 29, and Set Free member Michael Alan Timanus also pleaded not guilty Thursday to felony weapon and gang charges.

Prosecutors say Phillip Aguilar is the leader of a criminal motorcycle gang disguised as a Christian ministry for recovering addicts and ex-convicts. The court denied the District Attorney's office request Thursday that Phillip Aguilar not be allowed to associate with members of the Set Free group outside of his own family.

"We are not your normal motorcycle club," the club states on its website. "Some say we are too good for the bad guys, and too bad for the good guys. We don't argue that."

Court documents state that a high-ranking member of the Orange County chapter of the Hells Angels confronted Phillip Aguilar at the Newport Beach bar Blackie's By The Sea on July 27 about Aguilar and other Set Free members claiming association with the Hells Angels. The confrontation escalated into a brawl in which two Hells Angels members were stabbed. Attempted murder charges against seven men involved in the fight were later dropped.

Law enforcement officers seized large caches of weapons and ammunition from four homes where Set Free members lived in Anaheim during a raid in August.

The three men are scheduled to return to court for a pretrial hearing Dec. 4.

BRIANNA BAILEY may be reached at (714) 966-4625 or at brianna.bailey@latimes.com.

# CHAPTER 39

# THREE DAYS IN THE BELLY

The first two days after my release from jail, I borrowed a car for my family to get around in and helped my family fix our homes that had been abused by the police. They tore family pictures off walls and threw everything off of every dresser and out of every drawer. They put holes in the walls and broke so many articles of our property. It took several days and a lot of money to get our homes back to their original condition, I was just so happy to be at home with all those who I love so dearly.

My wife and I have been together for 34 years. All of our children love us and we love them. Twenty-two of us have all lived together for the purpose of sharing our lives and our faith in Jesus. My children and grandchildren squeeze into two homes so we can be together. We don't have much money but we have so very much love. I have always learned in life that "all things work together for good for those that love God". I didn't understand all that God was teaching me at the moment but I was sure that He had a wonderful plan for all of this.

As I reflect back to my three days in the Orange County Jail I think about Jonah in the belly of the whale. God told Jonah to go speak to the people in the city of Nineveh but Jonah chose not to go and instead headed the other direction. I saw myself as Jonah--not preaching to all the people I was suppose to and just going into relax mode. God had to get my attention and He did a good job of it. I was planning on retiring from the ministry because I wanted to spend more time with my grandchildren, and ride more often with my Set Free Soldier brothers. I was full of good intentions, but more than once I have said the road to hell is paved with them.

The second day I was locked up in the county jail I looked over at my friend and Soldier brother, Dave, and told him these words, "I allowed us to get in this bad situation, and by the grace of God I will lead us out of it." I was a prodigal son who had come to himself and was ready to go all the way back home into Daddy's arms.

On the third day I had one of the jail guards come ask me if I was the famous Pastor Phil Aguilar, I told him I am just regular old Phil Aguilar a sinner saved by grace. He said he had some friends who had been helped by the Set Free Church; he then asked me if I told the Hells Angel about Jesus before I killed him. The rumors were flying everywhere and the press tried to make the Set Free Soldiers some type of criminal gang. I knew in my heart that all the allegations; I mean all of the allegations about me were a lie. I knew that God would reveal the truth one day. I knew it wasn't the whole police department that felt I was a criminal. I also recognized the man who was heading the charge and I have prayed every day for him to know Jesus and to open his eyes to the real picture of who Pastor Phil is.

The Bible teaches us that to some people all things are unclean, meaning that everything is in the eye of the beholder. Since the day of my release I have given my total effort to getting back to my first love one more time. The police had no idea that they were putting fuel in the tank of this old Soldier for Jesus. I realized how much I loved our Set Free Church and the Set Free Soldier brothers.

On September 25' 2008 we had our first day in court since we were bailed out. It took place at Harbor Court Newport Beach. As we entered the parking lot that morning the placed was filled with police units from all over. We got out of our cars and proceeded to walk to the courthouse and then up the stairs to a hallway full of sheriffs and policemen.

The press and law enforcement were making us look like we were the head of the 5 families in Chicago, or New York City. I knew in my heart they had the wrong people, but I also understood that God saw fit to allow this drama to unfold. The judge called us forward and asked how we plead to the crimes we were being accused of. MJ, my son-in-law Michael, and I pled "not guilty," and our next court date was set.

Since that that day we have been to court several times and at each hearing our case was postponed. Each time we went to court, our attorneys requested that the belongings that were confiscated be returned to us. The police took all of my children's clothes, their computers, and their work materials that they made a living with. They took our livelihood and laughed in our face. I had to turn bitter feelings in to better feelings. I had to forgive from my heart in order to be able to serve the Lord one hundred percent.

I felt like Samson in the Bible who had his eyes poked out and was imprisoned, but saved his last bit of strength for the last spiritual show of his life. I knew in my inner spirit that it could not end like this.

The words and the scare tactics the police used on my family just fired me up to serve God like never before. I was determined again that I would rest on Gods word that I had learned to lean on so many times before. Acts 20:24 says, "But none of these things move me, neither do I count my life dear to myself, but I am going to finish the course God had given me, and I am going to finish it with joy, the ministry of telling the whole world about Jesus Christ. " Yes, the day I saw the whole army of Orange County come against me was the day I saw how much Jesus truly loved me. He was willing to allow all those terrible things to happen to me to get my attention. God never sends evil our way, but he allows it to happen so we can let our light shine in the darkest hours.

I remembered back to the happiest days of my life, living with Jesus in state prison. It wasn't about circumstances or things that made me happy. I use to be a drug addict and a man who hated life. It took state prison to bring me to Jesus and now it took me being locked up and facing four felony charges with a life sentence over my head to bring me back to my first love.
People ask me "was it all worth it?" yes; it was worth it all and even more. The head detective's goal has always been to get me out of town, but there is no way I will ever stop doing what God has called me to do. I am not fighting this case for me, but for every tattooed, bald-headed character, that has been judged by the way he or she looks on the outside.

# CHAPTER 40

# THE GOOD FIGHT

It's the beginning of May 2010 and I have been rebuilding our lives for the last 18 months since we were arrested. I have lost vehicles, property, and friends throughout this ordeal. The finances to get bail, hire lawyers, pay the mortgage has drained every bit of savings and more from our lives. I started having church in our backyard until we found a local hotel banquet room to utilize. I have never despised small beginnings, and with the new fire in my bones I know that God will restore even more than I had before.

My family of twenty-two people had to trim down from living in four homes to two houses. Sandra and I moved into our living room and spread the grandkids around so we could all stay together. I don't mind living this way because we are going to fight for what we know is right.

We lost a lot of our congregation due to the fact that the newspapers persisted in capitalizing on a great story. By now we were known by many as the bad ass biker gang who used the church as a front. I am very secure and know who I am and whose I am as I walk through this valley of the shadow of death.

In the valleys of life you get to see who your real friends are by the actions they take. A friend loveth at all times, and is closer than a brother. My dearest friend, Glenn deserted me and I have not seen him since. It hurt because he and his wife were our very best friends, so we thought. Many were afraid to come to church for fear of retaliation from those who hated us. Our livelihood had been taken with all of our work materials and machines being confiscated, but we have made do and totally trusted God for providing a roof over our heads. I have had countless Christian friends judge me and crucify me through their blogs and gossip to people everywhere. Many people are shocked to know that I am out on the streets preaching Jesus, thinking that I was already doing time in prison. The rumors were flying and growing and myths of Pastor Phil were getting bigger and bigger. People love to believe the worst, and the spirit of imagination can get way out of control.

I dove into God's Word and started planning a strategy of rising up again, and making my ministry and family the top priority in my life. When your back is against the wall the creative juices given from God can flow like never before. I faced my enemies of fear, lack of faith, and I was ready to do battle. I put on the full armor of God and was ready to fight the good fight of faith.

My first message after my release was about loving our enemies and forgiving anyone and everyone. Upon approaching the throne of grace, God requires that we get things right on the horizontal level before getting the vertical one right. Each and every week church and weekly bible studies and life itself has gotten sweeter.

Our Set Free Soldiers who have remained are into God's Word and they are standing shoulder-to-shoulder with me. We have lots of new blood that have heard the call from above and joined forces with us. I have so many great friends who have held my hands up when I had no strength on my own. It has been a long good journey heading up the spiritual mountain of God.

During the first few months after my arrest Set Free was harassed over and over again by the local police. One of the head officers involved in the raid on my home said she was bothered with the picture I had of one of my son's and said he looked like a big thug. I told her that thug is one of my sons who loves his wife and family, and is our worship leader. I have Bible studies and prayer meetings at my home on a daily bases, and every time a car has left my home they have been tailed and pulled over and questioned about their reason for being at my home. It has been difficult to know some of our neighbors have been part of the reason for our raid. I am learning more how to love people right where there at. I make sure to give everyone love even when I know they have been so ugly to me and my family. God is so cool, and He is so very patient with us as we grow in our relationship with him.

Over this last year and half since our arrest we have moved into a larger hotel room to make room for the influx of people that believe in our cause for Jesus.

God says we need to sing a new song. Set Free still rocks out with hip hop and rock 'n roll at church. Our church is filled up with street people, business people, ex-cons, and all the others in between. The Noah's Ark church is slowly but surely building back up. By the Grace of God I have the fire of my youth coming back to me. I am turning 63 years old and feeling like a youngster. Read about Joshua and Caleb and when Caleb was 85 years old he still had the fire of his youth. God is bringing back what the enemy has stolen. I often wonder how much of the taxpayers' money has been spent on me by the Anaheim police and the District Attorney's office in Newport Beach. I wonder how much money the raid cost. I wonder how much overtime all the detectives were paid to keep my house under surveillance for three years. I know it was way too much for sure.

I am preparing for the finish of my pre trial on all of my felony charges. The only deal they have offered me is to end Set Free church and the Set Free Soldiers. They were willing to let everything die if I would admit that I was a gang member. Like I said before, Set Free is a way of life, not just a name. I will not let anyone but God stop what he has started in my life. Set Free is me and what God has begun only he can finish. I just recently returned from a trip to Richmond Virginia to visit my sons Geronimo and Phil Jr. Phil Jr. needed a change of pace and saw a opportunity to enhance his gift of doing music with his brother Geronimo. I took my 2 other sons Matthew, aka MJ, and Roc, aka Hebrew with me to have a family reunion. Geronimo is doing great and just celebrated the grand opening of his new church facility. He had close to 5 thousand people show up and the Governor of Virginia was his special guest speaker. Phil Jr. aka Chill is his new worship leader for the church and is doing a mighty work for God. I had such a good time in Virginia getting to visit with 9 of my grandchildren. Geronimo's 2 children from his first marriage have recently moved in with him. I only had memories of them since they left with their mother Stacie 16 years ago. Geronimo wanted to show his dad that he has applied all the good things I had taught him. Chill has just begun to blossom and I see him being used of God to lead multitudes to Jesus.

The hand of God is all over my family, and its all by my Heavenly Father's choice. I am the happiest man on earth knowing I have the greatest family in the world. To top things off my one and only daughter Trina and my son n law Michael just had twins. What more can a man ask for in life?

My wife Sandra and I are so in love and having the best time serving God together. I am so very proud to know that all of my children are serving Jesus and involved in full time ministry. I have made a lot of bad choices in life, and I committed some very ugly sins, yet God has seen fit to bless me with some beautiful offspring. Yes, if you delight yourself in the lord you will receive the desires of your heart.  Are things with my family just how I would want them to be? Hell to the no! I am like any parent that would pray that all the family would be together sharing the Love of Jesus in person. I am content in the fact that they will all go to Heaven one day and live for eternity in a place that words cannot describe with tongue.

I don't know if I am going to prison or not. I am writing this book in part to leave a legacy to my children and their children. I want them to know that I didn't always do right, but I had a heart to do right. When you read the accounts of King David's life in the Bible it is just amazing to see all the sins he committed, yet how God said he was a man after his own heart. I am able to say with a pure heart that since my conversion to Christ I have never returned to the vomit of my lifestyle of drugs. I have never raised my hand to cause injury to anyone. I have done my best to serve God with all my heart. If my children and grandchildren are evidence of a changed life, then I am happy with that. If God took me to Heaven today I could go in peace, knowing I fought the good fight.

# *P.S.*

It's May 13th 2010. While most people are at work, school or the beach, I'm driving my son and me from our house in Anaheim to the courthouse in Newport Beach. As we journey to what has been our second home for the last two years, I begin to share with my son that I would have never finished writing this book if it was not for this trial in my life. I told him how even at this age of my life I'm still learning to put my complete trust in the Lord and that whatever happens today, God is in full control. If Papa thinks I need to go to prison, then I will go back to where it all started. As we approach the courthouse it's a beautiful day in Newport Beach, California. One of the nicest and wealthiest cities on the planet, but for my son MJ and myself, we had to rely on the weather in our hearts and pray that are future would be more sunny then cloudy. This is the final day of our Pre-Trial. The day where the court decides after almost two years if we, Set Free Ministries, Set Free Soldiers and Pastor Phil Aguilar are guilty of being a gang and street terrorist.

I'm sure a few of you reading this can relate, but there's something about walking in a courthouse not knowing your fate that makes you feel a little funny inside. We walk through the security check point and head up stairs where we meet up with my son-in-law Michael, who is on trial as well. We pray up and head into room H6. There are no reporters along the wall, begging for comments and no longer are there a dozen sheriffs in the court room just for us, like in the beginning. All that drama died after the first year, but still as the three of us walk in, it is here that we will be judged, judged by our look, our conduct and our past. The reason why all three of us are on trial together was not for the incident at Blackies, which none of us had charges from, and is what most believe, but because the "District Attorney" thought it would be good for their case if the judge saw three "thugs" instead of one. That is the honest-to-God truth and that might help you understand what they were willing to do to take us down.

Court is an intense place and never a comfortable setting. As the three of us take a seat behind our lawyers, we remain quiet. Soon after is when the voice of an older female judge is heard asking us to arise. A judge who happens to be a woman can be interesting, not knowing what she has experienced in her own life or what prejudices she might have. Then there's the typing that you hear constantly recording every single word that can in some cases, come back to haunt you and of course let's not forget the one sheriff that constantly stares in your direction and because there is three of us, looks really worried being that he's outnumbered. All of this plus the young hot shot D.A. who is aiming right for us, but I truly believe he is a decent guy; he just has the Anaheim Police Department breathing down his neck. I think I can relate. Besides, the small talk between our attorneys, we have to sit there for hours and listen to nothing but Police and D.E.A. speak on what they found in our homes during the raid, what we told them during interrogation and their own opinion of what they think of us in general. So after hours of hearing what they think and most of it being a waste of time because our lawyers were well prepared and caught them on many details which helped the judge be very fair and reasonable, we finally take a recess and prepare to hear from the man who started this whole situation.

As we stand in the hallway waiting for court to return to session, I see a man walking towards us from the other end of the hall. As he slowly approaches, I start to notice this person more and more. He is short, chubby not stocky, his eyes have dark circles under them. He is a police officer with power and he hates what I stand for. A lot of us have problems and issues, but most of it we can't physically see and look directly in its face, when needed. Well this time I saw my problem and my issue in real life and let me tell you, it wasn't pretty. The officer shakes hands with the D.A. and they head inside the courtroom, we follow moments after. Sergeant "Hater" walks up to the stand wearing his freshly dry-cleaned uniform that looks like a football letterman jacket that he hasn't worn since his senior year in high school. He takes a seat, I take a seat and we all take a deep breath as we can only imagine what this so called "outlaw motorcycle gang expert" has to say about us.

The district attorney is up first to speak to the witness, and you have to remember, every witness that has been called up to the stand so far has been part of law enforcement. Not one person was a civilian and none of them knew us personally or were on our side whatsoever. He begins to ask the officer about his history on the force, what qualifies him to head up this task.

The officer talks about how he has been undercover many times, he has spent hundreds of hours studying gang culture and what all the patches, colors & signs really mean. I know he's supposed to be an expert, but to me it sounded like he just watched the TV show Gangland. Regardless of what I think, he is the one on the stand and he is definitely the one with the badge and gun. He goes on for hours talking about how he thinks we're a criminal organization and that we only use God as a cover for our illegal lifestyle. He explains to the court that Set Free Soldiers are an outlaw group and only help troubled people so that we can train them to be a part of our criminal organization. He then goes on to say that there is no way that they could be helping or servicing other motorcycle clubs in their area without it being for something illegal. The sergeant doesn't speak of the numerous times I have married, buried and counseled members from every major motorcycle club in California. God has placed me in a position to be there for people that would never come inside a church, and share with them about the love of Jesus, but this officer didn't quite see it that way.

One of the things that brought the case this far were the so-called informants they had acquired over the past few years, without them they would have no case. The so called informants never made it to the stand but the sergeant spoke of them many times. He said that the informants told him that we deal drugs through our ministry home, that we are enforcers for other clubs and that we run a prostitution ring. None of those things are true and on the record the sergeant said that after doing surveillance on our group, our home and my family for three years, he never saw one illegal activity take place.

Did that stop him from lying on the stand? Did that stop him from raiding my family's homes? Did that stop him, even after searching our homes inside & out and still not finding anything illegal to call this whole thing off? As a matter of fact, when my lawyer was cross examining the witless, excuse me the witness....he asked him, "after you tore apart Phil Aguilar's home and found nothing, no drugs or drug paraphernalia and not one illegal weapon, did you maybe think that you got the wrong guy?". The officer thinks for a minute and answers, "slightly". He continued to say that there is no possible way that they could have all those motorcycles and two homes right next to each other without it being from some illegal enterprise.

This one man who started this trial, could have stopped it all that day, but after all that work and hype over the big bad boogeyman known as Pastor Phil, there was no way he could go back to his side with his tail between his legs. He is trained to profile and be one sided, all he could see was the way we look and not anything else. This of course is not anything new, all my life I've been judged by the way I look. I'm used to people profiling me and my group, especially by Christians and Police. When profiling can come inside your home, traumatize your family and break your bank account, that's just not right. My grandkids will never forget that horrible day.

After hearing all the hearsay and just his own opinions for hours, we all knew that he had it out for us and didn't even really know why anymore. Was it the way he was brought up? Was it what he learned at the academy or just his own pride stopping him from seeing past the black leather? What was it?

Opinions rarely matter on the streets and they definitely do not work in court. So him saying over & over again, things like "they have loud bikes", race up the street and hang on the corner didn't go over so well. He say's I live in a compound, but you tell me what compound has a white picket fence and a playground on the corner of a highly populated neighborhood. He says I have all these new & expensive vehicles, but I only have one motorcycle to my name and no cars newer then 2005. Our three lawyers were letting him have it. When something is just not true it's hard to prove that it is, even if you're a cop. If you're trying to spread lies about God's children, then you have a lot more to be scared of, than the Set Free Soldiers.

After cross examining the witness for what seemed like an eternity, you could tell that he was dying up there. He was shooting himself in the foot every time he'd open his mouth. He could not keep up with the lawyers and I was beginning to realize that this job is how he got those dark circles under his eyes. They have been offering all of us deals since day one. "Admit you're a gang and no jail time" is what they said. "Snitch on your dad and you'll go free", they offered. These were the so-called deals that they offered us individually. I refused over & over again to plea to a deal that first off is not true and secondly, will destroy our ministry and stop me from helping anyone with a past ever again. I would love to have the money just so I could challenge the reasoning for what ended up being one of Orange County's biggest raids ever. I would love to take this to trial and let my people take the stand to give the court, the police and the world a better understanding of "Our" kind of people. Or, for a chance to have the world see what the raid did to my family and our homes.

The one thing they did find in my home during the raid was one single bullet in a keepsake jar filled with coins &

candy....yes; it was one of those jars that we all keep at home. I had no weapons, I had no drugs, I did no wrong, and even at Blackies I broke no law. I know I'm a convicted felon from 1976, but I never in a million years thought this would all come down to one stinking bullet!!! There was absolutely no good reason to come and tear my house apart. The so called informants were never produced and I don't believe they ever will come forward, because they don't exist. In life good things happen to bad people and bad things happen to good people. It was nearing the closing hours of court and none of us wanted this to carry on any longer than it already has.

The officer was repeating himself, the judge was restless and I was drained emotionally. We all knew that this case would never hold up in court if it went to trial. At the end of the day I was still a felon with a bullet in my room. The witness was free to step down from the stand and the judge gave the counsel some time to talk things over. The district attorney and my lawyer called me into the back room a few minutes later and asked me if I would admit to having the one single bullet in my home. I didn't have the finances to pay my lawyer to continue to fight the case so I had no choice. I agreed and plead guilty to a misdemeanor possession of a bullet. After years of surveillance on our home's, my phones tapped, our houses raided, grandchildren traumatized, reputation destroyed, no cars, no money, treated like a criminal and many lies told....I was asked to admit that I, a felon was in possession of a bullet.

I do not have the words to describe the pain & suffering that myself, my family, my ministry and my club had to go through. I wouldn't wish that on anybody, not even the Anaheim Police. I sign on the line and make a deal for the misdemeanor, my son MJ makes a deal as well for some collectible brass knuckles (a gift) they found in the illegal search of his home. It was not easy making this deal knowing how wrong it was for them to come in our homes with no concrete evidence and use this against us just because they had nothing else to convict us with. In the end it is a victory for all of us. No Prison time for me, no more court every month, no more paying lawyers, money I don't have and most importantly, no, we are not a GANG.

Was it printed on the front page of every newspaper and website that Set Free Soldiers and Pastor Phil are not guilty and the police made a mistake? Of course not. Is there still many that think we're bad boys looking for trouble and are using this "God Thing" as a front? Unfortunately yes. Hopefully the words on these pages will change the minds of all those have judged me. Did we get our money back for proving our innocence or at least for the lost wages we suffered during this whole trial? No, not one dime. We do have the fulfillment in knowing that we proved to the court and hopefully to others, that we never have and never will do illegal activities in our ministry or our club.

Ultimately we have the victory in Jesus. He was our attorney, our defendant, our supporter and the witness who was silently on the stand the whole time. Even though the trial is over, he is still all that and more. Knowing that the way we serve the Lord is okay and not illegal or even weird in our father's eye's, is all that really matters. Would we like others to feel the same way, especially cops & other Christians? Sure! But that's just not reality... at least not mine. I'm back on the streets doing what I do best and that's sharing the love of Jesus Set Free Style. I still have the police visiting my home often to speak of some new thing I am doing that irritates some. I put up a "honk if you love Jesus sign" a couple of my same lovely names have called the police. I have a public Bible study every morning on the front lawn of my house that has some eye brows raised, and blood pressure going up. The apostle Paul provoked a revival to take place, or a riot to happen. Guess Pastor Phil, aka Dr. Phil Good, aka the Chief will keep on keepin' on telling people to get high on JESUS!!!!!

# CHARACTER REFERRENCE

(All information listed on this page is based on public information listed on Wikipedia or through Google)

Anaheim, California

- **Anaheim** is a city in Orange County, California. As of January 1, 2009, the city population was about 348,467 making it the 10th most-populated city in California and ranked 54th in the United States. Founded by fifty German families in 1857 and incorporated on February 10, 1870, Anaheim developed into an industrial center, producing electronics, aircraft parts and canned fruit. It is the site of the Disneyland Resort, Angel Stadium of Anaheim, Honda Center and Anaheim Convention Center. In the 1920s, the Ku Klux Klan, at the height of its influence and popularity, decided to make Anaheim a "model" Klan city. In 1924, the Klan secretly managed to get four of its members elected to the five-member Board of Trustees. Nine of the ten members of the police force were also Klansmen. The four Klan trustees served for nearly a year, until they were publicly exposed, and voted out in a recall election in which 95% of the population participated. In the late 20th century, Anaheim grew rapidly in population. Today, Anaheim has a diverse ethnic and racial composition.

Tommy and Matthew Barnett

- **S**enior pastor of Phoenix First Assembly of God in Phoenix, Arizona. Tommy and his son Matthew, co-pastor the Los Angeles Dream Center, where the former

Queen of Angels Hospital and Angelus Temple was located. Before moving to Phoenix First, he pastored Westside Assembly of God in Davenport, Iowa. Mr. Barnett has been a pastor for over 30 years.

Paul and Jan Crouch

- **Paul Franklin Crouch** (born March 30, 1934) is the American co-founder, chairman and president of the Trinity Broadcasting Network (TBN), is the United States' largest Christian television network.
- **Jan Crouch** (born **Janice Wendell Bethany**, 1937) is the co-founder, vice-president and director of programming of the Trinity Broadcasting Network, or TBN, the world's largest Christian television network. She is the daughter of an Assemblies of God pastor who was also the founding president of Southeastern University (Florida). Crouch is noted for her flamboyant makeup and dress when appearing on TBN. She typically sports a large pink bouffant and heavy make-up, somewhat reminiscent of another televangelist, the late Tammy Faye Bakker.

Oden Fong

- Born in the USA. He first rose to prominence as lead vocalist and songwriter with the highly-regarded Christian rock group, Mustard Seed Faith. As he once explained, "I don't see myself just as a professional musician because I'm not a Christian music entertainer". Currently, Fong is the Poiema Christian Fellowship Pastor.

Chuck Smith

- **Charles Ward "Chuck" Smith**, (born June 25, 1927), is the senior pastor of Calvary Chapel Costa Mesa. He is widely credited as founding Calvary Chapel Costa Mesa, though he was the second pastor.

Benny Hinn

- **Toufik Benedictus "Benny" Hinn** born December 3, 1952) is a televangelist, best known for his regular "Miracle Crusades" – revival meeting/faith healing summits that are usually held in large stadiums in major cities, which are later broadcast worldwide on his television program, *This Is Your Day*.

Fred Hunter

- Mayor of Anaheim, California from 1988 through 1992

Bill Taormina

- William C. "Bill" Taormina Born in 1951, resident and business owner in Anaheim his entire life. Bill and his family built their Anaheim-based business, Taormina Industries, into the largest privately owned solid waste and recycling firm in the nation.

Tom Daly

- Mayor of Anaheim, California from 1992 through 2002

Lonnie Frisbee

● **Lonnie Frisbee** (June 6, 1949 – March 12, 1993) was an American Pentecostal evangelist and self-described "seeing prophet" and mystic in the late 1960s and 1970s. Frisbee was a key figure in the Jesus Movement and eyewitness accounts of his ministry documented in the 2007 Emmy-nominated film *Frisbee: The Life and Death of a Hippie Preacher* explain how Lonnie became the charismatic spark igniting the rise of two worldwide denominations (Chuck Smith's Calvary Chapel and the Vineyard Movement)–It was said that he was not one of the hippie preachers, "there was one." Frisbee, evangelical preacher, also privately struggled with what he called the evil sin of homosexuality both before and after he was born again.– He made it repeatedly clear in interviews that he believed homosexuality a sin in the eyes of God. Both Calvary Chapel and the Vineyard ministries later distanced themselves from him because of his homosexuality; he was removed from leadership positions.– As part of his ostracism from his former churches his work was maligned, but he forgave those who tried to discredit him before his death from AIDS in 1993. Frisbee lived in the Set Free Ministry homes during the last years of his life

FORGIVE ME FATHER FOR I HAVE SINNED

Made in the USA
Lexington, KY
17 October 2011